NOT LOSING FACE

NOT LOSING FACE

ACTUALITY AND POTENTIALITY OF POWER WHEN FACING UP TO ONESELF

RICHARD MICHAEL HEAD

COMMON GROUND

First published in 2024
as part of the *Interdisciplinary Social Sciences* Book Imprint

Common Ground Publishing
2001 S. 1ˢᵗ St., Suite 202
University of Illinois Research Park
Champaign, IL
61821

Library of Congress Cataloging-in-Publication Data

Names: Head, Richard Michael, author.
Title: Not losing face : actuality and potentiality of power / Richard Michael Head.
Description: Champaign, IL : Common Ground Research Networks, 2024. | Includes bibliographical references and index. | Summary: "What power is, can be, or is imagined by human reasoning. This topic is essential, even vital, because what power is and how it is used is the energy that determines the social and cultural fabric of life. Power is understood in many ways, an existence too complicated to be conveniently rationalized from a compartmentalized methodology. But there is also a paradox at play, for power can be reduced to the simplicity of acting or not acting in a certain way. This "acting" can be self-induced or due to pressure from others and societal expectations. Thus, power is multifaceted, but also binary, yes or no, in its potentiality and actuality. "Not Losing Face: Actuality and Potentiality of Power" interweaves this versatile nature of power within the space of its binary disposition"-- Provided by publisher.
Identifiers: LCCN 2023053470 (print) | LCCN 2023053471 (ebook) | ISBN 9781963049138 (hardback) | ISBN 9781963049145 (paperback) | ISBN 9781963049152 (adobe pdf) | ISBN 9781963049169 (ebook)
Subjects: LCSH: Power (Social sciences)
Classification: LCC HN49.P6 H42 2024 (print) | LCC HN49.P6 (ebook) | DDC 303.3--dc23/eng/20240105
LC record available at https://lccn.loc.gov/2023053470

Cover Photo Credit: Kayla Head

TABLE OF CONTENTS

ACKNOWLEDGEMENTS

To all who are drawn into the powered game and simultaneously trying to keep a straight face.

An anonymous and meticulous proof reader.

A generous review by Professor Wayne Cristaudo

Book dedicated to my mum Christine Mary Patricia Head

INTRODUCTION

One's face retains the essence of who a person is. In most encounters and lived contexts, it is the public persona one makes visible to the rest of society. It can be thought of as a mask of deception and creativity through purposeful acting, to allow oneself to get through life. This is not to say that the path of least resistance is achieved, for sometimes, to maintain one's face in a manner that is acceptable to oneself, paths of great resistance are chosen. However, the process "chosen" may misinterpret the actuality of what a person must do, since choosing can be an unattainable luxury or not even an option one can apply to a situation. This is because there is really only one course to follow, however painful, to maintain one's face. Although many, if not all, in society do mislay their face, be that of momentary duration or during the whole of one's existence. This is due to surviving and maintaining what one has or is accumulating in the societal system one is in, when competing with other faces. Thus, one's face is compromised and conflicted.

Since facial public persona is the surface of one's embodied face, the rest of oneself remains hidden and only perceived by others through visible behavior and of how one perceives others. This "rest" is the invisible face that drives performance in a never-ending game of power play, and consequently always risking one's face in the hope and intention that it will not be lost. From this, one's face can be thought of as one's identity or one's sense of self and self-worth. However, as one is of an embodied form, of a corporeal disposition, one's sense is governed by this and, hence, judges oneself accordingly. As well as being restricted in movement to the physical environment lived within, there is also the no small matter of the social and cultural structure that has been constructed over countless generations, and that also supplies restrictions on the oneself. So, not only is the oneself physically bound to one's environment, one's physicality adds to that confinement of movement of what is possible, as well as one's mental, emotional, and spiritual capacities curtailed by the sociocultural system in place. Therefore, it follows that one's face is under tremendous pressure to not become distorted or too distorted from its unworried and unconcerned pure representational form.

For instance, the physical face is the representation of one's inner face, and it is not coincidental that the physical face begins life as a smooth surface, carefree and fresh. Purity of intention and outlook accompanies the smoothness, but as time weaves its constant challenges, conflicts, and contagions, the face becomes weatherworn through the nature of immortal time and of human mortal time. It is the worn(ing) and worn-out face that tells its own story of how one has played the game of power and for how long. The "how" may have been reflected in a series of "victories" or "defeats" according to the extents of one's movement in the physical and sociocultural environment. Of the amount of self-expression one expresses along the course of one's life, which equates to one's capacity of power. The victories and defeats along this pathway of life are in quotes since they incorporate the same experience or movement (physical and mental) at the same time when powering up the oneself. For to gain victory in power involves a self-sacrifice of part of the essence of oneself, a defeat of sorts; i.e., there is always a price to pay for losing part of oneself to win, and the longer one plays the game, the price of victory is shown in the lines of defeat.

The lines of defeat are retained in the surface face and in the inner face. The inner face will retain mental scars of how life, essentially the process of power that one goes through, has treated the person and of that person's reactions to it. Depending on individual character (both bodily and mental capacity), what one has learned in life, the experiences gone through, one's sociocultural standing from whatever levels one found or finds themselves, life changes and chances, and the ability and drive to take advantage of these, potentializes and actualizes power encounters. Since individuals are of their time and space and evolve through these two through a combination of unique (of how the self, lives) and common group (e.g., members of a particular society) influences, there would be innumerable ways and means of how power was and is encountered. For example, selected heritages and histories of the past in combination with the complexities of social contemporariness produce perspectives and practices that create meanings for power and the resultant power that comes from those meanings. These meanings or abstractions or potentialities can either remain in an insubstantial form or, in some instances, when the physical environment is right, the sociocultural opportunity is right, and the person's capacity to act is right; this combination of "rightness" is the time and space to transform the potential into an actuality of immaterial and material power.

From this immaterial and material hybrid, power can take many forms and thus be understood in many ways. Although this does not imply that power can be comprehended in absolute terms, it is enough to construct processes to power life. Consequently, some of these constructions may be far from perfect in terms of group efficiency or for the "good" of the many within the societal space on the receiving end of power but may be nearer to "perfection" of the individual or "elite" minority of how they think power should be and exercised. Since power is understood in many ways, it shows that power is too complicated an existence to just conveniently rationalize from a compartmental methodology. However, there is also a paradox at play here, since power can be reduced to simplicity of to act in a certain way or not act in a certain way. This "acting" may be self-induced or take place due to the pressure applied by others and societal expectations. Hence, power is not only of a multifaceted nature but also of a binary yes or no within its potentiality and actuality.

It is the versatile nature of power within the space of its binary disposition that the book interweaves with. When "interweaving," several "faces" have been selected to put forward their perspectives of what power is and what it does. This cross-section of faces of power is by no means exhaustive since all in society, both past and present, would have practiced their version of power and what it is believed to be. However, to avoid an infinity of perspectives that would be impractical to address, eleven faces have been highlighted to provide a meaningful cross-section of power at rest and in action, which covers much of what power is that the infinity cohort would recognize. There may be other power perspectives that are not investigated, but since the book retains its own powered limits, in terms of word size, that is unavoidable. This limitation is understandable because power itself is of an infinite quality and quantity and no method of investigation could cover all its potential and actuality.

Of the eleven faces, eight are prominent social thinkers or "simply" thinkers who consider what life is, as it may be incorrect just to restrict or label them to the social aspect of living, as being of and in existence is more than that. Another face is of the physical evolving environment that all living beings enjoy movement through. As for the remaining two faces, one participates with power through religious filters of production and the other is an artistic appreciation of how to power. All these faces of power are filtered through my face of power, which offers extra perspectives. The irony here is that I am as much a prisoner of the powered process as these eleven faces are, but that is the point of power in that while trying to explain and understand the powered performance, the oneself is simultaneously an intimate part of that performance and, hence, viewing and doing power from the inside. Thus, it is a challenging proposition that one's perspective on the issue is generally fluid and the indulgence of being a "space apart"....'
However, one can still try and get as close as possible to the purity of power.

The book's pursuit of the purity of power begins with **Chapter 1: Aristotle**. It was deemed appropriate to commence with one of the founding fathers of modern Western philosophy to plant seeds of power understanding. This does not imply that the faces that follow grow their powered interpretations solely from these "beginnings," but there will be some connectivity to their powered perspectives and an historical connection between them. So, this history or heritage "reference point" provides context to what has evolved, in terms of power comprehension. Also, this point in time and space is the product, or a particular product, of what had evolved prior to Aristotle's time and place of being. Essentially, each face retains this quality of prior human exposure to power, and what the face offers from this to those of their time and space and those humans yet to exist. Aristotle's offerings range from societal space; universal of living systems; time; five elements of the universe; four causal factors (circular causality); actual and potential; Ladder of Life (Chain of Being); memory; ethics, happiness, and virtue; city; Law of Nature; Rule of Law; ambiguity of human nature; human self-centeredness; balance of power; and education.

There was an unavoidable obligation to include **Chapter 2: The Bible (and God)**. This is because the power of religion and the associated belief of an immanence beyond the Earthy realm, who it is believed by many to have caused the Earth and Heavens to be, is such a significant aspect of human history, both past and present. Also, again for many, the "God" presence is the epitome of power or where all power originates from, and the Bible (within all its versions) is the "earthly" narration of God's deeds on Earth, as well as the immense testimony of the existence of Earth and the Universe as a major evidence piece of God's deeds or God's powered work. This chapter looks at the potency of words; transcendental entity; text of divination; Constantine (religious doctrine helping to run society); powerful catalytical driving force; comprehending the Bible (filtered comprehension of the Bible); theocentric world view; anthropocentric positionality; individual pathway to goodness; dunamis of God; symbolism of the Bible (God as beyond the Earthly symbol as God does not need symbols); State as God; Good of God; This Entity baptized God; and the other end of Genesis (openness and ongoing-ness.

As God enjoys such intimacy with the Earth and Heavens, basically of the living space that humans move within actually and potentially (this space includes the heavens or universe), **Chapter 3: Nature** was the next logical face to include. Since Nature is the infrastructure that has the power to sustain life and take it away, it cannot be overlooked when considering the powered game. For if it ceases, the power which those living on it also ceases, just as they would cease. Therefore, the power of Nature should not be ignored, and to do so would be imprudent. To avoid being imprudent, the chapter covers the colors of nature ceasing nature; self-invention; only constant is nature; unlimited nature; human natures (borrowing power from nature); wrestling power from nature; building the social of nature; societizing nature/naturing society (distancing and togetherness); political and economic struggle; ecological political struggles; nature as a plurality of power perspective; and nature is the present moment.

From the first three "grounded" chapters, grounded in the sense of having a powered background (physical and metaphysical) for the subsequent faces to express themselves from, Chapters 4 through 10 incorporate the remaining seven prominent thinkers. The first of these, **Chapter 4: Foucault**, allows for some of Michel Foucault's considerations of what power is, to be expressed. Since living life incorporates many structured and unstructured encounters, reflecting the stillness but fluid motion of society, Foucault's deliberations add a rich mix of critical thinking to the powered question. Consequently, this chapter contemplates the limited spaces of knowing; problems of power polemics; genealogy (tweaking, errors); errors through time; archiving materiality and nonmateriality (conscious and unconscious); science as power; episteme (thought frameworks); truth of power; objective subjectivism; disempowering the body; knowledge of power; disempowered resistance; and complex strategical situation.

Complimenting Foucault's unstructured structuredness of how societal processes perform is input to the powered societal equation from Pierre Bourdieu. Hence, **Chapter 5: Bourdieu**. Just like Foucault, Bourdieu looks beyond or through the surface veneer of society and its established physical and mental powered symbolism of society as a "naturally fair" and "pleasant" land of "opportunity," to where the real of sociocultural power resides and hides. It is this probing that opens and expands one's awareness of the power performance, both within its covert and overt state of being and application. Bourdieu applies himself to the speaking (voice); articulating language; emblematic (primacy of relation); emblematic violence; provinces of power (fields); biased field power; capitalization (economic, cultural, symbolic, and social); political capital; professional access to capital; doxa (implies common opinion and belief); class or classless; civilization; class (less) as difference and sameness; embodied culture; and inhabiting power (habitus: blueprint residing in the subconscious that behaves the conscious).

Beyond the "structured rigidity" of society is its unstructured aspect or post-structural, but differentiation between the two may be too rigid as society can be thought of as simultaneously structurally unstructured; i.e., society over the course of its evolution has been, and still is, a structure of movement.

Chapter 6: Giddens reflects this movement of stillness through the apparent dichotomy of agents and the structures they exist within. "Apparent," because it is the agents that create their sociocultural structures and over time discard or adapt them to the requirements of changing power requirements of the agents' own making. Hence, the two are not opposite but intimately related. The relationship is investigated through the tension and compromise between structures and agents; social structure; structuration (social practices ordered across space and time); duality of structure; structuration as limiting (the unlimited quality of the virtual space and its abstract nature allow thinking to reach beyond the substantial limits of structure, even if in practice the concrete of structure and other agents' realities prevents that unlimited space from being attainable); self-identity (reflexive self); class (biographical decision-making, life politics); rules (overridden by the power of the practical moment); ontological security sustainability (the ongoing maintenance of one's identity of self, essentially to empower oneself within the power disempowerment of societal structure); and power (relations of autonomy and dependence between actors in which these actors draw on and reproduce structural properties of domination).

To own the fluid structures of society and having the capacity to construct them to one's requirements is a power journey visibly expressed by economic profit. It is this monetary medium, the extent one possesses it, and the means to accumulate more of it that provide social leverage over others of "lesser" economic standing to go along with these economic owners. Consequently, in capitalist systems or societies, of which the world is generally made up of, owning money and the means to get it is the currency of power. **Chapter 7: Marx** looks at the economics of power through class; political state (ruling economic class interests, social relation; insulated from society); alienation (loss of oneself, commodity); capitalism and attendant economy; primitive accumulation (historical process of divorcing the producer from the means of production); maturing the embryonic; timing and spacing capital (constraining); and currencies of actual and potential power (essentially, power is ever present, and by its very nature creates a hierarchy based on ownership of property).

To do power and create materiality of power, a level of consciousness to be aware of power's existence has to be present, and also that awareness has to be of a critical nature to do something with this thing called power. This "something" can be of minute proportions, but that does not imply it holds no significance within the powered scheme of some(things), for this seemingly diminutive powered act can be the starting event of something much bigger that becomes the established powered face of society. Accordingly, **Chapter 8: Gramsci** looks at ideology consciousness (individual and mass, knowing oneself, ideal, man as historically determined and as a process); speech (produces difference); law (as the Law of Society, which the closed exclusivity shuts the general demographic outside of law creation, construction, and implementation); time of the now and history (coercive and consensual power structures of the now, similar to law, retain a timed dual face, a face of the present and a face of the past(s) or faces of the past); faithful (State/Church); State and Civil Society (fluid); war (narratives on state and civil society incorporate a significant connectivity to military language); and hegemony ("group" of society).

However, being conscious of power may not be enough to supply oneself with the critical capacity needed to meaningfully move from one's potentiality to one's actuality of doing power. For instance, the extra of one's unconsciousness can be thought of as an essential ingredient to achieve that pure sense of meaning and integration between oneself and one's power, in which both become one; i.e., one is power. The perceived illusiveness of this "not quite real" grasp of power—but at the same time it could be the "really real" of how power manifests itself—is "purified" by **Chapter 9: Husserl** while emphasizing that power is not located anywhere (natural attitude to phenomenology); giving to the pregiven (adding to throughout life); powered horizon; phantasie; bracket ("phenomenological epoché"—phenomena as they are originally given to consciousness); how of the world (utmost thematic focus is on the *relations* between the structures of the object as it is given and the structures of conscious subjectivity which are necessary conditions for the object thus to manifest itself); essence (being at one with the purity of pure power, in that the What of an individuum, of the individual, is the actuality of that person); spirit (one's spirit is one's essence, one's soul, life, life force, and inner self, so one's spirit is one's center and one's centerpiece); and time.

Negotiating through the pathways of one's consciousness and unconsciousness when tapping into power or becoming power and how much of that power should be exercised and the effects it can have on oneself and others can depend on one's attitude. An attitude that has been trained to believe, act, and behave in a certain way acceptable to societal expectations. However, what if the expected attitude is transcended to create alternative versions of how power should be, as the "willingness" of the individual and collective in society moves in that direction and moves society in that direction. Willing the attitude is considered in **Chapter 10: Nietzsche** in terms of morality (good/evil, inner/surface, customs, values); nihilism (no limit or boundary, or no goal or destination, is one suggestive of ongoing expansiveness in human perceptive capabilities); perceiving instincts (milieu, ego, happy, dissimulation); good and evil (gap between first and second nature, falsehoods); Zarathustra will to truth (freeing of one's expression of self beyond religious limitations of expected behavior and cognitive development, returning to one's natural state, overcoming power); and will to power (the will is required to power one's life and in a sense the will to power is simply being alive, being alive provides the power to will, the will within and without, multiple wills within).

To play the powered game of potentiality to actuality involves a mixture of theory, imagination, knowledge acquisition, and resultant practical implementation. Also, to do the powered game well—in terms of flexibility, effectiveness of action, and the sustainability to retain gains made—becomes an art form. An art form of a mindfulness and responsiveness to those that have performed the powered game previously and have thought about the most essential ingredients for success in power and applying these principles for oneself to emulate powered success at one's level of potential to actual. **Chapter 11: The Art of War or the Art of Power** offers thirteen ingredients or directives to be good at doing power, but not always for the common good as the oneself may hold sway at times. The thirteen are laying plans, waging war, sheathed sword, tactics, energy, weak points and strong, maneuvering, variation of tactics, army on the march, terrain, the nine situations, attack by fire, and the use of spies.

The combined face of these eleven faces offer up potentialities and actualities of what power is, does, and aspires to. For instance, its illusiveness and directness, its visible and invisible, its consciousness and unconsciousness, its presence and absence, its inclusiveness and exclusives, its singular (the oneself or individual) and collective (society); its structure and unstructured; its miniature and universal, its…power of being power. It is time to face off with these faces.

CHAPTER 1

Aristotle

The Greek philosopher Aristotle or Ἀριστοτέλης (384–322 BC), from 18 to 37 years of age, was part of Plato's Academy in Athens. After Plato passed away, Aristotle moved from Platonism to empiricism (pragmatism, experimentation, observation, practicality) (Barnes 1995, 16), judging that people's ideas and thoughts and knowledge base were centered on perception. Since what is perceived and how it is perceived are a process of filtration, empiric disposition is already colored by what societal system one lives within, so what one perceives is filtered by that system. An implication is no one can possess "pure" thought in the context of thinking outside or beyond societal space; hence, thought is subjected to the influence of how one lives. Therefore, thoughts replicate that living system, which causes repetition, adaptation, enhancements, and reductions but not anything "purely" new.

Universal

The universal of living system, life, or of society is a philosophical purpose of Aristotle, as it was with Plato. Diverse interpretations of how the universal plays its part saw Aristotelian ontology seeing the universal in particular things, the essence of things, whereas Plato saw the universal existing separate from particular things but connected as their standard or model. Aristotle's way of seeing is a duality of induction and deduction, whereas Plato is deductive from a priori principles (Jori 2003). However, whatever way the universal is performing as the benchmark of life in terms of its involvement, the fact that it is the reference point of how things are as they are indicates the universal as a powerful presence. This should not be surprising as universal implies worldwide, widespread, collective, total, complete, and unanimous. Also, time is on the universal side and not on the human side. For instance,

As time never fails, and the universe is eternal, neither the Tanais, nor the Nile, can have flowed forever. The places where they rise were once dry, and there is a limit to their operations, but there is none to time. So also of all other rivers; they spring up and they perish; and the sea also continually deserts some lands and invades others. The same tracts, therefore, of the earth are not some always sea, and others always continents, but everything changes in the course of time. (Lyell 1832, 17)

So, from this "earth time," humans cannot gauge universal space meaningfully by human time and its rigid digitalization or making use of one or two generational first-hand memories. Or appreciating fully the bigger picture of human behavioral patterns demonstrating repetitiveness of action, inaction, struggling for control of resources and what are perceived as vital resources. This is because human performance of power is only of short-term duration over the universal of the earth, which is understandable, as human lifespan dictates that this is so. As Aristotle says, earth changes are imperceptible when measured against life duration, that they are not noticed, and the migrations of people after great catastrophes and movement to other regions ensure the event is forgotten (Lyell 1832).

Empedocles (a Greek pre-Socratic philosopher) offered four elements that make up the space of life and its universal: Earth, which is cold and dry; a solid. Water, which is cold and wet; a liquid. Air, which is hot and wet; a gas. Finally, Fire, which is hot and dry; plasma and heat. Solid, liquid, and gas are states that can be changed with the introduction or withdrawing of fire. It is the elements of earth, water, air, and fire, the four powerful sentinels of life, that determine life quality or lack of it, as these four in combination or in isolation can abruptly cut short one's life or subject one to a slow demise. Thus, an autonomy of fourfold power that can be beyond what humans attempt to aspire to in their dominion over nature. Aristotle spoke of a fifth element, aether, which is a substance of divinity that is the heavenly bodies and spheres, namely stars and planets. Hence, the universal expands to the universe, in which the mysticism of the seen but untouched visions of the skies creates curiosities and imagined explanations of what they are and why they are. Essentially, trying to understand the universal through these five filters of power explanations of prescientific "rationality" was seldom far from the comprehension of what life may be about.

Causing Power

Aristotle fathomed that the reason for anything happening/occurring is influenced by four diverse concurrent active causal factors. Firstly, *Material cause*, i.e., the material of which something is constructed from. This is the material that makes up a thing, live or inanimate, giving it its structural space and sense of permanence within its eventual limited temporal nature. A materiality that is almost a token, symbol, representation, a simulacrum of the universal actuality within that actuality of physical presence, since it is only a fleeting flame of power expression that is all too soon extinguished along universal time. Secondly, *Formal cause*, is form, i.e., how the material has been assembled. This gives the material a sense of uniqueness, an identity, a flag saying what it is, adding another layer to the tokenism. Formal cause can be present as of itself created by nature, but it can also be created in the imaginations of those who create form. For example, transforming one material into another or revealing another form cloaked within the surface form of a thing or indeed a person. This is because the surface character is not necessarily the "truer" character beneath, but it may be revealed by power manipulation as one human encounters another; through performance, ritual, or base intimidation; and both stakeholders in the "partnership" revealing another or other forms hidden beneath. Summing up, the formal cause is the idea existing originally as exemplar in the mind of the sculptor/agenda setter/life manipulator, and in the second place as intrinsic, determining cause, embodied in the matter of the "alive" and by association the "dead," which in a sense is an extension of life as an altered form. Or perhaps vice versa.

Thirdly, *Efficient cause*, the primary source. It is that from which the considered change progresses, revealing what makes of what is made and what causes change of what is changed. These relate to the input of the "dead" and "alive" of those influencing their particular "dead" and "alives" of matter, as all these types of agents are the source of change, movement, and inertial. Hence, causality as the performance of cause and effect. The performance is portrayed as the visible happening, occurrence, and agent or agency of particular events or state of affairs or affairs of state. It is a process of involvement of the visible power solution and resolution, from its invisible instigation of those of dead and alive dispositions causing other deads and alives in matter creation and recreation or that "matter" within creation. The *Purpose cause* or cause of the purpose is the fourth, i.e., the sake of which a thing exists or is done, incorporating both purposeful and instrumental actions and activities. This teleos is the purpose, maybe functional, that something is intending to serve, e.g., be of service. This is a motivational cause of wants, needs, and desires and of ethical considerations and beliefs of a spiritual nature.

Things are also reciprocal to each other, causing each other, "causing" Aristotle to consider a circular causality as a relation of mutual dependence/ influence of cause on effect. The same thing can also cause opposing effects. In addition, being there or not being there creates diverse outcomes, and either way the aim or purpose can result in an event. Also, placing energy or will of purpose toward a particular goal may result in that goal's realization, and the goal of power acquisition would be part of that. Aristotle discerned two means of causation —proper (prior) causation and accidental (chance) causation. A chance occurs by one's will of purposeful intention producing an unintended result, and the trick is to push for that unintentionality, see it as a fortunate developing circumstance. Thus, sometimes, power acquisition is not always the result of cold calculation, but acting toward that power gain is essential, i.e., the power of the acting and of the fact that action is taking place. Aristotle suggested that luck must involve choice (deliberation is taking place), a trait reserved for humans; e.g., "what is not capable of action cannot do anything by chance" (Aristotle 1983, *Physics*, 2.6). Whether it is only the human species that retains the "rights" for deliberate choice is questionable; however, it is deliberation that produces difference on what was before to what is now, with potential for change into the future.

Actual and Potential

All causes, proper and supplementary, can be viewed as potential or as actual. Potential of a thing is its capacity to be transformed into something else or trans-forms something else. Potentially beings can either "act" (poiein) or "be acted upon" (paschein), which can be either learned or innate, and the conditions of change should be favorable and uninhibited. The key thing here is change, from one form into another—Becoming. In Physics (Book III) (Aristotle 1983) and On Generation and Corruption 319b–320a (De Haas and Mansfeld 2004), Aristotle saw the becoming from growth and reduction (a quantity change), movement (a spatial change), and adaptation (a quality change). Change implies motion from one state to another, of which Aristotle expressed motion as the actuality of a potentiality (Aristotle 1983). Actuality is the accomplishment of the finished motion of the potentiality:

> For that for the sake of which a thing is, is its principle, and the becoming is for the sake of the end; and the actuality is the end, and it is for the sake of this that the potentiality is acquired. (Aristotle, n.d., *Metaphysics* IX 1050a5–1050a10)

Power retains potentiality and, depending on causal interference or application, can produce an actuality of performance. However, it may be just as well that many power potentialities remain in a "dormant" state and do not experience an actual becoming, since these extra power plays would significantly add further layers to societal workings, causing greater marginalization and stratification of societal universals and particulars. Aristotle concluded that actuality is prior to potentiality in substantiality, time, and formula; the potential being (matter) and the actual one (form) are one and the same thing (Aristotle, n.d., *Metaphysics* VIII 1045a–1045b). In the context of power, its actuality is already of a form that can practice power performance, because it supplies the potential to be actual. In essence, the potential would not be so without the actual, and the actual would not be so without the potential. Thus, power cannot be generated out of thin air, as it has to have a substantiality, a retained capacity, to be.

A particular substance, including power, is a combination of both matter and form (Aristotle, n.d., Metaphysics VII). Aristotle differentiated the matter of the substance as the substratum or the stuff that composes it (Metaphysics VIII), and matter is what makes up something; i.e., for humans it would be the blood, bones, skin, organs, and water. The form of the substance is the actual human, the coverings of all the matter, and allows identification as "human." The formula that gives the components is the account of the matter, and the formula that gives the differentia is the account of the form (Aristotle, n.d., *Metaphysics* VIII 1043a10–1043a30). Considering power, this would be identified as the account of the form it overtly displays and impositions, and the account of the power matter is the constituent parts of power. What these constituent parts may be will retain not only a sense of uniqueness, depending on the context and scale of power being applied, but also a sense of commonality with all types of power plays, since all types would replicate certain causes and effects, which is the essence of power.

Scala Naturae

Nothing is more remarkable than [Aristotle's] efforts to [exhibit] the relationships
of living things as a scala naturae. (Singer 1931)

Aristotle's History of Animals graded organisms along a hierarchical "Ladder of
Life" (scala naturae or Great Chain of Being), locating them depending on structural and functional complexity, so that "higher" organisms demonstrated greater
vitality and movement ability (Singer 1931, 44). Similarly, Aristotle assumed that
creatures resided along a graded scale of perfection from plants on *up* to man (Mayr
1982). His system consisted of eleven grades, arranged according to the degree
to which they are infected with potentiality, expressed in their form at birth. The
scala naturae is based on an assumption that the immense schematic that is life and
all species that exist within its space of being are subjected to power differentials.
For instance, this thing called power exists but is divided up on an unequal basis
depending on how a species is classified in the great scheme of things.

  With Aristotle being a human, his perspective on how things are is biased from
the said human perspective. His "natural" naturae sets the human at the pinnacle
of power on Earth and seeing its potential as the leading force. Consequently, the
constructed Chain of Being reflects dominant tendencies within the human psyche,
but it must be wondered if all other animal and plant species see it that way. They
may have their own Chain of Being versions, setting themselves at the pinnacle,
and perhaps not even acknowledging humans at all. Within the human version of
the Chain of Being, the pinnacle position would be subdivided into different human groupings, depending on cultural background, creed, and color. This human
hierarchical system would "naturally" be reordered depending on who is charged
(and in charge) with setting out the human "order of things," i.e., different orders
of cultural elitism vying for the top spot to enforce their version of power.

  The version of power may be militaristic to intimidate by force or show of force,
i.e., the potential to do force. Or the version may be intellectual. Aristotle deemed
that intellectual purposes, i.e., final causes, channeled all natural processes. Such
a teleological (relating to or involving the explanation of phenomena in terms of
the purpose they serve rather than of the cause by which they arise [philosophy]
or relating to the doctrine of design and purpose in the material world [theology])
view gave Aristotle cause to justify his observed data as an expression of formal
design. The formal design served phenomena and purpose in the material world,
being one of manipulation and control over others. Also getting and retaining
control over oneself to allow a strong base to exert influence over one's other.

Natural processes, if not natural to begin with, become so over the course of time as people lose the memory of initial or original constructed behavioral patterns, and, hence, what may have been there before is forgotten. So, this new way of thinking and doing becomes the natural normal and the resultant power differential is accepted as that is the way things are. Perhaps this "natural" way is the way of things, in that a power differential will happen anyway. For instance, Aristotle may be right in observing natural processes as natural—or at least as natural as one can perceive of what is going on around them—based on the trappings of societal learning from birth, of which will be skewed to certain ways of intellectual thinking, viewing, and doing. Also, Aristotle may be remarkable in constructing an imaginative Great Chain of Being, but not so remarkable in feeling the necessity of actually doing so, as this is just another example of creating a living environment to apply standards and rules to, with the aim of realizing one's power potential and hoped-for actuality.]

Memory

According to Aristotle,

> memory is the ability to hold a perceived experience in your mind and to have the ability to distinguish between the internal "appearance" and an occurrence in the past. (Bloch 2007, 12)

Memory as mental picture (phantasm) is defined in De Anima as an appearance that is imprinted on the part of the body that forms a memory. The imprinted mental picture on the bodily organ is the concluding outcome of the whole sense-perception process. It is irrelevant if the experience was seen or heard, as every experience ends up as a mental image in memory (Carruthers 2007). Aristotle utilized "memory" for two fundamental abilities —(1) preserving experience in the mnemonic imprint resulting from sensation and (2) emotional concern that happens concurrently with the imprint due to significant happenings at a specific time and managing distinctive content and context. This results in memory being of the past (Bloch 2007), responsiveness of the present, and the future as speculation, manipulation, and calculation.

Memory is a never-ending imprint acquisition, and, through all the types of sense perception, people incessantly construct fresher imprints of experienced things. To "extract" these imprints, people search the memory itself (Warren 1921). When people recall experiences, they stimulate certain previous experiences until they have stimulated the one that was needed (Warren 1921). When setting a sociocultural agenda, memory recall can be "trained" to certain ways of thinking, being, and doing, and the process of recollection is the collecting of imprints that provide a person with an identity, a history. This so-called self-directed process of bringing to the surface recollections depends on the scope of mnemonic capabilities of a being (human or animal) and the abilities the human or animal possesses (Carruthers 2007).

Self-directed is partially questioned since what people know is through a combination of the immediacy of the space they live within and the overall space of society and beyond, i.e., beyond in the context of blurred boundaries of sovereign place, particularly when capitalism is involved. The self-directed aspect may appear to be of the self, and taking direction from the self, but the pure weight of capitalistic processes and training people to commodify in ways that advantage profit encourages an acquiescence of this is the "right" way to be. For instance, the power of memory persuasion and repeated similar capitalistic imprints to reinforce particular belief systems and memory experience maintains the capitalist monopoly. Accordingly, memories of the past are reinforced by similar memories of the present, which in turn encourage future memories of a comparable disposition and positionality. When an "imprint" is recalled, it may bring forth a large group of related "imprints" (Warren 1921, 296).

People manipulated to be "influenced" can only work effectively if memory recall is possible. Also, of certain types of memory recall, Aristotle considered that the thought chain finishing in recalling certain imprints brought together three associations: similarity, contrast, and contiguity (the sequential occurrence or proximity of stimulus and response, causing their association in the mind). These three were Aristotle's Laws of Association. Association is the power innate in a mental state, which operates on the unexpressed remains of former experiences, allowing them to rise and be recalled (Warren 1921). Retrieving imprints is not an instant process, since an in-between conduit is required and placed in past experiences to acknowledge the previous and present experiences. This delayed process is mitigated by the "placed" memories of those that power.

Ethics

Aristotelian ethics is to discover the purpose of human life, stressing a teleological approach. This teleology may be separated into cause and serve, or these two may be a continuation along a same theme of production. For instance, the original cause may have been constructed to serve the purpose, which reinforces the original, consequently reinforcing the ongoing service. Thus, a teleology of intentional power, a potential and actuality relationship. An ethical environment is produced because ethics would not be of the same regard or itemized from the same list for every individual. This is where ethical tensions would emerge between spatial combatants jostling for position in the finite of society and trying to be that society.

As Aristotle saw happiness as life's purpose since regarding it as the ultimate good, whereas all other goods are transitional, these others being tools, levers, manipulated events, or structures to get to this thing called "happiness," they are desired and acquired to reach the happy state. The uncertainty within this pursuit of the contented life is that the happy space and its "goodness" may contain undercurrents of "badness" that paradoxically are intimate aspects that create the good. For the "good" is not necessarily decent, moral, noble, worthy, and wholesome. Although for the protagonist, she or he may regard themselves as all of these, but others may have different ideas of what "good" actually implies. In this manner, one may experience happiness or what is imagined to be of a happy disposition, while others may not be so happy as their unhappiness feeds the happiness of the "good" guy, i.e., who controls and who is controlled. Also, maintaining the euphoria and sustainability of the happy place can cause anxiety and unhappiness, and a desire to get back to that heavenly feeling, once again subsuming the potential happiness of others to do so.

The previous paragraph creates happiness as a hierarchical skewed system of happy and good at the pinnacle, descending to unhappy and bad, and degrees of that along the slippery slope of power effects, and of all being two sides of the same coin. To protect against, or at least limit this duality of good/bad and happy/unhappy, Aristotle deduces that the means of happiness and to make happiness mean and ultimately the purpose of human life is virtue (Aristotle 1934a). Virtue contains choice and habit, and "correct" choices can add to and sustain a virtuous habit, powered by one's character and temperament influenced by past decision-making. Of course, the viability of the whole depends on what sort of decision-making accumulates to the present place of virtue, because again like "good," what are the measurements of virtue to achieve a level of integrity, honesty, and morality.

Aristotle recognized the difficulty in delimiting what virtue and, by association, good, may be. So, he adopted a broad range of acceptability, as the virtuous choice was a mean residing between extremities—defect and excess. From this, perhaps being good and virtuous is problematic to pin down or it is of common occurrence, when staying away from extremes. The commonality suggests that feeling good and virtuous is widespread, with its existence also appreciated in a widespread manner. Thus, being and feeling "good" and "virtuous" is a matter of perspective that may involve not only some collective consensus but also individual consensus. As a result, it is the power plays in a society that backdrop people's search for happiness and virtue but which do not necessarily result in the "common good. "

Considering continence and incontinence, i.e., in this context the weakness or strength of the will, all wrongdoing came from ignorance according to Socrates. However, Aristotle saw "right" is acknowledged, but people do not act on it and do the "right" thing. In this fashion, an incontinent person retains potential knowledge but in actuality does not apply it. Aristotle sees desire as a prohibiting factor in stopping the potential to become actual at the judicious moment. This is because desire overrides the common good, as individual advantage resides within desire and forms a potential aspiration toward an actuality of "bettering" oneself, or the materiality of oneself. In essence, acquiring a bit more for one's self of power." However, this may not be recognized as such, as in the process of absorbing more power, as it is simply what humans do, i.e., to try and improve their lot in life and of life. When "improving," power is not necessarily a finite product or resource, as it may have an infinite quality about it, but what is available at any current moment in time will fluctuate between the power players. So, some will gain more absorption, while others will lose some of their power capacity, as power is not a loyal servant or loyal master of societal ceremonies. Hence, people need to work to maintain what power they have or wish to gain, since the tendency is to lose it, if one is not careful and prudent in planning.

Ethics is practical as opposed to theoretical, according to Aristotle. The target is to become and do good rather than knowing, in and of itself (see the Nicomachean Ethics), although the knowing assists with the practical harshness that life can be. It is significant that the actuality takes precedence over the potential in this ethical performance. Perhaps to be ethical in a meaningful way does involve dealing face-to-face with the everyday demands of life. A reality check! Aristotle postulated that virtue relates to the proper function (ergon) of a thing, and humans must have functions specific to and for themselves. This function is an active aspect of one's psyche (one's soul) in harmony with reason (logos). In his discourse *On the Soul* (De Anima), Aristotle offers three soul perspectives; the vegetative soul, the sensitive soul, and the rational soul. Humans are "rational" and connected to the vegetative and can develop and sustain. Also, like the sensitive, can undergo sensations and enjoy movement in the immediate space. What the rational does offer, which stands apart from the other two, is the reception of forms of other things and applying comparison to them. Ultimately, one's ethics can be one's subjective motivation to seek power, be that at an unconscious or conscious level of self-awareness and may be for the "good" of the person rather than the good of society. Although one may inadvertently contribute to the other.

City as Political Society

for the whole must of necessity be prior to the part. (Aristotle 1998, *Politics*, 1253a19–1253a24)

The city, for Aristotle, was regarded as a natural community. A total asset that held the highest importance in terms of being prior to the family, of which the family was prior to the individual. It is the wholesomeness of the city that generates its power, the aggregate of all that belongs within its spatial and, hence, political influence. "Man is by nature a political animal" and humanity's defining factor among others in the animal kingdom is its rationality (Aristotle 2009, 320–321). It is this human form of rationality labeled as such—for other species would retain their own rational behaviors—that creates the existence termed *politics*. Aristotle viewed politics as more of an organism and not so much as a machine, and, as a grouping of associated components, which left on their own would cease to exist (Ebenstein and Ebenstein 2002).

An organism can be considered under an assortment of labels—animal, plant, virus, bacterium, being, beast, entity, system, organization, cooperative, coalition. From these, an organism is not a "clean" and "pure" place to live and do business and retains layered challenges to ensure the "city as society" performs. The "natural" in Aristotle's version of the city tilts toward the cleansing end of the organism definition spectrum, since the city (polis) as political "community" or "partnership" (koinōnia) is there to negate injustice, encourage economic constancy, and allowing some citizens access to the "good" and the performance of beautiful acts; "The political partnership must be regarded, therefore, as being for the sake of noble actions, not for the sake of living together" (Aristotle 1998, *Politics*, 1281a1). Here, hints of exclusivity are apparent, as some in the city or, by extension, the society, enjoy a privileged existence and can aim for these "noble actions," which may not benefit the "common" people or be of concern to them.

Part of a speech by the character "Aristotle" in the book *Protrepticus* illustrates the exclusive "intelligent" nature of the "natural" city:

> For we all agree that the most excellent man should rule, i.e., the supreme by nature, and that the law rules and alone is authoritative; but the law is a kind of intelligence, i.e., a discourse based on intelligence. And again, what standard do we have, what criterion of good things, that is more precise than the intelligent man? For all that this man will choose, if the choice is based on his knowledge, are good things and their contraries are bad. And since everybody chooses most of all what conforms to their own proper dispositions (a just man choosing to live justly, a man with bravery to live bravely, likewise a self-controlled man to live with self-control), it is clear that the intelligent man will choose most of all to be intelligent; for this is the function of that capacity. Hence it's evident that, according to the most authoritative judgment, intelligence is supreme among goods. (Hutchinson and Johnson 2015, 22)

It is questionable that "everybody chooses most of all what conforms to their own proper disposition," as one's perceived position in the city and its accepted norms and values to enforce that would be influenced by what everyone can conceivably "choose" to do or be. For instance, during Aristotle's time and space only citizens could be involved in the running of the city-state. Those excluded from political decisions were slaves, resident aliens, women, children, and occasionally the working class who had little or no leisure time for ongoing and full involvement. Alternatively, the included were the intelligentsia who were regarded as the superlative of the city, the ones possessing the capacity to run the show. However, the characterization shown is perhaps too simplistic, as "man" would not just possess one attribute. Also, it may well be that society conveniently emphasizes particular qualities or quality as "special" to advantage some individuals over the rest.

Additionally, the Law of Nature helps with inequality as well as quality, and in a sense overrides the intelligentsia, and the city as a natural community is central to the Law of Nature. To illustrate, the implication of "law of nature" from an Aristotelian context is not a system of rules or statues created by intellectual origins but as repeating inequalities and equalities in the nature of things. These justify the uneven dissemination of actions and things, for Aristotle regards the Law of Nature as above the Law of Man (Pakaluk 2011):

The Law of Nature is so unalterable, that God himself cannot change it. For tho' the Power of God be infinite, yet we may say, that there are some Things to which this infinite Power does not extend, because they cannot be expressed by Propositions that contain any Sense, but manifestly imply a Contradiction. For instance then, as God himself cannot effect, that twice two should not be four; so neither can he, that what is intrinsically Evil should not be Evil. (Aristotle 1934b, *Nicomachean Ethics*, II.6, 1107a8–1107a17)

The paradox here is that the Law of Nature is constructed from the Law of Man in terms of interpreting what nature may actually be or mean, understood by the only way humans can understand, i.e., from a human perspective of nature. Also, by the only way humans can act and perform, from a human perspective of themselves within and without of nature. Relating to the "natural" act, Aristotle believed imitation is natural to mankind and constitutes one of mankind's advantages over animals (Aristotle 2004, *Poetics* IV). However, the effectiveness of imitation depends on what is being repeated and who benefits from the repetition.

Imitation in the Rule of Law or at least following its intended message was appreciated by the American Founding Fathers (Pakaluk 2011), who valued Aristotle's doggedness on the Rule of Law, particularly where law is said to be reason or intelligence (nous), free from passion, and, as it were, the governance of God (Aristotle 1998).

Rule of Law

Aristotle's beliefs in how society or the city should run politically was utilized as moderating guidance by the American Founders

- Government should govern for the good of the people, not for the good of those in power.
- There is a natural aristocracy, and skilled statecraft arranges things so that this element acquires authority, or, failing that, blends democratic and oligarchic influences in society to approximate to that outcome.
- Mixed regimes are better than pure regimes, because they are more stable.
- The best form of government in nearly all circumstances involves the balancing of aspects of all three pure regimes (kingship, aristocracy, and timocracy).

- A pure democracy can easily turn into a tyranny of the majority (Pakaluk 2011, 1)

Aristotle advocated a calculating act of how power is used, recognizing the vulnerability and instability of how power can be performed in terms of maintaining an extended period of power sharing for most societal members as possible. Hence, many, rather than the few or one, benefit, but if not monitored and policed at a virtuous level of inquiry, the tendency of exercising power is toward the minority and the minority of that minority. As such, the instability of power for the masses gravitates toward stability of power for the few, if not governed by checks and balances.

As within the majority of societal movement, people practice business. They are in the business of doing business, and power acquisition drives business processes, allowing for a greater choice and scope to do so. These greater business processes attract greater power to complement and enhance the process, thus potentialities becoming actualities. When people become business professionals in a successful sense, they graduate to expertise in business that, "there is held to be no limit to wealth and possessions" (Aristotle 1998, *Politics*, 1257a1). Aristotle regards this as a predicament since a limitless environment evolves to aim for this thing called wealth, negating the actuality of virtue and "real" happiness. Thus, these "wealthy" people

> proceed on the supposition that they should either preserve or increase without limit their property in money. The cause of this state is that they are serious about living, but not about living well; and since that desire of theirs is without limit, they also desire what is productive of unlimited things. (Aristotle 1998, *Politics*, 1257b38)

This results in the nonwealthy as limited in their life choices to perhaps an absolute nonmaneuverability of expression, performance, and movement. A life relegated to the margins. A powerless life. However, in a sense, all in the unequal power system, both the wealthy and nonwealthy, retain power and powerlessness, respectively, without each possessing quality of life or living; however which way one measures what quality potential and actual implies and also what wealth infers.

Between the wealthy and nonwealthy, Aristotle regards partnerships as a significant component to make society work and one linking "persons who cannot exist without one another" (Aristotle 1998, *Politics*, 1252a27). For example, within the demands of "pure" nature and the survivability of species, humans included, one essential link is of the female and male. Another example, from a human perspective, although other species (plants and animals) do practice subordinate linkages of other species and within the same species to maintain the species sustainability and enhancement, is of "the naturally ruling and rules, on account of preservation" (Aristotle 1998, *Politics*, 1252a30), i.e., slavery. In this context, preservation means both the naturally managed slave and naturally governing master require each other, to be, and this state of affairs advantages both the master and the slave.

It may appear odd that the slave enjoys advantage in this centralized and marginalized relationship, but in a warped sense she or he does. Warped in that a place in society is given, one has a place, and one "knows" their place, although they may not be "happy" about it. There is some form of shelter, food, security, and protection, be these of a precarious disposition. Also, of a precarious connectivity between the two parties involved. For example, in the modern take on this, the wealthy could be regarded as the "factory" owners, the business owners, the major corporation shareholders, and the "slaves" could be the unemployed, fixed-wage earners or small business owners relying on big business for their livelihood. Hence, the "slaves" in a sense are still connected to the wealthy and working directly and indirectly for them. So, with the ancient Athenian societal space and the modern connecting in their partnership of structural repetition, perhaps only the technologies of their times create a surface veneer of difference and the type and intensity of the slavery space influencing the beneficial "sharing" of resources.

Within this symbiotic system of uneasiness, Aristotle looks to those that are beyond the city and society:

> He who is without a city through nature rather than chance is either a mean sort or superior to man. (1253a3)...(and) One who is incapable of participating or who is in need of nothing through being self-sufficient is no part of a city, and so is either a beast or a god. (1253a27) (Aristotle 1998, *Politics*)

Consequently, those without a city who are positioned separate from it can be of the lowest or the highest status. The lowest in terms of having no appreciated functional contribution to society, seen as valueless, and the highest in terms of running and manipulating society for their own gain. However, to do the "highest" in an absolute successful way, if absolute can be ever fully realized, control from a position "outside" of the city/societal space is paramount. To illustrate, the conductor of society cannot be part of the societal orchestra and yet cannot be completely disconnected from it. This is another example of Aristotle's necessary partnership—that the one cannot exist without the other. Existence would still be possible, but the level, in the case of the conductor, would be more of a potential than an actual or actuals. Achieving the level of divination/conductor is only available to a select few or the One, so an unlikely scenario for the vast majority, but man becoming the beast is far more likely and happens: "For just as man is the best of the animals when completed, when separated from law and adjudication he is the worst of all" (Aristotle 1998, *Politics*, 1253a30). Thus, there is ever a need for power control to regulate and limit the beast within the human!

The Ambiguousness of Human Nature

Since politics and moral knowledge originate from human construction and sociocultural filtered interpretation, these produce ambiguity of what they are:

> Problems of what is noble and just, which politics examines, present so much variety and irregularity that some people believe that they exist only by convention and not by nature…Therefore, in a discussion of such subjects, which has to start with a basis of this kind, we must be satisfied to indicate the truth with a rough and general sketch: when the subject and the basis of a discussion consist of matters that hold good only as a general rule, but not always, the conclusions reached must be of the same order. (Aristotle 1934a, Nicomachean Ethics Book 1, 1094b14)

This ambiguity allows freedom of movement and spaces of occupation for how power is appreciated and manipulated, of which the variety and irregularity that are produced can only be steered toward generalities that allow for a commonality of negotiated acceptance. This is because a precise definition of what is "just," "good," and "truth" is an elusive concept. Therefore, Aristotle avoids rules that are set and, as an alternative, advocate's the "knowing" and "whys" of the correct course of action when considering political and ethical challenges:

> The end [or goal] of politics is the best of ends; and the main concern of politics is to engender a certain character in the citizens and to make them good and disposed to perform noble actions. (Aristotle 1934a, *Nicomachean Ethics*, Book 1, 1099b30)

Aristotle saw partnership in politics and ethics and restricted entry for those accessing ethical and virtuous life to those "doing" politics. For example, "Citizens" had access to political power and noncitizens did not, and this political community voiced moral education over the city from positions of privilege. However, the ambiguity of this power differential is ironic. Ironic in the sense of the community of politics not practicing what they are preaching, in terms of equity for all, of politics allegedly producing a living environment for people to entertain complete human, ethical, and happy lives, which reinforces political involvement in the correct manner:

> We become just by the practice of just actions, self-controlled by exercising self-control, and courageous by performing acts of courage...Lawgivers make the citizens good by inculcating [good] habits in them, and this is the aim of every lawgiver; if he does not succeed in doing that, his legislation is a failure. It is in this that a good constitution differs from a bad one. (Aristotle 1934a, *Nicomachean Ethics*, Book 1, 1103a30)

From this, the lawgivers require a consciousness of restraint in the type of legislation fabricated to avoid accusations and actualities of "mis-use" of power. Within the city network of relationships,

> It is clear that all partnerships aim at some good, and that the partnership that is most authoritative of all and embraces all the others does so particularly, and aims at the most authoritative good of all. This is what is called the city or the political partnership. (Aristotle 1998, *Politics*, 1252a3, III. 12)

The strength of the "authoritative good" is in its acknowledgment and embracement of the "others," as all like to feel they have a voice that matters and is heard and considered in decision-making. However, there would be "others" and other "others," both in ancient Athens and modern society, who were/are not heard and effectively silenced.

Since humans are of diverse stock, this encourages the formation of cities, as these places grant specialization and a heightened degree of self-reliance, i.e., wholesomeness of the city. This autonomy is maintained by "reciprocal equality," especially in cities where "persons are free and equal." However, in these places of apparent uniformity of expression and performance, "all cannot rule at the same time, but each rules for a year or according to some other arrangement or period of time. In this way, then, it results that all rule" (Aristotle 1998, *Politics*,

1261a30). But, on an ancient Athens day, the "all" are a select and preselected breed, an ambiguous usage of grand claims that in actuality are restricted to a set few members of the city.

The Not So Much Ambiguity of Human Nature to Possess

Within these annual rules, Aristotle recognized the self-centered aspect of humans:

> What belongs in common to the most people is accorded the least care: they take thought for their own things above all, and less about things common, or only so much as falls to each individually. (Aristotle 1998, *Politics*, 1261b32)

These acts are shades of the beast, and Aristotle accused human depravity (Aristotle 1998) of encouraging conflict, rather than blaming the availability of common property. For to counter depravity is the already-mentioned moderation of desire, shown overtly by those "adequately educated by the laws" (Aristotle 1998, *Politics*, 1266b31), and dangers of desire of material acquisition points toward troubles as common people crave limitless prosperity (Aristotle 1998, *Politics*, 1267b3). Also, those of less common stock, the elite, get involved in dispute due to inequality of honors (Aristotle 1998, *Politics*, 1266b38), resulting in an attitude of conceit and superiority over the "common" people. Control through ownership is key here, for who owns has power over those who do not. From this, Aristotle plays the moderating card to smooth the rough edges of power:

> Thus it is the greatest good fortune for those who are engaged in politics to have a middling and sufficient property, because where some possess very many things and others nothing, either [rule of] the people in its extreme form must come into being, or unmixed oligarchy, or—as a result of both of these excesses—tyranny. For tyranny arises from the most headstrong sort of democracy and from oligarchy, but much less often from the middling sorts [of regime] and those close to them. (Aristotle 1998, *Politics*, 1295b39)

To moderate "ownership" leverage, Book III advocates for the law to rule, summarizing much of what has been said so far in Aristotelian philosophy:

> One who asks the law to rule, therefore, is held to be asking god and intellect alone to rule, while one who asks man adds the beast. Desire is a thing of this

sort; and spiritedness perverts rulers and the best men. Hence law is intellect without appetite. (Aristotle 1998, *Politics*, 1287a28)

Since the law is created by humans, there is an inbuilt bias. An inbuilt desire to construct society and the city to preordained courses of action and heading, but the prior of law over present encounters allows a neutrality of sorts, allowing the judge a limited lack of prejudice when "judging"…"For where the laws do not rule there is no regime" (Aristotle 1998, *Politics*, 1292b30); however, a regime of moderation stays in place longer. This is the power of the passiveness of moderation, but if there is not an ongoing moderating presence "in place," then:

> the lesser engage in factional conflict in order to be equal; those who are equal, in order to be greater. (1302a29)…As for the things over which they engage in factional conflict, these are profit and honor and their opposites…They are stirred up further by arrogance, by fear, by preeminence, by contempt, by disproportionate growth, by electioneering, by underestimation, by [neglect of] small things, and by dissimilarity. (Aristotle 1998, *Politics*, 1302a33)

So, there is an emotional/emotive motivation and competitive nature to grasp at power and yet at more power, but to counter this is essentially that the key to power moderation is "balancing" power.

The Balance of Power

Aristotle outlines half-a-dozen regimes:

> monarchy (rule by one man for the common good), aristocracy (rule by a few for the common good), and polity (rule by the many for the common good); the flawed or deviant regimes are tyranny (rule by one man in his own interest), oligarchy (rule by the few in their own interest), and democracy (rule by the many in their own interest). (Aristotle 1998, *Politics*, Book 111, chap. 7)

He also arranges them in terms of what is "good"; monarchy at the summit, aristocracy second, followed by polity, democracy, oligarchy, and tyranny (Aristotle 1998, *Politics*, 1289a38). It is noteworthy to see democracy in fourth place, as in present-day considerations, at least from the Western powers, it is advocated as the most desirable form for equity of potential for people. Nevertheless, perhaps it is the most efficient form for those in big business to maximize the potentiality to actuality of profit, control, and possession of power, and the democratic rhetoric disguises this, so all think they have opportunity to express themselves, materially and personally.

To realize a "balance" of power, a delicate state of affairs to reach for and sustain, the challenge for those of particular political persuasions to do so is the influence of their own inbuilt ideological bias. For instance, Aristotle offers perspectives from the oligarchs and democrats. The former is a power structure residing with a small number of people (Wikipedia, n.d.-a), and the latter favoring the masses involving egalitarianism and social equality (Wikipedia, n.d.-b), essentially a realm in which the power is spread more evenly. However, when both groups retain their perspective concerning the dissemination of political power to "obtain" justice, both are incorrect, since "the judgment concerns themselves, and most people are bad judges concerning their own things" (Aristotle 1998, *Politics*, 1280a14). For instance, oligarchs insist that their weightier wealth equates to superior power and, hence, they govern. Whereas, democrats see everyone is free equally; thus, all have the same proportion of political power, and, as the majority have little or no wealth, essentially the poor govern. Working within these two extremes of power acquisition, one can return to Aristotle's connectivity to allow for a "best fit" societal political system. This being that "the defining principle of a good mixture of democracy and oligarchy is that it should be possible for the same polity to be spoken of as either a democracy or an oligarchy" (Aristotle 1998, *Politics*, 1294b14). In this way, the system is seen as one of neither and both, which will maintain it, "because none of the parts of the city generally would wish to have another regime" (Aristotle 1998, *Politics*, 1294b38). Hence, a power complementary act.

This is a potentially theoretically nice "dwelling space" (Heidegger 1962), "where the multitude of middling persons predominates either over both of the extremities together or over one alone, there a lasting polity is capable of existing" (Aristotle 1998, *Politics*, 1296b38), but in actuality difficult to accomplish over the long term. Thus unhappily, as Aristotle observes, this dwelling space is very rare, as the reality is more to do with which group, poor or rich, who wields power at the time, bias dealings to their agenda. Since

> whichever of the two succeeds in dominating its opponents does not establish a regime that is common or equal, but they grasp for preeminence in the regime as the prize of victory. (Aristotle 1998, *Politics*, 1296a29)

For this one-sided space to endure, "the part of the city that wants the regime to continue must be superior to the part not wanting this" in quality and quantity (Aristotle 1998, *Politics*, 1296b16). "And it is for this reason that, when either [group] does not share in the regime on the basis of the conception it happens to have, they engage in factional conflict," which can lead to civil war (Aristotle 1998, *Politics*, 1301a37). However, to avoid this,

> instead of hostility between the oligarchs and democrats, whichever group has power should be certain always to behave benevolently and justly to the other group. (Aristotle 1998, *Politics*, 1309b18)

Final Words

Although Aristotle's power balance is admirable, it has its challenges to achieve fruition, but it would be one of the most stable political regimes since all are acknowledged and respected; i.e., all would feel valued and included, which is important, as everyone likes to feel a sense of belonging and having a share of societal potentiality. In view of that,

> those regimes which look to the common advantage are correct regimes according to what is unqualifiedly just, while those which look only to the advantage of the rulers are errant, and are all deviations from the correct regimes; for they involve mastery, but the city is a partnership of free persons. (Aristotle 1998, *Politics*, 1279a16)

The emphasis on "free" persons shows the narrow definition of Aristotle's time, as it equates to the "citizens," who are "men" "similar in stock and free" (Aristotle 1998, *Politics*, 1277b8), and who rule over their "same citizen" men as they are equal in status, and this is termed *political rule*. The narrowness is apparent in the separation from the political rule of masters over slaves, men over women, and parents over their children. For example, a keystone of Aristotelian belief is, "when [the regime] is established in accordance with equality and similarity among the citizens, [the citizens] claim to merit ruling in turn" (Aristotle 1998, *Politics*, 1279a8). Consequently, the workable political environment for the citizens is

> in similar fashion to participate in ruling and being ruled in turn. For equality is the same thing [as justice] for persons who are similar, and it is difficult for a regime to last if its constitution is contrary to justice. (Aristotle 1998, *Politics*, 1332b25)

In this context, constitution is contrary to justice from a democratic perspective, as only the "Oligarchs" retain the "voice" of power.

Book IV says the correct regime of polity is under political rule, whereas divergent regimes are masters overseeing slaves. Aristotle interestingly states that in political rule:

> For in the case of persons similar by nature, justice and merit must necessarily be the same according to nature; and so if it is harmful for their bodies if unequal persons have equal sustenance and clothing, it is so also [for their souls if they are equal] in what pertains to honors, and similarly therefore if equal persons have what is unequal. (Aristotle 1998, *Politics*, 1287a12)

Interesting in the sense that "unequal" persons struggle to cope with being "equal," and vice versa. Since, for both the oligarchs and democrats, being or adopting the other's persona is difficult and perhaps not possible, and tentative connection between them is perhaps the workable solution for the benefit of the majority. However, there are always those who cannot become meaningfully involved in the political power processes, for "those who are outstanding in virtue do not engage in factional conflict to speak of; for they are few against many" (Aristotle 1998, *Politics*, 1304b4).

Education is key to sustaining a polity:

> But the greatest of all the things that have been mentioned with a view to making regimes lasting—though it is now slighted by all—is education relative to the regimes. For there is no benefit in the most beneficial laws, even when these have been approved by all those engaging in politics, if they are not going to be habituated and educated in the regime—if the laws are popular, in a popular spirit, if oligarchic, in an oligarchic spirit. (Aristotle 1998, *Politics*, 1310a13)

Education goes hand in hand with the dominant ideologies of the rulers, as teaching people in a certain way may less likely cause resistance, although this is questionable. The purposeful teaching agenda set advocates that

> those who are going to rule in the authoritative offices ought to have three things: first, affection for the established regime; next, a very great capacity for the work involved in rule; third, virtue and justice—in each regime the sort that is relative to the regime. (Aristotle 1998, *Politics*, 1309a33)

"Relative to the regime" is a loaded term; nonetheless, putting these elitist citizen perspectives aside, Aristotle was aware of abuses of power. For instance, Book III addresses the difficulties of citizen accountability. Also, laws written down enjoy superior authority than the ruling-class authority, which is a legacy brought forward to today, with its aim as countering power abuse.

The name Aristotle means "the Best Purpose" (Behind the Name, 2023), which is apt, for he thought about and advocated for the "best" living space in the city; hence, this can be extended to the "best" living space that is society; fittingly a balancing power act!

CHAPTER 2

The Bible (and God)

Potency of Words

Words of singular representation, such as "no" or "yes" or "perhaps," the latter to keep one hopeful, can dictate what movement and decisions are to be consequently applied next. Also, words in multiple representation, from phrases, sentence, and sentences strung together in a tight to lose formation of tone, sound, and expression, can make one's immediate and distant long-term aims and aspirations intimately and remotely related to what the words express. The context of what the type of words are in relation to their purpose will act on a reader in diverse ways, from self-help literature, academic offerings, fictional imaginative works, legislation, to directions on how to use, behave, and socioculturally "belong" in social media as well as texting and, more importantly, knowledge acquisition. There are more applications that can be added. Also, how effective the context is will depend on the sensitivity of a reader of words by what they are experiencing within their time and space along various moments. Consequently, vulnerability to the strength of words, in relation to how they influence, varies within particular times and spaces. However, what if a singular word and their adjoining words, sentences, paragraphs, and chapters group together to form a book, but not just any book, but the "One Book." The bestselling book in history to date, with over thirty varieties in English and beyond one hundred in other languages (Segall and Burke 2013). This numerical evidence suggests the potency of words within that particular book's covers may be regarded as something beyond the ordinary.

The "One Book" is the Bible; although depending on religious and "nonreligious" perspectives, it is possible for the "one" aspect to be deemed an arbitrary label, for some its context is the seminal text and for others there are other texts to report on how power is structured, formulated, and applied on Earth and in the Heavens. "Nonreligious" perspectives are highlighted, since the formative religious text and what it communicates to create and reflect as the irrefutable and unquestionable historical, social, and cultural facts and ideals will still influence texts of "no" religious intention. For instance, returning to the Bible as the primary text of potency (in numerical terms, if not acknowledged by all through its human history), it in conjunction with the classical of Greece and Rome reflects the infrastructural grounding of Western thinking and culture (Segall and Burke 2013). So, the Bible is much more than the sum of its parts, as it takes on the function and role of the source of Judeo-Christian thought processes, both secular and religious, incorporating education, law, and culture (Segall and Burke 2013, 308):

> Bible, as the Word of God, is two books, Jewish and Christian: Old (first) Testament and New (second) Testament. (there is)…what we may justly call the third testament, the Koran, in which the prophets, together with Jesus and Mary, are explicitly acknowledged to be divinely inspired figures on whose spiritual insight the revelations of Mohamed are founded. (Polka 2015, 564)

Thus, the Bible transcends national identities, it being a transcendental entity and identity in itself. It was produced in a time, about 2,000 years ago, give or take a hundred or two hundred years, to achieve the coming together of an array of stories from various authors. The timing was important to the modern formations of the then-fledging Western and Middle Eastern cultural and associated language groups, as the writings in this classical work of art can be thought of as a guiding hand or "light" of ways to behave, think, be, and do. A crucial consideration is, when did the Bible become a text of divination, showing the way of how people should live? For example, adopting the role of the devil's advocate, it is possible to see that, given the process of time and space of putting together the "separate" contributions that became the original Bible (before the numerous versions evolved from that, or maybe more than one version manifested at a similar or same time of origin!), it would not initially have been elevated to the position of sacred, holy, supernatural, otherworldly. At the time its component parts may have been regarded as unremarkable text or text as unforeseen potential before the actuality of the finished product took shape and figuratively and literally took off.

Or perhaps those who wrote the text and those who played with the jigsaw puzzle of these various texts when faced with the challenge of putting them together into some form of coherent order had divine guidance all along, this being (exactly in terms of the creative "Being" of life) the catalyst for successful and ongoing completion. That is a significant, if not the significant essence of what the Bible is, or what it is purported to express and represent, as it is the throne behind which resides "The Power," to which all other powers are subordinate and originate from. For instance, the Bible from the conception of its first letter, word, words, sentences, scriptures, books within the Book, actually the first thoughts prior to the first letter, and so on may have already been on a divine footing already. Hence, its potency and success already pre-ordained with the actuality preceding the potential, and actually the potential not even being necessary, since the potential was a foregone conclusion. In other words, as it would be with anything to do with the Word of God, since the actuality of the Bible was and is simply an actuality—an actuality of God and an actuality of God's power.

Returning to the ability of the Bible to create a cultural identity, one can surmise it ought to have been assisted by a city or society favoring the influence of religious texts and beliefs to guide how these places and spaces are and what they are to be in the future. Without that accommodation, religion would not be an integral part of societal existence, and would not exist, at least within the forms recognized 2,000 years ago and prior to that and today. However, perhaps it is inevitable that human society enjoys a natural affinity with acknowledging something beyond the visible, every day, grounding and grounding out of what the harshness of life offers. There is always this human need to imagine and wonder possible existences that can be realized that offer a "better" way or a way out of the challenges and fatalistic apparentness that the end of life presents and, in turn, knowing or comforting oneself with the thought that the end is just another beginning. A beginning of goodness that is of a higher order to the "good" advocated by Aristotle when "alive," because "alive," as living after death, may be another form of "alive" or the "truer" form.

Constantine and the Ministry

Constantine was an early proponent of including religious doctrine as part of how society should be run. Since economic well-being and profit is integral to societal functionality, in 313 CE he sought to encourage religious participation by offering tax breaks for clergy (Clarke 2013). Today in Australia, churches are regarded as charitable organizations, thus benefit from the modern version of tax incentives, so carrying on his decree. Constantine's rationale for making such a declaration was not solely for the benefit of the clergy in an act of benevolence, as although he regarded worship as the pinnacle endeavor, he envisaged such a move would create affluence and happiness for the state. Accordingly, the city thrives when worshipping God:

> On you, then, I call, who are best instructed in the mysteries of God, to aid me
> with your counsel, to follow me with your thoughts, and correct whatever shall
> savour of error in my words, expecting no display of perfect knowledge. (Con-
> stantine's Speech to the Assembly of Saints, Clarke 2013, 3)

Constantine was willing to share authority and partial power and bow to theological and biblical clout. Thus, recognizing the seen and probably more influential unseen potential of God. As anyone is a product of their time and history,
Constantine was not an exception, and his speech merged the voices of Roman
and biblical space (Schott 2008). He used scripture to advise political judgments
and societal evolvement, because the disclosure of Christ and, consequently,
Christian faith, served to educate the populous (the paideia) as an integral
part of this evolvement. As a comparison, the Greek paideia was the place of
intellectuals and philosophers (Aristotle's domain); an exclusory space, but the
Christian paideia was for all; an inclusive space rising above cultural and ethical
limitations. Therefore, the power of religion and symbols, such as the Bible, is
fed by the limit of no limits of how societal spaces and places are represented
and moves within and beyond these representations. Consequently, the Christian
paideia is "the victorious sign...the rule of self-control that brings harmony to
all peoples" (Schott 2008, 118). Here, there is an aspect of attempting societal
cohesion, producing a sense of societal identity, a sense of belonging to a group,
and a sense of unification to make the system stronger.

    Religious intent is thus so as it draws people together from their apparent
aimless wonderings to provide purpose to their lives. It supersedes their partially
independent spirit, partial in the sense of society controlling that spirit to an
extent, and dwelling performance to date, with a "new and improved" version.
"Aimless" is questionable, as people would have possessed purpose to their
wonderings, but perhaps not in accord with the purpose of the ruler which may
equate to society. To ensure this accord is met, the expectation is to follow this
new way of believing and living to harmonize their lives and self. Therefore,
becoming in agreement and synchronicity to the will of scriptures of biblical
proportions, which happens to work well with the will of the ruler. Hence, it
provides the ruler with a powerful tool to control and manipulate the population
and to enhance efficiency and actuality of the said ruler's purpose. Constantine's
liaison with the biblical space reflected the Byzantine symphonia, i.e., mutual
comprehension of the Church and human ruling at a discrete distance from
each other, to nurture the will of God on Earth, e.g., "Thy Kingdom come, Thy
will be done on earth as it is in heaven" (part of the Lord's Prayer). This textual

prayer could be literally read as "Thy will be done"; i.e., My will, as God, will
be, and whoever holds center stage as the "voice," holds the reins and direction
of power. God's voice is the ultimate exemplifier of this.

During Constantine's time and after the Byzantine Empire, also referred to as
Byzantium or the Eastern Roman Empire, carried over the Roman Empire in its
eastern provinces during Late Antiquity and the Middle Ages, when its capital
city was Constantinople (Encyclopaedia Britannica, n.d.). Thus, a time and space
of societal evolvement, as Constantine envisaged. However, the harmony aspect
of the evolvement may have been left wanting between the biblical and social
performance. For instance, the word Byzantine is characterized by a devious and
usually surreptitious manner of operation (Merriam-Webster), which has left a
modern legacy of Byzantine-induced various meanings, prejudiced by what its
more ancient performances are remembered by, e.g., the mentioned devious, but
also scheming, underhand, deceitful, secretive, plotting, dishonest, calculating,
complex, intricate, tortuous, convoluted, and complicated, Actually, some may
say, a typical human settlement. As well, speculation arises as to whether the
scriptures contained and retained in the Bible would have contributed to the
dis-harmony intentionally or inadvertently, as human interpretation tends to
distort and continues to distort biblical texts to advantage individual and group
societal position. Either way, the Bible and its contents can be thought of as
a powerful catalytical driving force. So, the "beast" of humanity, as Aristotle
mentioned, continues.

Constantine's "colonisation" of his people to biblical ends extends to the
modern and postmodern versions of colonialism. For example, considering the
Bible translation in Africa, the discourses of colonialism reflect

> the understanding of the representation and categorization of the African identities
> produced and reproduced by various colonial rules, systems, and procedures, in
> order to create and separate the Africans as "Other." (Kinyua 2013, 59)

This was related to Bible translators' aspiration to dominate and restructure the
colonized reality. Again, is this process part of the Bible's intent, or is the beast
of human intention distorting scriptural meaning? Kinyua continues by observing
that the translating performance was not separate from the restructuring power
of decolonization:

> An analysis of colonial relationships reveals not just the individual or social
> groups but also a historical consciousness at work. For this reason, the place of

language, culture, and the individual within the political and economic realities have to remain at the forefront for a fuller comprehension of the evolution of Bible translation in Africa. (Kinyua 2013, 59)

So, the power of the Bible is used to benefit rulers, be they the ancient pre-modern Constantine or the modern colonists, but the Bible can also benefit the populous.

Comprehending the Bible

"Reading" the Bible does not have to be filtered through the interpretations of religious "professionals." They may have had access to formal training and ongoing exposure to the whys, wherefores, and hows of biblical wordplay and act as a conduit between the Bible and the laity, but the paradox is in the human aspect of the training. This is compounded by the authors of the Bible also being human. The point is biblical construction was and continues to be through human endeavor. This is not necessarily a negative practice and performance, as how else could the word of the Bible come into existence, but it would be heavily weighted, perhaps totally, toward the human way of things. Also, some in the laity would not have the time or intellectual prowess to engage effectively with the Bible, so the assistance of the said professionals is advantageous within degrees of interpretation, so their input should not be discounted. However, since humans cannot avoid retaining the bias of their time and space, the Word of God may also be subsequently biased. So, its "truth" may never achieve absolute interpretation and reflection of God's message. Another component to add to the complexity of interpretation is the nonstatic nature of language, since over time meanings and implications change, and the original messages in the narrative take on different appreciations, which may not have been part of the initial intent. Added to this is the translation of the Bible into numerous languages, where some of the translation may be lost in transit. Essentially the religious professionals are faced with a challenging remit to get things as "right" as possible, in whatever forms "right" is realized, as the "right" and power practices are intimately entwined.

It is these "right" forms that need to be guarded against, with the laity readership having an awareness of the "non-purity" of God's word as it is filtered through professional voices, although direct engagement with the reader to the Bible would cut out the professional "middle" person. Of course, these nonfiltered readers would still be filtering the Bible's text through their sociocultural time and space, but a personal, direct encounter would be performed, which may form a purer interaction with the One Book and the individual self. For instance,

> Textual reading and interpretation, like all other human activity, is goal oriented. It serves the personal, social, cultural, religious, and political interests of the reader. We engage in an activity in the hope or expectation that we will achieve desirable results. (Greenstein 2009, 294)

This purer experience would allow direct exposure to the power of God through God's word, which may produce a profound power experience. That, in turn, would allow a feeling of being powerful within one's self, hopefully in a "good" way, benefiting those who come into contact with that person. However, the potency of "powerful" reading will be different for each person, and, consequently, numerous methodologies of how the Bible is understood are created with each propounding stratagems to be utilized for the process (Yee 2007). For example, deconstruction reveals fundamental and implicit assumptions (Derrida 1991); ideological criticism that looks at power struggles between classes and other groups (Clines 1995; Scholz 2003); gender and feminist criticism (Bach 1999); and the new historicism that comprehends how people have felt and constructed history (Hens-Piazza 2002).

Adding to the mix of strategies, literary appraisers regard the Bible as a unified composition, regardless of its prehistory, and seen as a singular piece, although perhaps inconsistent (Alter 1981). Alternatively, source appraisers argue that to comprehend the biblical word is to straighten the editorially tangled textual strands and singularly unravel them prior to studying implications that are drawn from their combination (Friedman 1987). Others see the Bible as the source, helped by supporting texts from Christian, Jewish, and Muslim input (Kugel 1997). Another type of source is the Bible residing in its first space of historical/culturalness of ancient Israelite texts (Greenstein 2009), in which interpretation is applied through cultural artifacts and texts from the Ancient Near Eastern place that Israel evolved from (Keel 1978). So within these ways, to state one's power is not easy since multiple interpretations dilute the powerful voice somewhat. The message can get lost on the way or reproduced to means and ends not originally intended. So, the effectiveness of delivery of God's word through these interpretations can run along a continuum of powerful advertising of God's power to a perhaps absolute deconstruction; a sense of rendered powerlessness.

The one-to-one of intimate communication between the reader and the Bible omits powerful forces that wish for the reader to understand the Bible and "act out" biblical guidance in particular ways. This "soul" searching and researching connects to Puritan reading of concentrated self-scrutiny (Hall 1989), Protestant individual study aiming for salvation (Reilly and Hall 2000), and St. Augustine's innovative function as a silent, contemplative reading (Bielo 2009, 110). However, all readers in this solitary endeavor aim for purity within

> a community of two—the Christian and God…practical piety is private, indeed it must be for good Christians who want to become great Christians. (Forbes 1997, 125)

To illustrate, Luther's "sola scriptura" does not depend on a hierarchy to read the Bible. It supplants rituals and creeds, and "within this tradition, religious reading is central to religion itself, and to be reliant on 'sola scriptura' is to be 'solus cum scriptura': alone with sacred texts" (Ronald 2012, 325). Although going solo is an admirable intention to be at one with the power of God, a sola scriptura model is difficult to attain, since "there is a network of authorities and commentaries that surrounds the solitary reader and shapes his or her interpretation" (Wolfe 2003, 71):

> "Religious" reading is no longer an objective assessment, based on the use of a canonical, sacred, authoritative text championed by a religious tradition, but a subjective process marked by the reader's intention. As the figure of the solitary reader of sacred texts fades among the examples of religious group readers and nonsacred texts used for religious purposes, the boundaries of what constitute "religious" reading come into question. (Ronald 2012, 337)

So, the interpretation of religious professionals is a powerful influencer of how to read the Bible. Consequently, to ascertain how the power of God is regarded inevitably leads to competition between the various professional religious groups as to what is the "optimum" God and Bible interpretation.

Bible Is the Product of a Theocentric Worldview

To maximize the Bible as a tool of power for human utilization, it is written from an anthropocentric positionality. The human is located at the center of things and create their place in the world and beyond to universal space, as enjoying prime connectivity to God. However, God may not see this "power play" in such simplistic terms, as since the Bible claims that God is the creator of all things, humans would just be one part of that whole. So consequently, within the natural that is Earth,

> the world, inclusive of humans and animals, trees and plants, land and seas, belongs to God because it is God's creation, and it is in relation to God that each part of creation has its value and worth. (Simkins 2014, 397)

Accordingly, the anthropocentric perspective is a case of "spin doctoring" to justify behavioral patterns, such as the Western Christian Genesis 1 of humans created in God's image. Here, the implication is that the human rises above nature, and being without, not within it, to perform power over it; e.g., "no item in the physical creation had any purpose save to serve man's purposes" (White Jr. 1967, 1205). Apparently, God has provided a mandate for this, as Genesis 1 "insisted that it is God's will that man exploit nature for his proper ends" (White Jr. 1967, 1205). As a result, an efficient and unquestioned space of human progress is set up to exploit the potential of resources—land, sea, plant, and animal—by the backing of the ultimate power, and it is difficult to go against this type of "total" ideological performance. Essentially, this is power by proxy, and if one objects to it and complains to the perpetrators, they simply respond by saying the responsibility that allows for this comes from "on high." To exemplify the defending of this privileged position, "evidence" can be drawn from the Bible:

> When I look at your heavens, the work of your fingers, the moon and the stars that you have established; What are human beings that you are mindful of them, mortals that you take care for them? Yet you have made them a little lower than God, and crowned them with glory and honor. You have given them dominion over the works of your hands; you have put all things under their feet, all sheep and oxen, and also the beasts of the field, the birds of the air, and the fish of the sea, whatever passes along the paths of the seas. (Psalm 8:3–8)

Hence, evidence that places humans in a "good" place of advantage, a place of power. Yet, when hanging on the coat tails of the one in power, caution must be sought as to what is the intention of those "hanging" on:

> Rise up, O LORD! Do not let mortals prevail; let the nations be judged before you. Put them in fear, O LORD; let the nations know that they are only human (Psalm 9:19–20). In arrogance the wicked persecute the poor—let them be caught in the schemes they have devised. For the wicked boast of the desires of their heart, those greedy for gain curse and renounce the LORD. In the pride of their countenance the wicked say, "God will not seek it out"; all their thoughts are, "There is no God." (Psalm 10:2–4)

For it is interesting that other humans, by countering those humans who wish to dominate, offer the accusation that these latter renounce God, thus negating their power source, for how can these say it is God's will to control nature if God is not acknowledged as being in existence. Also, the other humans could be regarded as manipulating the power of God to strengthen their own agenda.

It is the beast in humans, or their weakness to resist power opportunities, that encourages "reading" the Bible from a prior agenda. From this context, the power of God is simply made available through biblical text, and it is up to the individual to how it is received. To illustrate, the character Job directly engages with God by questioning God's way of acting. However, God respects Job's challenge by listening to him and engaging with him (5:1–27), by stepping back as Job debates with his friends (8:1–37:24) and by taking him on "man-to-man" as the book closes (38:1–39:30) (Jaensch 2014, 186). In other words, perhaps Job's encounter shows the true purpose and power of God, which is for each individual to find their own pathway to "goodness." For example, "anyone who has surrendered their reason at the foot of the cross will discover that Christ hands it back again to be used more appropriately and insightfully in the search for truth" (Crump 2013, 112). This leads to that "once we admit that the Bible, as divine discourse, is accommodated to various human viewpoints and contexts, then we will listen with more care to all that it says" (Sparks 2008, 358). These "powerful" individual "meetings" with God "involves going beyond explicit ideological systems and clear boundaries of identity…(and) accepts as axiomatic that truth is more multidimensional and organically independent than most theories or accounts of truth can grasp" (Fowler 1981, 186). So, powering oneself by individual effort is fraught with challenges when negotiating its pathways, especially when sourced from a theocentric origin.

Powerful Quotes from the Bible

One's imaginative creativity can be applied to this section as to what divine power implies in conjunction with what Fowler stated about multidimensional truth and organic independence.

Psalm 62:11

Once God has spoken; twice have I heard this:
that power belongs to God,

The Bible (and God)

Job 26:14

Behold, these are but the outskirts of his ways,
and how small a whisper do we hear of him!
But the thunder of his power who can understand?

1 Corinthians 6:14

And God raised the Lord and will also raise us up by his power.

Isaiah 26:4

Trust in the LORD forever,
for the LORD GOD is an everlasting rock.

Jeremiah 10:12

It is he who made the earth by his power,
who established the world by his wisdom,
and by his understanding stretched out the heavens.

2 Timothy 1:7—For God hath not given us the spirit of fear; but of power, and of love, and of a sound mind.

Philippians 4:13—I can do all things through Christ which strengtheneth me.

1 Corinthians 6:14—And God hath both raised up the Lord, and will also raise up us by his own power.

1 Corinthians 4:20—For the kingdom of God [is] not in word, but in power.

Ephesians 6:10—Finally, my brethren, be strong in the Lord, and in the power of his might.

Colossians 1:11—Strengthened with all might, according to his glorious power, unto all patience and longsuffering with joyfulness; https://www.kingjamesbibleonline.org/Bible-Verses-About-Power/

1 Corinthians 1–Christ is called the power of God, as through him and his gospel, God displays his power and authority in ransoming and saving sinners.

Matthew 24–The powers of heaven may denote the celestial luminaries.

Hebrew 4–The Word of God is quick and powerful.

God is Omnipotent in Creation: Isaiah 44:24–"This is what the LORD says–your Redeemer, who formed you in the womb: I am the LORD, the Maker of all things, who stretches out the heavens, who spreads out the earth by myself."

How do you respond to God's omnipotence? 1 Peter 5:6 says, "Humble yourselves, therefore, under God's mighty hand, that he may lift you up in due time." We realize that without His almighty power, we can do nothing. "I am the vine; you are the branches. If you remain in me and I in you, you will bear much fruit; apart from me you can do nothing" (John 15:5).

Dunamis

These quotes focus God's power, to show God is in control in religious belief systems and intimately relates to dunamis. Dunamis is the philosophical concept of potentiality and actuality in ancient Greece; in other words, power (dunamis [duvnami]). The Greeks saw dunamis as a significant cosmic principle, with God and cosmic principles corresponding, but in the Bible God is a person and not purely power (Meadors, n.d.); therefore, power of God takes on new meaning because a person who possesses the characteristic of power is the prime mover of the universe. "Moving" the universe may consist of the dunamis strength and ability of:

a.   inherent power, power residing in a thing by virtue of its nature, or which a person or thing exerts and puts forth
b.   power for performing miracles
c.   moral power and excellence of soul

d. the power and influence which belong to riches and wealth

e. power and resources arising from numbers.

(Bible Study Tools 2020)

Perhaps the most important of the five power scenarios is the *dunamis* "inherent power, power residing in a thing by virtue of its nature," since it is the innate, inborn, natural, inbuilt, and fundamental dunamis of God powering the quotes.

This section portrayed an array of power quotes from the Bible depicting God's status as the origin of all things, narrated from multidimensional perspectives. The organic independence of truth can be viewed as God separate from carbon-based life forms on earth, the limited autonomy of humans "independent" from God, or the individualism when "speaking" to God one-on-one. All encounters are subjective to God, and all are affected by social power. Sociologist Michael Mann designates social power as "the capacity to get others to do things that otherwise they would not do," and as power creates movement for people, Mann's social power of ideology "derives from the human need to find ultimate meaning in life, to share norms and values, and to participate in aesthetic and ritual practices with others" (Bossman 2014, 66). Symbolism assists this social power.

Symbolism of the Bible

Symbols are powerful representations. They are denoted by signs, characters, figures, icons, and pictograms, both animate and inanimate. The Bible, as an entity, would be among the foremost if not the foremost known symbol in the world. That makes it powerful, even if it was never opened and the pages turned, for the presence of the Bible is enough to make it noticeable and eyed with degrees of respect, curiosity, and wonder. This awareness is due to the longevity of its existence and to those who have read it, or read select parts of it, and passed on their perspectives to others, i.e., a process of compound awareness spreading out like the ripples on a lake caused by a cast stone and a metaphoric biblical talisman transmitted by God.

It makes one speculate why God felt it necessary to encourage the creation of the Bible symbol. For instance, was not the symbolism of the creation of the world and universe an infinitely far more statement of intent and show of power, since the existence of the Bible pales into insignificance when compared to the endless space of nature? Indeed, the Bible is made up of parts of nature, i.e., wood trans-formed to paper, and ink in Roman and Greek times produced from soot, glue, and water, sourcing plants and animals as part of the process. One may speculate that perhaps humans, rather than God, felt the inclination to construct a symbol that was far easier to comprehend of God's power, rather than to take on the universe and try and work that out. Thus, something that could be held in the hand within a reductive space of comprehension, contemplation, and contact, along human terms of God, rather than God's overwhelming immensity of terms, e.g., a symbolism of God's presence that can be coped with at a human level of intellect. Essentially, a "placed" symbolism of manageable decoding, be that within a limited narrative set, for perhaps it is an impossibility to understand fully the One power.

Within humanity, social relations and ideologies drive the long history of contact with the Bible and what it symbolizes. Since societal structure and ideals are fluid, biblical symbolism will also be fluid. There may be an inner core to the text that remains, but other narratives will be subjected to newer ways of reading as time and space move ever onward. The "assemblages" of Deleuze and Guattari (1988) look at arrangement and layout and modes of ordering, seeking to chart these assemblages of regimes of signs, tracing how they come together, mingle, and reform (Boer 2013, 300). Also of how they evolve into the dominate characteristics of any composition of people, language, or time. In this causal context,

> we may still speak of people, periods, or languages, or even "a given style, fash-ion, pathology, or miniscule event in a limited situation," and we may even go so far as determining "the predominance of one semiotic or another." (Deleuze and Guattari 1988, 119)

The predominance of the semiotic Bible is a case in point in assemblage formation over time, as one assemblage supersedes another, and so forth, with the Bible ever present in the background. Each assemblage experiences political tensions with biblical text, both within one's internal outlook and externally to what society is at the time and also in movement and what is manifold in character. From this tension with what the Bible represents:

> The Bible and the religions that claim it as a sacred text do not have a default setting for cosy and corrupt deals with power and the state, even though it often seems to be the case. Instead, there is an internal dynamic that constantly tempts them to make such trysts as well as oppose them. (Boer 2013, 316)

The symbolic power of the Bible is also a beginning, a starting point or comparison point to expand human imagination. For example, natural science associated
to evolutionary theory utilizes the behavior of biblical text to create alternative
textual interpretations (Nielsen [2009] 2012), but not discounting the Bible as
transformative consultant and used intertextually by both religious and nonreligious appropriators. The "cross" (over) appeal of the Bible for religious and
nonreligious followers lies within its typological symbolism, which:

> operates on four levels: literal, allegorical, moral, and mystical. Typological
> symbolism provides a way of understanding the Old and New Testaments of
> the Christian Bible as the unified story of humanity's sin and redemption with
> applications to moral conduct in this world as well as to the quest for eternal
> life. (O'Neil 2015, 91)

Hence, the power of the Bible and what it symbolizes as a guide of how to live.

State as God

> In a crucial early modern compromise, the Bible graciously gives up its role as
> theocratic oracle and consents to become the indispensable foundation of the state.
> Biblical authority does not disappear but changes its shape. (Sherwood 2008, 316)

Constantine recognized that in running the state, religious support is a useful and
perhaps indispensable tool to achieve state aims or his aims. Whether utilizing
the theocratic angle or "simply" utilizing the presence of religion as a familiar
doctrinal text to limit human behavior to certain ways, religion is useful, especially the power of the word written down, which takes on a special status of
"biblical" influence. This is particularly useful if people believe what the Bible
says in relation to laws of living and associated morality. Therefore, combining
God with man/woman in a joint venture of state-sanctioned control is an effective
lever of persuasion. England thought so:

> The laws of England (as all just and righteous laws) are grounded originally
> upon the divine law, as their foundation or fountain. The supreme and sovereign
> God among the heathen is supposed to have the name of Jupiter, quasi "Juris
> Pater"—But more immediately human laws have their force and authority from
> the consent and agreement of men. (Atkyns 1688)

Thus, the Christine Bible decentralizes power tactfully to human government, the compromised accord between Christianity, law, and politics that is the infrastructure of the modern (Christian) democratic state (Sherwood 2008). A tactical maneuver, since the religious professionals recognized a shift of emphasis to Enlightenment of how the world works, as significant competition to their version. So, at the risk of losing power and influence, it is better to run with the illumination and stay close to the new power on the state block. As a consequence, the modern Western state as a "secularised theological concept" has experienced movement from "a nominalist model of the singular transcendent God to a kind of secularised deism, in which God is immanent in the world's lawfulness" (Schmitt [1985] 1922, 36). Within this biblical/nonspiritual partnership, state and its law achieve their own God status, allowing the Rule of Law, i.e., democracy, to dispense special decrees for self-protection (Sherwood 2008, 335):

> Given that democracy is now the "sovereign" sacred, god-like notion, the ultimate G[o]od (capital G) for which we must sacrifice, then it follows that no sacrifice is too great for democracy—least of all the temporary sacrifice of democracy itself. (cf. Derrida [2003] 2005, 33–36)

The "good" for people becomes the "good" of the state, returning to Aristotle's notion of the city as primacy over the family and individual. Achieving the "stated" good is a ritualistic performance and, within this ritual, power is locational, imprecise, relational, and organizational, and power is distributed all over the social body (Werline 2014, 7). Thus, it is "a matter of techniques and discursive practices that comprise the micro politics of everyday life" (Mitchell 1999, 88). For instance,

> Ritual does not disguise the exercise of power, nor does it refer, express or symbolise anything outside itself. In other words rituals do not refer to politics…they are politics. Ritual is the thing itself. It is power. It acts and is actuated. (Bell 1992, 195)

So, the state as God also acts, and is, as an actualized ritual of power.

The Good of God

Is it intentional that the selection of the name of "God" was purposely chosen to be stretched to form Go(o)d? This is a close association suggesting that God is

Good and Good equates to God, thus attaining a sense and realization of God's "quality of existence" performance and touching and being touched by God's power to achieve well-being and being well. This sense of being well can involve a complete transformation of oneself, which includes the physicality of humans "being" in the image of God (Walton 2011). This is an ultimate state of being that corresponds to uncontaminated power free from material vices and desires to control others to one's aims. Accordingly, a self-less power not a selfish power, but, paradoxically, it is also a power of the self as the one takes center stage into becoming a self-less being. In this way, power of the non-self of self may be the highest form of power.

Hence, it is raising oneself above human limitation into an infinity of everlasting choices and non-choices. Moving on to new stages in evolutionary existence free from the shackles of Earthly sociocultural pressures and competitiveness, and its historical behavioral power struggle of repetitiveness of greed, destruction, and exploitation. This is a state of being not necessarily of corporeal form, as one can move at will or be stationary in the immensity of the universe. Or whatever space God has in store for the after human life. For instance, perhaps a heavenly space or a space beyond the Universe of Space, changing into another image of God to function comfortably within these heavenly spatial contexts. Additionally, it may be that the heavenly space is not a type of physical space at all, but a state of mind, soul and spirit; a spatial nonmateriality.

To create power, a sense of order from disorder is normally the performance direction flow, i.e., order from chaos. Within this shift of emphasis, attaining "good" equates to order and should be functionally feasible (Walton 2012, 883) to the grasp of human intentionality. The functionality aspect is God's intentions for human progression/evolution toward the good, and even though absolute order may equate to absolute good, attaining the absolute is challenging, since only New Creation will nullify disorder and non-order (Rev. 21). Speculation arises of why the original creation included disorder. To answer this, Genesis 1 comments that the ongoing-ness of disorder and non-order is not a flaw in God's power capacity—in his wisdom he has chosen a process and has chosen to involve humanity in the process. Nevertheless, is God carrying out a longitudinal power experiment, with life and those in it as the "guinea pigs," to see if good is achievable? But, would God not know the answer anyway? Perhaps God wishes that life, including humans, would benefit far more from finding out for itself, rather than providing the punch line. It may be that since God is Good, God cannot be bad or experience bad but can imagine what bad looks like by utilizing the opposite of good and create this life form labeled human and the Earth as the laboratory, both with their goods and bads, to see what happens in the relationship. Indeed, a biblical theological/philosophical "Good/Bad" experiment:

> We are no less at the heart of the Bible as philosophical, at the heart of philosophy as biblical. The human subject is, as a willing, self-determining, desiring, thinking agent, the source of all value, of both good and evil. Good and evil belong to subjects, not to objects. Good and evil are not natural but human (and divine). (Polka 2015, 565)

After all,

> the Bible contains invaluable lessons about the purpose of life, about human nature, about how to attain happiness, wholeness, and love, and advice upon a whole host of other issues that have been the perennial concerns of philosophy, literature, psychology, and jurisprudence. (Goodman 2013, 227)

This Entity Baptized God

But what of this entity called God, who has the starring role in the Bible, and indeed the starring role in life (and death) for many people. There are multiple perspectives of belief of what God is or may be:

- Monotheism: Supreme Being and primary faith object
- Theologians: God concept involves omniscience (infinite knowledge), omnipotence (unlimited power), omnipresence (present everywhere), divine simplicity, eternal and necessary existence, omnibenevolent (perfectly good), and all loving
- Theism: creator and sustainer of the universe
- Deism: creator, but not the sustainer, of the universe
- Pantheism: God is the universe
- Atheism: God does not exist
- Agnosticism: God as unknown or unknowable
- Also, incorporeal (immaterial), a personal being, the source of all moral obligation, and the "greatest conceivable existent"

(Swinburne 1995).

This is quite a role call. There would be no other being (alive or beyond life) that could be awarded such adulations or even come close. Consequently, there has to be very powerful reasons for the existence of such status, from "rational" to nonrational, and one that significantly pervades the immaterial and material that is life, and from certain beliefs regarded as an absolute (and more than) pervasion.

God's power is of binary character according to Pastor Mizzi (n.d.), i.e., absolute and ordinate. Absolute implies power that can be used but is not, and ordinate is used. These two are shades of potentiality and actuality; however, the binary powers are still unified within divine power, returning to oneness of power that is God:

> My Father can send twelve legions of angels (absolute power); but how then shall the Scriptures be fulfilled, that thus it must be? (ordinate). (Matthew 26:53, 54)

So, even God seems subject to the mores of potential and actual when performing, which can be regarded as a self-monitoring entity protecting created life forms and life itself from the dangers of disorder due to self-excess of power production. Potentially, God could be intentionally performing self-protection to limit potential, for the actuality maybe too unbearable to bear. For instance, God's own power would be the only thing that would cause God's power to be no more. So, if God's power is no more, then what are the consequences for life, the universe, and the very small part of that termed *humanity*. Also, if the one with absolute/ordinate power is missing, does that imply the end of everything as is known, becoming nothingness and powerlessness, or a new creation event that occurs due to the power void? Or does disorder reign in those life forms that are left to fend for themselves, or something else occurs that is beyond human imagination such as a hidden potential hiding from God that sees an opportunity to actualize and to take over the role? Whatever the outcome, a reordering from the disorder and order that was, may result.

Anyway, at the present time, the source of all power is God (Missler 2012). It's *His* saving power, *His* pardoning power (Matthew 9:6), *His* infinite power (Matthew 28:18), *His* power over nature (Luke 8:24), and His life-giving power (John 17:2, 10:10). Romans 13:1 tells us, "For there is no power but of God." He is the One who places rulers in positions of power, and He is the One who controls our lives and our destinies by His power; a baptism of power of foreseeable ongoing-ness.

Other End of Genesis

The genesis of how words are formed can grow into something far beyond the original intentions of their selected written text. For example, the quiet energy that drove the Bible authors to feel it was the right thing to do to volunteer their time to scribe down words, and not knowing that these words would explode into a global energy that still reverberates 2,000 years later. These reverberations vibrated and continues to vibrate the cultural (historical and modern) and religious aspects of societies, actualizing of how one is often expected to read the word and the world (Aichele 2008; Orosz 2008). As there were Bible authors, not author, it is inevitable that numerous perspectives and interpretations characterize its pages. Thus, the Bible may potentially be seen as not only an inherently complicated, inconsistent, fractured, multilayered, and contradictory text but also an overt text of inconsistencies, contradictions, and ambiguities (Segall and Burke 2013). Since the Bible does not hide behind a veil of dogmatism, at least not from the array of its authors, but perhaps from the filtered performances of religious professional commentators over its history (although not all), it summons up opportunities to challenge, question, and produce alternative interpretations:

> After all, even for those believing that everything in the Bible has a purpose, that all is directed from above, orchestrated by some all-knowing hand, what, one might ask, could that hand have intended by forwarding multiple accounts of similar events? It surely does not seem like a desire to establish authority, to stifle questions, discussion, and interpretation. (Segall and Burke 2013, 321)

Therefore, the all-knowing hand of God allows the individual to make their own minds up, an empowering process. Although, paradoxically, if God created all, God's hand will be the human hand, so comprehending the Bible "will" be weighted toward God's will of thinking and doing. This intimate connectivity of God's hand and human hand, in a sense, being one and the same, is demonstrated through Spinoza showing, dispassionately, that the Bible is a human fabrication from beginning to end (Levene 2011, 549). For example, the already-indicated "faulty, mutilated, adulterated and inconsistent" and "God's eternal Word and covenant" is human (Spinoza 2001, 145) found in the mind, "the primary cause of divine revelation" (Spinoza 2001, 10) and "divinely inscribed in men's hearts" (Spinoza 2001, 145). In his discussion of the divine law, Spinoza notes that this law is "common to all mankind" and thus "does not demand belief in historical narratives of any kind whatsoever" (Levene 2011, 549). However, it is precisely the human input being God's input that allows for biblical acceptability and a sense of authenticity of God's word or words. Accordingly, Spinoza's absolute human contribution to the Bible ironically can be seen as its strength, its power base, since in religious terms the base is God, e.g., the ultimate character reference of acceptability and honesty:

> The Bible can always be corrupted is the one incorruptible thing about it, the one thing that has reached us uncorrupted, the one thing without which it would not be what it is, namely, nothing. Nothing without us, as we are nothing without it. (Levene 2011, 571)

Of course, the power of the Bible is undermined if God does not exist, as its main sponsor is discovered as a fraud. However, the existence or the nonexistence of God does not depend on the proof of human beings, for what matters about the ontological argument proving the existence of God is that it is not a logical but an ontological, an existential, proof (Polka 2015, 569):

> The transcendental, the metaphysical, and the rational together constitute the heavenly kingdom of God that human beings necessarily will to bring into existence as the kingdom of ends. (Polka 2015, 573)

Perhaps all that matters are enough people believe, which is "Good" enough to power the process to biblical proportions, even though the belief is not a constant across people, as "fathoming" God produces disagreement to conceive and understand God (Fiorenza and Kaufman 2008). As a result, imaginably it is beyond human capacity to conceive and comprehend God, but at least people are open to try. Openness and ongoing-ness of interpretation is the other end of Genesis, involving a constant beginning-ness as the Bible reveals more of its power to the faithful and curious potential to actual believers.

CHAPTER 3

Nature

Scaling the Power of Nature

Nature to the lay person may be regarded as what is "out there" beyond the urban sprawl to the authentic colors, i.e., nature free from human interference. To illustrate, for those dwelling in the cooler climates and regions of the world, green and white are the colors of choice laying their comforting blanket over the land, producing a landscape of familiarity, reassurance, and identity building and sustaining. For those in the warmer and hotter humid and dry parts, reds and browns are the expectations and realizations. Additionally, coastal region living would imply various shades of blues and greens, but greens of filtered liquid rather than the greens of solid rainy dryness. Temperature and precipitation fluid levels and exposures over time through the seasons and years would transform these colors in the majority of "localized" weather systems, if not all, as the Arctic and Antarctic are being subjected to generalized global temperature increases, which will and does rearrange their "surface" landscapes to generate color beyond their traditional whites.

   Nature of many colors, or the infinite color of a "natural" disposition, is a powerful presence that everything in the world—plant, animal, and all life forms, material and immaterial—is exposed to. However, the term *exposed* in a sense is an inadequate verb, as everything in the world owes their time, space, and place and, indeed, existence, to this thing called nature. As verb means a "doing" word, all who reside on Earth "do" their performance because of nature and within nature, the performance that is birth, life, and death. From this, conclusions are reached that without nature and its life-giving properties, all species, including humans, would be found wanting, to put it mildly; firstly, if nature ceased being the land with its accompanying plants (including trees), fertile soils, stream and river systems, underground aquifers, mineral deposits, mountains and canyons, deserts, arid, semi-arid, tropical, subtropical, and life forms. Secondly, if nature ceases to be with its associated seas and oceans (solid and liquid forms) and their flowing currents acting as the world's thermostat and pathways to transport freight too large for air carriage and to transport self-propelled life forms. Lastly, if nature ceases to be of the "air" for those that can fly, but that would be the least of Earth species' trouble for those that require oxygen to function. Accordingly, the solids, liquids, and gases that make up the "nature of things" is vital for the survivability and sustainability of "all. "

"All" is in quotes since nature has ample potentiality and actuality to reinvent itself from local to global scales of production and reproduction. Therefore, not all may suffer extinction, as life forms have potential to adapt to new environments if given enough time and space to "do" so. Also, if nature does reinvent itself, some of the previous life forms may have been beyond the reach of its changed space as nature as a whole entity may have places within it that are "outside" of the present change. For example, perhaps in the vast depths of the ocean or land mass which are not affected by "surface" re-presentation. Surface is a significant imagery of what nature is and means to those that live on the surface, simply because that is the space where they live. However, direct or immediate appreciation of spaces beyond the senses of surface species, of what is below, above, and beyond sight, is perhaps not regarded as essential nature. This is because it does not hold that necessity of nature is so important for ways of being and "sense of place" (Seddon 1972).

From a human perspective, due to technological advancement of flowing global information and image availability, direct and immediate spaces can be global. These "far off" places of nature are seen through the digital screen, although the quality of appreciation, as compared to the physicality of actually being there, may be less so. That would depend on an individual's past experiences and limits of imagination, and their extent of mindfulness of one's nature other, as opposed to one's nature own. However, the present technology assisting one's gaze does not imply that current generations have a privileged access to the world's nature(s), as human history is saturated with expansion of movement to newer places and spaces, i.e., a colonizing character of humans to populate and "own," which is a commonality of all species to expand to the limits of their inherent capacities of what "nature" gave them. Also, what nature can limit them to in relation as to what time and space is "allowed" for species, when both indicators run out, with history showing these potentials are actual and, hence, absolute in their finality.

The only common constant over the whole history of the Earth, i.e., Earth history—not just the minuscule human contribution to that history in terms of time and space change over the surface landscape—is the presence of nature. For instance, nature in its ongoing-ness combining permanency and fluidity of physical expression and living expression is always there. It may appear to be in the background, quietly ticking along, trying to mind its own business, but instantaneously can come to the fore. Either way, its power is a mixture of passivity and activity. Time is on its side, as it will eventually outlast all Earth dwellers. Even though humans have conquered gravity and extended their reach into very localized space as compared to the vastness of the universe, walked on the Moon, and tentatively probing Mars as a fledging colony, with a long-term view to expand their reach beyond this, nature is there already. Waiting, watching, and adapting.

If nature is there already, how deep does one go into the Earth and beyond the skies to space and outer space to the end of the universe, and further than, before the blanket term *nature* ceases to have meaning? In an absolute appreciation, nature equates to the universe, perhaps beyond. It is a concept of abstraction and reality that echoes the God concept of abstraction and reality. Therefore, from select religious filters, God and Nature (capital N intended) is or are one and the same. Nature also equates to the microcosm, the atom, and smaller to perhaps an eventual space of "nothing," as the infrastructural unit of life and beyond life (both prior and a prior). Basically, nature as nothingness but also nature as everything-ness, equating to Nature as an immensity of power of which a part of it powers humans.

Human Natures

Just as religious doctrines and associated religious professionals acquire and practice power by claiming God is the sponsor of their endeavors, i.e., absorbing and transfusing *the* divine power source to provide authority and a sense of unquestioned performance, nature can be seen to perform a similar role. For instance, the power of nature is absorbed and transfused by humans to power their performance, and humans gain power by the existence of nature and how it can be exploited to further their aims. These aims are guided by whatever socio-cultural system one happens to be a part of, historical as well as contemporary, along varying levels of development generally within a capitalist-based system, which is becoming more and more dominate. How nature is utilized facilitates the capitalist project and can and does reflect it in physical form, as the landscape is reshaped into human images of what they think it should be. For example, urban, rural, and remote environments with their accompanying residential, industrial, farming, mining, pastoral, tourism, and inevitable waste products. Seas and oceans are part of the imagery of overlaid human representation from freight and military, to depleted fish stocks and increasing plastic presence. Also, skies filled with commercial jets, satellites, and, in places, pollution gases, i.e., more waste production from human invention.

The inventive characteristics of humans are fed by imaginations of how something can be of advantage, regarded as its potential, to producing an actualization of that potential. For example, considering altering nature is fundamentally a potential to actual process of physical change, and, in the background, the imagination process is quietly working away, overlaying the physical with abstracted change, which can be a more powerful image than the original physical object, i.e., powerful in the sense of exploitative capacity deemed greater than the original physical state left to its own devices. First, Second, and Third nature conceptualizations are the abstracted tools that create the physical, and more than physical, usage and understanding of space and place. First nature is that which has not been touched by human hand and imagination, e.g., being spaces and places of original, before human existence and, consequently, the existence of their being there. Essentially the Earth unreconstructed by anthropological performance, or the Earth untrans-formed by people (Brooks et al. 2011), now comprehended as merely mytholog-ical or historic (Hughes 2005). This anthropocentric view limits the contribution of nonhuman species prior to the human "invention" and the nonhuman species living alongside humans of how both contributes to the changing face or sur(face) of nature. Also, the influence of erosion and reformation of nature by heat, water, and wind. Fundamentally, all these factors contribute to a First nature of never was, as nature is constantly on the move within its sometimes-apparent stillness. A stillness of geological time behind the movement of Earth species.

Whatever convenient way(s) or imaginations "virtuous" nature is seen in its "original" state, potential and actual power that this chastely space offers are difficult and unavoidable to resist:

> First nature, which is "the result of autonomous ecological processes," is the source of natural wealth or "natural capital," such as soil fertility, abundant forests: "this was the wealth of nature, and no human labour could create the value it contained." (Cronon 1991, 205)

This power of the wealth of nature is beyond what humans can ever hope to produce, except by jumping on the back of nature, so images of First nature as abstract are manufactured in more concrete terms by Second nature. The regulated power deployed in the social world of culture and the city, society, and the market (Smith 1996) can be thought of as second nature. A "nature that is humanly pro- duced (through conceptualisation as well as activity) and that therefore partakes, but without being entirely, of the human" (Biersack 2006, 14). An environment "as worked by people and shaped by extraction, agriculture, markets and other anthropogenic factors" (Hughes 2005, 158). Additionally, Second nature can be thought of as nature of the human, a reflection of human nature in its physicality of intent. It is the most visible of the three natures, as the other two are more abstract, supported by and supporting physical presence. Second nature can be thought of as raw, brutal even, in how landscapes are changed from an assumed First nature or previously termed *Second nature*. This latter being an older Second nature of technological excellence of its time, with that time running and ran out, and subsumed within a newer Second nature of updated technology. Hence, a potentially repetitive process of Second-nature replacement, but in actuality the long-term sustainability of this will depend on nature itself.

The paradox of "borrowed" power by humans from nature is the more humans extract from nature's resources, and deplete those resources, the more the power pendulum swings back in nature's favor. Thus, nature does not dictate, but physical nature does, at any given time, set limits on what is humanly possible (White 1985), and humans can only create Second nature with the cooperation of nature, in association with non-manipulable natural conditions of labor processes, and being cautious of too much reliance of human intentional transformative powers vis-à-vis nature (Benton 1989). Accordingly, if the natural conditions become untenable, humans are rendered powerless to do much about it, then nature regains control, as it will do eventually in any human activity by sheer cold existence of timeless permanency, and creating its version of Second nature of First nature, e.g., an environment absorbing what was altered by humans from previous First or Second natures and, in turn, altering that. This "new" natural form may be an amalgamation of all that has been there before, producing landscapes that may not have existed previously, but there will be tinges of familiarity about it, as previous natural ingredients (multiple First and Seconds) have been mixed and can be perceived through the latest nature layer, i.e., be that "Fifth" nature, "Twelfth" nature, or whatever. In this fashion, there is a power struggle and power resistance of nature and human nature(s).

Continuing this power struggle enters the virtual real of Third nature. This is a nature of movement, of "information flows...an information landscape...almost layering over old territories" (Wark 1994, 120). An immaterial nature generating theoretical economic value, becoming real, based on speculation that echoes speculative beginnings of Second-nature space potentiality for exploitation, so nothing new there, but a speculation of different emphasis. To illustrate, speculation of how nature should be, or potentially can be as an exploitation of indirect directness, as opposed to the direct exploitation of Second nature, by and for human inaction/action within and without localized environments (Hughes 2005). Thus, a nature speculation reflecting conceptual abstraction. The intention being that "nature" reproduces and extends itself as new capital, which is the basis of "third nature" (Dressler 2011, 538). In this way, the monetary Third nature reinvents the spaces of Second and First natures to ensure there is further life in these tired and worn environments, to keep capital circulation flowing. Hence, to revalue nature as capital according to modern ideals, needs, and concerns to conserve a newly imagined, reconstituted "nature" (Garland 2008). Principally, a kick start to liquefied nature that pours information onto targeted landscapes to keep them producing and keep the profit happening.

The Abstraction of Third Nature Works with the Abstraction of First Nature to "Place" a Price on Nature

> The conditional and speculative encourage financial revaluation of elusive nature. Consistently connected to first nature, the elusive/abstracted nature is discursively produced, disembedded, contained and subject to economic valuation. (Dressler 2011, 538)

Since placing prices on land for real estate purposes or industrial or resource usage has been going on for centuries, this process is not new. The difference now is between the more "concrete" existence of Second-nature material and the more insubstantial and indeterminate Third nature, immaterial. For instance, firstly, the former appears quite overt when visualizing and appreciating; i.e., Second nature can be touched and appreciated and compared and contrasted with other physical Second natures in the hierarchical price scale. Also, there is an abstract part to the "Secondary" process of costing, as all pricing assessment is arbitrary, but is based on something substantial. Secondly, the latter flowing Third nature cost analysis utilizes potential imaginings to actualize a profit, and potency of voice of the seller of the Third product is key to price fixing and return on investment. To exemplify, the "Third" is not past, present, or future, but conditional; not a tense (of time), but a mood of speech (Hughes 2005, 158).

As with the power of information flows, i.e., the Third nature of propagation and propaganda, it is only effective when the targeted population of a place acquiesces. This is realized by "applying pressure through extra-local comprehensions and dogmas of superimposed images, symbols, brands, and replicas of things in and of nature as mediated, valued monetarily" (Dressler 2011, 538). From this application, those on the coal face of local actuality are "required" to go along with these external definitions of what "their" place is, and act in favor of this new actuality, to ensure this artificial reality conforms to the structures of abstract reality (Carrier and West 2009, 7). Nevertheless, producing Third nature is a risk investment for the Third nature-ers, reflecting a speculative process to

> perceive a virtual reality, seemingly real but dependent upon the conceptual apparatus and outlet that generate it. (Carrier and Miller 1988, 2)

To ensure profitability of Third nature, a commonality of identity with the "social and cultural expectations that bind" (Dressler 2011, 534) is central to the process. In other words, the abstraction has to bind to the more concrete of particular meanings, norms, and beliefs (Brockington, Duffy, and Igoe 2008; Bryant and Goodman 2004) that signify society and nature. This is because abstraction in and of itself is powerless without something tangible to hook into, implying that Third nature "flows" back to the Second and First when it is reinterpreting, which in turn flow back to it. Consequently, a blurring of the First, Second, and Third into a tri-nature of power representation. These layers within their configurations of fluidity also play with nature's ongoing configurations of fluidity to make statements of power. These statements are there to be seen and experienced in nature, as human footprints attempt to walk everywhere that is humanly possible to access to what nature offers, but perhaps not so "humanely" in the quest to control, influence, and make power bases. Fundamentally, the three natures are understood, practiced, and performed by varying human perspectives that compete with each other, and sometimes themselves, when establishing how "best" to represent power in nature or over nature.

How to Wrestle Power from Nature

Positive (Progressive) Nature

The Bible chapter shows divine power and how God created life or the life of nature, with the catalyst of creation as a somewhat abstracted entity, even with the "evidence" of concrete nature. Thus, the uncertainty of abstraction creates doubt of actual existence within the parameters of how humans measure existence to be so. This doubt can reach a critical level of profound change in attitude, challenging the old order. For example, a sense of Second and perhaps accompanying Third nature of rationale thinking overlying the First nature of theology. This fundamental change of human nature directly connects to the Enlightenment. During the Seventeenth and Eighteenth centuries, the British philosophy of Enlightenment (Explanation, Illumination, Clarification, Insight), denounced theological world comprehension (Soule and Lease 1995) and replaced it with an expanding scientific knowledge potential that would explain nature and its natural order (Smart 1992). Positivistic science became the new "religion" of ordering and focuses on the encircling of nature, and "accomplishes" this by visual nature representation that is "consistent" (Figlio 1996), i.e., not ambiguous, and limits nature understanding to the limits of positivistic understanding, so borders between science and nature are uncomplicated and undemanding (Oudshoorn 1996). This science interpretation grew in power, in relation to its opinion, and has become the leading and almost exclusive objective knowledge creator, as opposed to The Creator. Consequently, as with all power performances, select voices are expressed, others not so much, and claims to knowledge are claims to power (Demeritt 1996).

Even though positivistic science claims of how nature can be perceived as limited in scope and therefore perhaps flawed in its encircling tendencies and not getting fully to the heart of the matter, no matter! For instance, this limited scope is ideal fertile ground to expand the scope of land and sea domination and exploitation, since positivistic science in a sense goes hand in hand with human power expansionist tendencies. Consequently, this filtered science of nonnegativity offers a "legitimate" ideological base to justify creating First, Second and Third natures and what to do with them to normalize the power performance as acceptable. Thus, reinforcing the positionality of the elite power brokers of nature and allowing them to be "progressive"; a derivative of positive.

Building the Social of Nature

However, nature power struggles and resultant tensions emerge when "positive" voices claim to be the only points of view, becoming the only ways that nature is regarded and treated. Plurality of voices and ways are deliberately stated, since ironically different positivistic perspectives can go up against each other when vying for the "top spot" of nature appreciation, while other nature understandings are marginalized. Ironic in the sense of demonstrating that there are multiple ways of seeing of what one is trying to understand, so being an antithesis performance of the "uncomplicated" positivistic doctrine, and driven by the complexity of the social, i.e., positivistics are part of society and its social and will be influenced by it. This process is not a same-size-fits-all experience and practice and, consequently, generating answers to what nature is and does and what it potentially and actually can do will produce differentiation. This is where social constructionism enters the nature debate, as it endeavors to go past these dictatorial and inflexible practices and assertions (Low and Gleeson 1998). Hence, a challenge of power.

Society is saturated in difference, and one of the essential differences is the diverse access to power. Paradoxically, this creates a societal space of "same-ness" or narrowness of "normality," as the differences are hidden behind the "official" doctrine. To hide does not imply that the differences have disappeared as they still exist and want to be heard, and in acknowledgment of this, social construction performs "truths," not "truth." These truths originate from social interaction and dynamics (Soule and Lease 1995), although incongruously, and the production of diversity of truths may undermine the power of nature more so than positivistic encounters with nature. This is because a whole range of truths about nature will be added to the mix of human understanding, making it much harder and perhaps untenable to find out "nature's truth." In other words, if there is not a uniformity of perspective regarding nature, it becomes fragmented in its understanding. On the other hand, a range of truths can strengthen the hand of nature, as the fragmentary can coalesce to produce an amalgamated nature. Thus, strength in depth, acknowledging all voices in the creation of nature knowledge. Essentially, nature is vulnerable to human ideologies and practices, as constructing nature is caused by the interaction and relationship of social forces (Scarso 2013) supplied from cultural knowledge systems (Escobar 1998). Therefore, what nature is and means to humans is generated from humans, both positivist and constructivist, but paradoxically nature is supposed to be precisely that which is not constructed (Scarso 2013).

Societizing Nature/Naturing Society

This paradox is the dichotomy of the constructed, non-construction of nature, as nature retains an immensity of power and can get along very well without the interference and absence of humans. Nature in essence is a power of adaptability, and has the potential to change when required, which is all the time. The change is from within and within/without. Firstly, within in terms of a self-generating capacity to induce change, for whatever reason, to achieve or flow toward a new equilibrium. The new equilibrium may be an instantaneous moment in time, a flirtation with static-ness, before evolving along a fresh set of fluidity seeking for the next equilibrium. Indeed, the natural state of nature is not stillness, but movement, and it is this movement that makes it a formidable player in the game of life and death. Secondly, within/without in relation to "outside" interference that causes a diversionary course from the intended self-made course. This would be the standard space it operates from, since nature is not a singular entity but a multiplicity. Thus, everything that shows life will cause interference with nature's performance, including humans, and it adapts to what they are doing, and they to it. The relationship is so close and intense that essentially all are of the same stock, the same family, and since nature bubbles with life it is unavoidable that it is in constant flux.

But here is the rub, as with many families, discord can arise between certain members and disassociation can occur. To illustrate by relating to humans, some see society as above, beyond, and detached from nature, while others see nature as part of the family unit. Thus, a self-governing social world, distanced from an equally independent and external nature or universal nature that incorporates human and nonhuman worlds in endless union (Smith 1996). Distancing is important, as it allows greater freedom of action and inaction when applying agended power aims. For example, separating oneself from nature and other humans affected by one's decisions enables a protective spatial barrier to be placed between them in case of resistance or consequential counter action; i.e., one removes themselves from the situation to lessen the fear of consequences and guilty conscience. As a result, nature is objectified and objects are easier to manipulate than subjects, which is a convenient place to be to exercise power more fully and, essentially, with minimized consequences.

Within the process of detaching society from nature, power exercising is shown on a global scale through economic speculation and practice. This "enlightened" way of things renders remote nature and human and nonhuman others, and all are peripherized through the Enlightenment project with only selected desires being applied, i.e., "what men want to learn from Nature is how to use it in order wholly to dominate it and other men. That is the only aim...Enlightenment is totalitarian" (Horkheimer and Adorno 1972, 3). The authoritarian attitude is necessary to maximize competitive edge, reduce costs, and maximize returns, e.g., an economy geared primarily to efficiency (Biesecker and Hofmeister 2010). Efficiency means performing within a narrow field of inquiry that best suits the powered agenda implemented. From this, collateral damage from nature wastage, physical damage, and human "casualties" (loss of livelihood and/or land) is an acceptable risk for the "risk takers," as the risk objections are minimized in the spatial manipulation of nature taking place. Therefore, for the attendant capitalist endeavor to advance economically and socially in society, the general populous is best served by disinformation on comprehending their connectivity to the environment (Dickens 1996). To counter this propaganda, thinking about what nature is should be practiced, and if not, "we abandon them (ideological and political struggles) to those who use nature to justify not only the domination of nature by humans, but also the domination of humankind itself" (Fitzsimmons 1989, 117). However, nature itself simply adapts and carries on, as it is the human adaptation on both sides of the economic divide that causes rifts (for humans and in and of nature).

Economic Political Struggles of Nature

Politics is concerned with power. The power to turn a situation, event, thing, place, and space to one's advantage through negotiation, coercion, intimidation, or covertly, all under the cover of language and non-language use. Politics is not just thought of as the "formal" kind of government performance, of those who are democratically elected or self-elected, but any interaction and encounter that demand communication between two or more involved stakeholders. The type and reason of interaction are only limited by human imagination and essentially involve only humans as part of the deal-making or deal-breaking process, with other nonhuman materiality and immateriality often being what is contested over. For example, what nature offers as exploitation potential.

Consequently, it is the tangibility of nature in its material existence that is projected onto abstracted imaginings of immateriality (shades of first Second and Third natures) and how much of these that can be "farmed" and owned that produces an economic framework. As with all processes, this machine of making money needs customers to purchase the goods on offer. For instance, the more money goods are sold for as opposed to how much they cost to manufacture or extract and refine to a predetermined use, the bigger the payout. In addition to this, it is the purpose of political voices involved in the economic money-making performance to speak out for better pay. However, not in the union way of better pay and conditions, although this would be an aspect of the payout equation but driven by "speeches of profitability." Speeches that drown out opposition; encourage fellow investors; groom potential customers to want, need, and desire (Shurmer-Smith and Hannam 1994) the production offered; and gloss over how this product is brought to the "table of consumption. "

The more economics one possesses, the more power one has in the world of political economic production. Hence, the greater the proportion of power, the greater the opportunity to get more and, consequently, a self-feeding system gaining momentum in the circulation of money. To ensure it is fed, markets need to expand and be invented and reinvented. To do this, nature is the commodity of choice; ultimately it is the only choice, since all products come from nature and, if they do not, they are imagined into nature. Thus, nature is changed into images that reflect imaginations of which can be sold in the consumer marketplace. For instance, political economic imaginings regard nature as "resource" and decide how this resource is owed. To assign this precious resource, political economics advocate appeal "to the theory of markets, to the goals of maximising utility, and to the centrality of money as the common means to measure heterogeneities of human desires, of use values and of elements and processes 'in nature'" (Harvey 1996, 150). So, political economy is a label of manipulation as it represents the connectivity of policy and technology and how these steer production and subsequent consumption, social integrity, and to where the social structure is headed for (Goodman and Redclift 1991).

Political economy manipulates nature as "rightfully" in the service of human-kind. This "right way" encourages acceptance of a social and wealth hierarchy and gathering private property, a power differential perhaps practiced prior to Aristotle (Coates 1998). Therefore, *servicing humankind* is not necessarily a blanket term involving everyone, at least not from an equitable manner. For example, when looking at practices of political economy, the practices are fundamentally of power distribution (Mosedale 2011); i.e., "In nature the allocation of power...control, access, extract, exchange, distribute and use of nature, ranges disproportionately across different social groups and space" (Mosedale 2015, 506). In essence, not only is power distribution inequality prominent among people, but even the power distribution of inequality is strategically allocated to the spaces of nature.

The modern and/or postmodern political economy is fashioned through neoliberalism. This coexistence acts as a corrective regulatory mode and accumulation system that redefines and co-constitutes socio-natures (Bakker 2010); e.g., nature's spaces are priced. The implication is that every space in the world, and perhaps the world itself, has been valued in monetary terms and within this globality (and globalization), nature is renovated to reflect economic and social movement (Adams 1996). Thus, nature is subjected, and nature is subjection as "capitalization of almost everything," and, consequently, the environment, or "nature," has increasingly been colonized (Christophers 2016, 9). Subsequently, the "remote" hand of the political economic players in the "world" of neoliberalism causes reaction in the immediacy of the local space and place that nature resource speculation falls on. This is because local experiences of the neoliberalization of nature reflect the interplay of inherited institutional lineages, policy landscapes, local economic and political dynamics, and the multiscalar dynamics of regulatory restructuring (Bakker 2010). In effect, neoliberalism creates inequality, which is part of its performance as it is a necessarily incomplete and fractured process where competing logics can persist and progressive opportunities can emerge (Higgins, Dibden, and Cocklin 2012). Thus, nature as fractured or "broken" is a by-product of political economic power, a "cracked" power system that nature puts up with.

Political economics draws its strength from a narrow agended power base, from a restricted attitude toward nature in terms of what nature can do for humans and not what humans can do for nature in terms of action and inaction, with both significant in influencing nature's subsequent reaction. Also, not considering the consequences of local people and cultures dwelling in targeted nature spaces and places ripe for resource extraction, and the effects on plants and nonhuman flora and fauna that are present. To consider these "unrecognized" consequences, another human power formation in the guise of political ecological filters of persuasion is added to the complexity of human–nature relations, to highlight the oppressed parties drawn into the nature as resource performance.

Ecological Political Struggles of Nature

Ecological perspectives act as a counterbalance to economic perspectives, a scene of human "natural" equilibrium between the two performances. It is equilibrium at the basic level of binary emphasis on how nature is regarded. For instance, a viewpoint dualism at a supposedly simplistic level of appreciation, for both would have shades of economic and ecological outlook along the positivistic to socially constructed highway of "realities," but not an equilibrium in how the extent of each one's ideologies and concrete practices are represented in the actualities of nature usage; i.e., the economics would enjoy the upper hand.

However, it is precisely the existence of power imbalances that encourage other ways of looking and being, since those who set the agenda and hold the reins of power should expect opposition. The paradox is if there is no opposition, ever, this renders power pointless, since power is not required to perform life's practices as everyone just goes along in the same direction, i.e., an absolute consensus. However, it is an unlikely scenario, as it would render society impotent and set in decay, for power is needed to power society. In effect, political economic outlook requires the existence of political ecological outlook to maintain its strength of purpose and primary position in the game of countering the other's perspective(s), and vice versa.

Political ecologists, in their bid for a slice of the nature pie, focus on political nature and political capitalism and related tensions of variance (Adams and Hutton 2007; Robbins 2012). Paradoxically, they create tensions too, just by questioning the status quo of political economy, as does the political economist by just doing what they do. So, all contribute to power struggles, with some more than others, as stakeholders vie within unequal power resources to access and control natural resources (Vaccaro, Beltran, and Paquet 2013). Of political significance is the nonhuman space of nature (Bryant and Bailey 1997), and the dehumanizing of those deemed not worthy of human status by those other humans Second and Third naturing their space. This is a result of the unequal power of external stakeholders to determine dialogues and land/sea usage that often marginalize local populations, due to perceptions of lost agency in determining and managing their own lives (Campbell 2008).

Thus, the pursuit of profit at the natural-resource-gathering stage tends to ride roughshod over those deemed to "be in the way," including both humans and the nature of the place. From this, the monetarist "development" of nature can be accessed any which way, including "risk nature" pricing from weather events, to ecosystems degradation, to species extinction (Christophers 2016, 9). The process of risking nature also extends to regarding it as just a money-making exercise, since "unless people feel the value of nature, it will be treated as a mere commodity, to be bought and sold, built and done away with as profit dictates" (Adams 1996, 172). So, ecologist advocates see "ecology" as more than biosystem balance concerns, by incorporating power/knowledge associations (Luke 1997).

Political ecology and political economy are similar, as both involve the human and their versions of the "good" for the human and engaging with nature through political filters. Indeed, is there any other kind or way to do so, since politics is whatever its user wishes it to be and to do in the resultant mix of different stakeholder negotiations. From these negotiations, nature has been defined within a plurality of perspectives in this political space. However, once something is defined, it can be difficult to go beyond that limitation as its potential has been curbed and its actuality becomes untenable, and the field of vision has been set with the blinkers on. In essence, the full power of nature will never be understood or appreciated by setting limits on how to gaze on it.

Nature as a Plurality of Power Perspective

There is a direct correlation between political economy in its relationship with nature and how society views and deals with nature. Also, similarly with political ecology, as each will use aspects of the other to advantage their own position in nature dissimilation. Thus, how society views and deals with nature is determined by cultural fields of life production, since it is the cultural that guides behavior and attitude, i.e., a practice of history up to the now of the "marriage" between culture and nature. This is an intimate and ongoing relationship (Arnold 1996), and one of complexity, meticulously developed through assorted human explorations (Colon and Hobbs 2015). However, as with the "nature" of marriages, breakdown of mutual communication between the two principal stakeholders can occasionally occur, sometimes resulting in divorce. Culture and nature are a case in point, since "the matrix of [the] opposition between culture and nature is the very matrix of Western metaphysics" (Benoist 1975, cited in Strathern 1980, 178).

As part of the metaphysics methodology looking at the dynamics of potentiality and actuality, the heart of the matter and resultant impasse between the culturally inspired humans and dogmatically inspired nature perhaps lie along the continuum of the potential of the actual and the actual of the potential. For instance, it is what resides within the power of humans to think about how nature is to them, dictated by cultural filters, which is where the power tension begins. This is not necessarily between human and nature but between human and human, as cultural performances sometimes do not travel in the same direction. Within this directional conflict, the "connectivity" between the cultural local and the cultural global plays an important role in saying what nature is, since due to a power imbalance the global can instill their cultural of nature onto the local, "encouraging" a "same" direction of nature usage "appreciation." A paradox here is the global cultural nature dealmakers would not consider compromising their own local regular living space and place in the scramble of cultural nature injection and extraction, unless absolutely necessary. Thus, the powerful can protect their place and reject the place of their others. Also, the potential and actual of two or more global cultural players targeting the same cultural local nature place add to the tension mix.

Nature in and of itself, within its ongoing reinvention, is thought to be a passive recipient of cultural usages as its objections to being violated are generally voiced by silence and a stoic attitude. Hence, its main role, to the cultural gaze, is of being there as a use(ful) value. Even though nature is an immensity of space as compared to the almost insignificance of human place, this quiet sentinel is assumed to be a thing of weakness (as it is exploited), but this is its strength. For instance, humans react to it, be that of preliminary conditions that fade into the background before the symbolic mind takes over (Scarso 2013), to recreate nature as cultural representation, but it is nature that actualizes the cultural potential. Fundamentally, without nature, culture would not have material to work with, essentially a voided metaphysics.

An egocentric culturalness that does not acknowledge the major shareholder in the living process, i.e., nature, imperils the "audacious arrogance of humanity not to recognize the raw physicality of the earth and its history of dominating rather than being dominated by humanity" (Franklin 2014, 265). Also, to minimize the role of how the more-than-human actors matter in this (Jönsson 2016) can result in forgetfulness of nature, which is an unwise place to be in the empowering and disempowering that nature can present, sometimes with devastating consequences. For example, the existence of nature and its power and mechanisms can operate clear of cultural discourse (Dickens 1996). For instance, species still retain distribution of their geography principally, beyond the human voice and touch, by climate, geological processes, and ecological tolerances (Soule 1995).

Human cultural integration with what nature offers to them and how nature and the human are altered in the enduring process can also place power relations and outcomes in a good light. For instance, the "good" of humanity may equate to the "good" of nature, perhaps not overall in the grand scheme of nature/human/ cultural history, but sometimes the Garden of Eden imagery, prior to the apple incident, can occur. To illustrate, both human and nature independent of human can modify environments of the same place and space, of which these have contributed to biodiversity and other natural values that have proven sustainable over centuries and are living examples of cultural heritage. Therefore, "they are rich in natural and cultural values not in spite of, but because of the presence of people" (Brown, Mitchell, and Beresford 2005, ix). Of course, these rich values are of human interpretive creation and not necessarily nature interpretation, but as the former is part of the latter, this supplies the perspective with some "goodness"; a sense of nature/culture well-being.

Nature as power needs to be considered in the world of human power relations and processes. It is of a power that has patience, an infinite capacity to wait for the right time to act as a violent reaction, or just slowly, but surely acting quietly to change environments. This "quietness" may go unnoticed by the human gaze, and this "silence" is powerful, since there is nothing that can be more effective in a power performance than the covert action, i.e., a hidden power that cannot be countered as awareness of it is negligible or nonexistent, for since this power "does not" exist it is convenient for the processes of nature to flourish without interference. Also, the human interference in the geological time scale of things may be found negligible, when the human postmortem of effecting nature is carried out, post-humankind.

Natural Conclusions

As there is no idealized version of what nature is, its true nature, and its gift of ability to react and adapt to any situation human and any other species (plant and animal) presents to it, it is problematic to assume it is "suffering." Since it is in constant change, movement, stillness, and existence, the "interference" from all that live within its spatiality would just be a "normal" part of its every day and night existence. Basically, nature's "others" that live in-nature are not separate from it; they are part of nature. Also, nature does not have a fixed identity; rather, it has an identity of nonidentity, a decentered identity. This makes it powerful. Alternately, when humans create their versions of what they believe nature to be, or should be, it is they who perhaps suffer. Suffer in the context of anxiety and stress caused by the practices and performances based on their fundamental beliefs of what nature is. This suffering is regardless of political economic or political ecological approaches, with the anxiety and stress of the former relating to how much of nature can be "dug up" to produce profit and power. As to the latter, they fret as to how much of this "digging up" "damages" nature within all its constituent parts, with paradoxically the vast majority of what makes up nature being indifferent to the angst of its human membership. It would simply stay calm and carry on as if nothing untoward is occurring, since essentially nature is as whatever the present moment is.

Whatever the moral position taken or not with nature, all humans use nature for their means and ends, it being an inevitable and unavoidable space of survivability. Those who agree with or object to the positivistic interactions of nature, and the related perceived environmental damage, resource depletion, and the consequent exercise of this power, would "benefit" from inevitability awareness from their constructed perspective. For instance, liked or not, realized or not, no one is outside the human performance of making a living, and life and living are about staying alive, and the only way to do this is to be at "one" with nature (whatever form that may take). Hence, utilize what is on offer and tap into the human ability to imagine new resources from nature, and from both, keep going.

In actual fact, being at one with nature is actually easy, since humans already are. Alternatively, if humans take it too far and "damage" nature irrevocably due to environmental degradation in the context of nature not sustaining human life forms any longer, the humans will cease to be, but nature will not. This is because nature has too much depth, breath, and capacity to be affected by the demise of humanity and has experienced countless species extinctions and extinction events and the emergence of new species on Earth. Also, in the "Heavens" with the birth and death of stars. Fundamentally, even though humans use nature's power to supply themselves with their versions of its power, which is "naturally" possible as they are part of nature's space, their segment of its power is temporary as all things will end, although nature may not be among those that do end since its power appears to be permanent and all powerful. God has competition!

CHAPTER 4

Foucault

Limited Spaces of Knowing

When appreciating what Nature and God may be and what they do and why
they do what they do and also incorporating all other related and partially unre-
lated life processes and performances, the human engagement draws upon the
knowledge and critical thinking capacities they acquired over their particular
individual lifetimes and prior sociocultural formulations of the ever-moving
present. Partial, since nature and what one thinks of as God will be part of one's
overall life appreciation project. Within this, both, i.e., knowledge and critical
thinking, combine to give a "picture" of what is going on, how to react to that, and
choice(s) of where to go on to or what is next. Thus, possessing an informed set
of perspectives and opinions guide behavioral patterns and non-patterns, which
is only as good as the quality of information served up. The implication is spaces
of knowing and knowledge creation and appreciation have restrictions or margins
to operate within. From this limited spatiality, Michel Foucault developed his
"restricted or marginal" version of how people come to know and be, and how
power "plays" and blows across the winds and flows of society. In this chapter,
selected margins of his perspective will be highlighted through the filters of
my marginable restrictiveness, as all in society(s), myself included, suffer this
inhibit-ness of understanding how life is, since all comprehensions of life are
products of power to reduce one's capacity of knowing, e.g., a space of polemics.

Problems of Power Polemics

The politics of polemics is a reductive process, a binary space of us and them
or us and the rest, with them and the rest not necessarily acknowledged as having a worthy voice of note, or indeed possessing no voice. Consequently, the

political canon of polemics agenda's "debate" with a one-size-fits-all structure, as discourse, discussion, and decision are based on this agenda. The implication is that no other outlook is either accessible or even considered accessible, and critical thinking is not part of the process and actively not encouraged. Therefore, any dissent from the agenda is treated as a threat, not as something that may assist in finding a solution (Gutting 2005), a solution of mutuality. Instead, a disagreeable solution is aspired to. Disagreeable from the perspectives of the other, and an agreeable disagreeableness from the self in this polemic relationship. To illustrate, polemics joins opinions and interests, is a group of like-minded individuals, and the "other" is an adversary and must be opposed until neutralized (Rabinow 1997). Essentially, one's self-interests are protected and sustained, and the poles-apart space is recognized and, consequently, removed, so the poles become pole. Accordingly, a fumigated and resultant germ-free performance, of which Foucault regards polemics as

> Sterilising: Has anyone ever seen a new idea come out of a polemic?…it is really dangerous to make anyone believe that he can gain access to truth by such paths and thus to validate, even if merely in a symbolic form, the real political practices that could be warranted by it. (Foucault 1997, EW1, 113)

Along these lines, Foucault sees significant restriction placed on people's thinking capacity within all time periods in determined, encoded domains. So, all thinking methods are filtered through implicit rules that materially limit the spaces of thought (Gutting 2005). From this, disagreeing with the other and agreeing with the self set up possible potentialities of power that extends to actualities.

The Foucauldian speak of "marginalising of the subject" in the polemic context can incorporate marginalizing of the other. For instance, it is through what the discoursed agenda offers as thinking engagement material for parties to "discuss," and, more importantly, what is not offered and what remains hidden that dictates the power arrangement and resultant consequential action or inaction. Hence, this beyond-individual-controlled space constrains the space of individual thinking. In this way, Foucault offers that "individuals operate in a conceptual environment that determines and limits them in ways of which they cannot be aware" (Gutting 2005, 33). Being unaware means that one cannot object or offer alternatives, just become a silent voice of unawareness; i.e., the unaware process produces the silencing of voices of dissent and silencing problematizations.

Society has its problems. These *problems* are defined as such by those who can, as an *arbitrary* state of affairs that is not random and left to chance. The polemic process that leads to problematizations creates tensions and societal limits of what is expected behavior, and it is within these spatial borders that individuals gauge their level of problem-ability. For instance, their defined self under the umbrella of being defined by social power relations, utilizing what ability they retain to cope with power behavioral acceptability constraints and thresholds. Therefore, attempting to transform themselves for the "good" of themselves and simultaneously tweaking societal belief systems to make its "goodness" incorporate more of its subjects, i.e., to reduce its problem of definition of what is "good," so more people in society feel good about being there. This is an ongoing challenging power issue, and an issue that can challenge power:

> we cannot chose between "an inaccessible radicality" and "the necessary conces-
> sions to reality." Rather, "the work of deep transformation [reform] can be done
> in the open and always turbulent atmosphere of a continuous [revolutionary]
> criticism." (Foucault 2000, EW III, 457)

Tweaking the Power of Society

Tweaking societal belief systems involves miniature power plays against the societal power play. These miniature power plays or little causes can change societal structures and, hence, power structures. The changes do not necessarily imply that the aggregate of "good" has risen in moral and practical virtue, as a reordering of power hierarchal performances may take the "little" changes as tools to be played with, to what opportunities and advantages these offer to one's power capacities. Unlike Marx's group consciousness of same directional salvation of one's subservient position in society, Foucault saw a general unawareness of others of their societal other in their reactions to polemic policy. This independent plurality of causes shows events to be a process of multiplication residing in a complicated field of relations (Smart 2002), an unconscious network of individual mini powers that Foucault termed *genealogy*. For a genealogy to be is

> to identify the accidents, the minute deviations—or, conversely, the complete rever-
> sals—the errors, the false appraisals, and the faulty calculations that give birth to
> those things that continue to exist and have value for us. (Foucault 1998, EW2, 374)

Through applying critical thinking in conjunction with personal experience, by means of the more unpleasant encounters remembered by oneself, the greater the learning curve is of the false and faulty and the resultant prominence in one's life of those things of continuation. Alternatively, pleasant experiences also have value when gauging a genealogical malpractice of society, as a comparison tool. So, one knows when the errors are occurring, and being self-aware of being part of the error space of problematizations.

Genealogy is also a hidden plurality of spatial influence. For example, hidden from the perpetrators are the potential consequences of their action and reaction to centralized or core power. It is this unknowable factor from within the individual hearts of the error performances, of changing power structures, that provides the unstoppable shots at power. For instance, if these shots or errors are undetectable to those holding the triggers, what chance has mainstream society of preventing it as awareness of the danger occurs a prior. Therefore, uncovering the hidden realization of the actualization is too late, which is a common conclusion of power ploys and plays. So, genealogy in its disjointedness does not consciously break open inequalities of social relations, but rather creates disorder or disturbs general perceptions about social performance and proceedings (Smart 2002), and it may be the momentum of subsequent events that change happens. Even though the perpetrators may be regarded as traitors to society, this is a matter of spatial perspective, or spatial power differential perspective, to be more accurate.

Thus, such a genealogical (perpe)traitor

> reveals disparity and dispersion behind the constructed identity of the origin; it shows historical beginnings to be lowly, and beneath "measured truth, it posits (theorizes/advances/imagines) the ancient proliferation of errors." (Bouchard 1977, 143)

The "origin" implies when, why, and how a particular power structure or domain came into existence. At its birth, it probably would not be an actual power representative, but the potential was there. To illustrate, genealogy of origin, according to Foucault, uncovers the potential possibilities of necessity, and necessity in the context of "divine will, human nature, or transcendental conditions of possibility is the general category under which fall all efforts to justify practices and institutions in terms of their privileged origin" (Gutting 2005, 50).

Placing the justification and valued presence of necessity within the genealogy framework, the place (and time) is a "history of the present" (Foucault 1979a, DP, 30–31), a "genealogy of the modern subject as a historical and cultural reality" (Foucault and Sennett 1982, 9). This is the ongoing, unfixed "final" product that connects with the birth of the current authority of "regulations, establishments and systems" (Gutting 2005, 50). Accordingly, to judge the history of the present authorities and the validity of the symbolized power on offer, one's place of position unavoidably resides within present history. This authoritative placement of immersion implies that to have an awareness of genealogical production one must have a realization that the power structures in place are not inevitable or have a timeless quality and permanence. Then from this platform of enlightenment current authoritarian practices can be questioned and revealed for what they may look like for the "realized" gazer. However, the leap of critical thinking faith from docile, compliant, and subject and subjective member of society to feeling uncomfortable about one's society is not an easy one to achieve. Consequently, many in society would have trouble going through the revealing process, to lay bare the base power of society, as the capacity to do so would be neutralized by the "necessary" presence of power processes and procedures, since these would have achieved their purpose of conforming the masses to not question the status quo. Also, many would not wish to, even if they did know or were suspicions, because they are comfortable in their ignorance.

Ordering Times Gone By

For Foucault, and for all concerned about the legacies of time gone by and producing the powered ongoing moments of the now, referring to historical processes is key. However, this does not mean referring to historical timelines that run along a tidy progression of events neatly signed off within a nonchaotic existence of life that does not exist in practice, at least in the long term, if not brief moments of stability over the short term, but instead referring to time lines of brokenness, essentially the errors already mentioned. Therefore, analyzing errors through time

> discover[s] that truth or being do not lie at the root of what we know and what we are, but the exteriority of accidents, (Bouchard 1977, 146) and it disturbs what was previously considered immobile; it fragments what was thought unified; it shows the heterogeneity (diverse nature of something) of what was imagined consistent with itself. (Bouchard 1977, 147)

The exteriority of accidents shows the power permanency of power, for it is significant that a "mistake" or "mishap" is required to break through the protective exterior of the powered space and place. In this fashion, its defensives are left temporarily vulnerable to the probing of "accidental" imaginings into the heart of its matter, as the defensives are designed to contain the mass of society, not individual abnormalities. To illustrate, powered norms, values, and aspirations experience difficulties with the abnormal, which can create accidents and errors of the powered core's own making, as the fragmented heterogeneity is revealed. This can lead the temporarily vulnerable powered formation(s) to become permanently altered to a new space of formation, which itself is of an impermanent nature as fresh accidents emerge.

So, the cycle of powered regeneration keeps turning over time as newer power domains overlay their old. Since power "placement" is a stubborn beast of its burden, the burden is once power is acquired it can become an inadvertent milestone and liability for the owner who fears to lose it, and radical courses of action may be required to wrestle it away. Radical in terms of an aggressive and vehement performance. Hence, from repeated forceful performances,

> historical change might be more appropriately conceptualized in terms of the
> continual institutionalization of forms of violence in systems of rules, or the
> succession of one mode of domination by another. (Bouchard 1977, 151)

Thus rules, which do follow human behavioral patterns, grant acceptability of the use of violence, sanctioning them as justified. Therefore, writing down in abstract form the concrete of offensive action denotes the existence and operation of a reciprocal power arrangement that strengthens the power project and its accompanying physical intimidation and practical application, when needed, i.e., when genealogically necessary. Systems of rules thereby "authorize and legitimate the commission of violence against violence, a corollary of which is the emergence of forms of resistance alongside what Foucault later conceptualized as relations of power" (Smart 2002, 50). Historical succession therefore

> becomes a matter of contests and struggles over the system of rules, success
> belonging to those who are capable of seizing…[the] rules, to…invert their
> meaning, and redirect them against those who had initially imposed them.
> (Bouchard 1977, 151)

To do genealogy is an ongoing awareness project and policing of power interpretation, which is no easy task since power representation and presentation would not be of a singular disposition, i.e., something that can be quickly revealed. Accordingly, there would be a multiplicity of coded and hidden stratums to fathom and decipher, a power defense in depth of which one tier must be understood and deconstructed before the next can be accessed. The point of this interpreted power performance or key issue for analysis is

> how men govern (themselves and others) by the production of truth (...the establishment of domains in which the practice of true and false can be made at once ordered and pertinent. (Foucault 1981, 9)

Genealogy experiences its own power rush when exposing the power processes of its other(s). It is a site of resistance pursuing and questioning origins of power, changeless and uniform truths, and persistent progress of humanity. Subsequently, the results of genealogical inquiry "uncovers the eternal play of dominations, the domain of violence, subjugations and struggle" (Smart 2002, 52). Therefore, a Foucauldian genealogy is a historical causal explanation that is material, multiple, and corporeal (Gutting 2005).

Archiving Materiality and Nonmateriality

Archive is a label used by Foucault to adhere to "the general system of the formation and transformation of statements" existent at a given period within a particular society (Smart 2002, 40). Describing the archive is the central tenet of archaeological investigation, in which archaeology is the examination of ancient cultures utilizing their material residue as evidence, e.g., the materiality of tools, burial sites, and built structures. The materiality is important, as it shows the surface, the physicality, the conscious level of what a particular sociocultural domain is, or was like, within particular time-spaces. It shows the power process and structure in action, in actuality. Hence, it is about how the society in any epoch was organized and constrained through the spatial materiality that was emplaced by those who were not "errored" and displaced from those of a genealogical persuasion. Foucault's archaeological investigation also draws from the nonmaterial. This is the more vibrant aspect of the material/nonmaterial connectivity, as it is the unseen, the unconscious, and the driver that makes the material; i.e., "It is the unconscious that is the more powerful for it 'ultimately' dictates the surface truths of the world and their 'conditions of possibility'" (Gutting 2005, 34). In this way of working together, the material and nonmaterial/immaterial are the statements of intent that drives the society and, consequently, the human behavioral patterns.

A statement is a declaration, announcement, speech, proclamation, assertion, and stating the spoken word—depending on what is being uttered, who is pronouncing it, and their symbolic status within a power domain—and can be very influential as to how others respond to it. For example, word usage, both through the spoken and written forms, speaks volumes about how power intentions are diffused through the population. It is the communication arm of power, with its varying volumes of sound intensity and volumes of written material, offering evidence for power to etch into one's conscious and unconsciousness; i.e., one is *persuaded*. One is also *dissuaded* as the word dictates power structures and hierarchies from the tone of their particular time-spaces, since the tone, or manner, attitude, and tendency, "sounds off" the power attitude in place. Thus, people become archived; recoded, documented, collected, filed—essentially controlled and manipulated. As a result, the object of archaeological analysis is then a description of the archive and

> literally what may be spoken of in discourse; what statements survive, disappear, get re-used, repressed or censured; which terms are recognized as valid, question-able, invalid; what relations exist between "the system of present statements" and those of the past, or between the discourses of "native" and foreign cultures; and what individuals, groups, or classes have access to particular kinds of discourse. (Foucault 1978a, 14–15)

The potentiality and actuality of discourse flow from the unconscious to the conscious. This is because the arrangement of interactions and rules that guide discourse formation and its constituent parts—i.e., statements, objects, theoretical options, and concepts—are not restrictions drawn from the consciousness, a society boss, or attendant materiality of institutions and social or economic relations (Smart 2002); instead, they originate from the unconscious, and these systems of discourse creations, comprehended by Foucault, are

> literally located at the "prediscursive" level…[where prevail] the conditions in and under which it is possible for a discourse to exist, of, what must be related, in a particular discursive practice, for such and such an enunciation to be made, for such and such a concept to be used, for such and such a strategy to be orga-nized. (Foucault 1973, 74)

For power plays to be generated in the unconscious, the question, a question of necessity, is, how did the power entity, with its presence or material/immaterial concrete abstraction, get there? For instance, did the unconsciousness energy capacity achieve a level of self "materiality" that formed into an idea or concept that, out of the necessity of life to be alive, instigated processes and performances to produce life? From this sense, power can be thought of (literally) as the Potential (capital P intentional) that actualizes life, and without it there would be no life or not as humankind knows it or maybe imagines it to be; a powerless void perhaps. Thus, it is the fundamental aspect of all living beings, including plants and animals, powering them up to get as far as possible along their time and space of existence, and, within this conceptual framework the power "spark" is prior to the unconscious, existing "independently. "

Independently is a vague positionality, since is it the conception moment in time that creates the beginnings of sentient beings and, in turn, creates the power spark that continues the life form and consequently giving rise to the power spark that is passed on from the old to the new generation and so on. If so, where did the original spark "originate" from to power the first generation, or does the power enter the body and mind from the outside, an omnipresence? Or is power simply energy within its potential and kinetic modes that occasionally take living form, suggesting also that power may be dormant and, if so, what is the dominant power state—is it sleeping or being awake or both? Essentially, it involves an array of powered questions and imagines to speculate on.

These questions may occupy prior space to Foucault's archaeology, namely a foundation space that creates the conditions for archaeological challenges to discursive inclusion and exclusion along the powered discourse. A space that already sets up the conditions of layered access to power. So, it should be relatively easy for the archaeological critical gaze of the task of recognizing how power is exercised within defined narratives of discourse and resultant disagreements with the stance adopted. This is because the blueprint of how power is runs through the whole living space, including the space of the archaeologist, thus gazing and recognizing the behavior of oneself, e.g., a mirrored power already acquainted with from birth. Therefore, it should be no problem to filter perception through the archaeological gaze that reveals discontinuities, gaps, ruptures, and, subsequently, the emergence of new forms of positivity of difference (Smart 2002, 42); Smart adds that repetitive, uninterrupted forms and numerous differences produced by transformations are also factored in and they, too, are vulnerable to positives. Positives return to the realm of "good," focusing on good things rather than bad, thus discoursing for the "good" and archiving the "bad".

Differentiating the good from the bad is a societal product, since each society has its regime of truth, its "general politics" of truth, i.e., the types of discourse that it accepts and makes function as true and says what counts as true (Foucault 1980, *Truth and Power*, 131). So, summing up the power investigation of archaeology and how it depicts the archive, it is literally what may be spoken of in discourse, i.e., which terms are recognized as valid, questionable, and in-valid, and what individuals, groups, or classes have access to particular kinds of discourse (Foucault 1978a). From this, Foucault removes the central position of the ruler(s) of society and re(places) them with analysis of the rules of formation through which statements achieve cohesion as a theory, text, or science (Smart 2002). Consequently, the societal network is re(placed) scientifically.

Science as Power

The implication of science is of a process, a method, that gazes on the "natural" and attendant physical world and phenomena from a systematized platform of experimentation and observation. This system of engaging adopts a central position of how life is and how humans should behave in it. The systematized aspect is significant in the creation and sustaining of powered places, spaces, and perfor-mances, since it produces a conforming human subjectivity. Part of this "powered" process involves archaeological filters of understanding in human sciences, which focus on the rules of organizations and formations that structure and distinguish thought discourse methods (Smart 2002, 23). These "thoughtful" approaches that ran through the Renaissance, the classical age, and up to today (modern/postmodern) demonstrate diverse thought frameworks or episteme. The episteme adheres to

> the total set of relations that unite, at a given period, the discursive practices that
> give rise to epistemological figures, sciences, and possibly formalized systems…
> The episteme is not a form of knowledge…or type of rationality which, crossing
> the boundaries of the most varied sciences, manifests the sovereign unity of a
> subject, a spirit, or a period; it is the totality of relations that can be discovered
> for a given period, between the sciences when one analyses them at the level of
> discursive regularities. (Foucault 1977c, 191)

The episteme incorporates a cautiousness of why a science enjoys status as just so—not its right to be a science but the fact that it exists (Foucault 1977c). Thus, reason is bypassed in favor of transformations in the "mode of being of things, and of the order that divided them up before presenting them to the understand-ing" (Foucault 1973, xxii).

Being presented to the understanding creates the conditions of understanding, but from intended agendas of a covert but also overt nature. For instance, the mass of the population is trained to understand, and the training may be over an extended period of time, an episteme, which constantly recreates the powered life processes and practices on offer. Furthermore, the training may also be of an abrupt nature when one episteme is overrun, subsumes, replaced by another, i.e., transformed by another. Then the training extends at a less volatile rate along the episteme's "allotted" time and space, until another replacement event occurs. However, essentially for the understanding to be effective, the general populous should not know about the archaeology behind the being of things but just see and experience the surface result of it, e.g., the covert and overt aspects working together.

However, this claim of not knowing may not be detrimental to the process, as only knowing the covert portion of the mode may not actually discredit it. This is because "good" intentions to produce scientific method from its original abrupt transformation on the boundary of one episteme to the next may be seen as good by the inventors and their users of the scientific product offered. Therefore, the not knowing claim is perceived as a necessity of change for the overall "good" of society. As a consequence, power does not necessarily produce benefit for a few or the one, to the neglect of the rest, since all may benefit to varying degrees of goodness. Also, the inventors of the scientific method may not have regarded it as a "power trip"; rather, they saw and sought the attractive properties of experimentation and observation over divine inspiration, as the latter could not explain all within the complexities of life and after life. For example,

> formation of knowledge in the human sciences were not attributable to immaturity, rather,…their uncertainty as sciences, their dangerous familiarity with philosophy, their ill-defined reliance upon other domains of knowledge, their perpetually secondary and derived character, and also their claim to universality, is not, as is often stated,…[because of] the extreme density of their object; it is not the metaphysical (abstract or theoretical/without material form or substance) status or the inerasable transcendence (otherworldliness/divine existence) of this man they speak of, but rather the complexity of the epistemological configuration in which they find themselves placed. (Foucault 1973, 348)

It is perhaps those who came after who saw potential profit and exploitation within the scientific space, adding economic value to the endeavor, so science became commodified. Accordingly, it is in this moneyed space that the covert performance can prove very useful to control the understanding of the population, including the inventors. Also, paradoxically, the commodity brokers would become controlled by the process as it becomes normalized and the original intent is forgotten.

Not Losing Face

Truth of Power

To construct a discourse is to construct a framework of thinking and doing that suit the intentions of the designers of it, i.e., suited to advantage their reasons for having a discourse and their truth of the matter that eventually extends to become the truth and not just one of a range of truths. As a result, the users of this truth are confined to the space of authority that it covers and, thus, are restricted in choice and deed by that covering. This creates an uneven contest of truths, a "strange contest, a confrontation, a power relation, a battle among discourses and through discourses" (Foucault 1978b, x). As a consequence of this, the textual truths to check their authenticity are filtered through truth of fact, truth of opinion, and truth of science (Barker 1998). However, this is a difficult thing to do, as facts, opinions, and scientific claims are not absolutes, and there is always room to maneuver. It is this space of maneuverability that is fertile ground for power and fertile ground for a discursive act, e.g., "a discourse in act, profoundly committed to the rules of popular knowledge...there was applied a question derived elsewhere and administered by others" (Foucault 1978b, 210). To illustrate, it is the remoteness of elsewhere and managed by the "other(s)" that creates the distancing of power construction that is so effective in ensuring behavior is followed "correctly." Hence, the intention is to limit the errors, and individual truths become the collective truth. Thus,

> what if understanding the relation of the subject to truth were just an effect of knowledge? What if understanding were a complex, multiple, nonindividual formation, not "subjected to the subject," which produced effects of truth? One should then put forward positively this entire dimension which the history of science has negativised; analyse the productive capacity of knowledge as a collective practice; and consequently replace individuals and their "knowledge" in the development of a knowledge which at a given moment functions according to certain rules which one can register and describe. (Barker 1998, 73–74)

Objective Subjectivism

The individual retains and is constrained by subjective outlook. The retention includes identity, character, behavioral patterns, ideas, and imaginings. All are expressed through performance and movement in one's "allocated" time and space, i.e., one's living extent. Everyone possesses these qualities, although inequalities exist in how they are expressed due to the competitive nature of life. Thus, this line of thinking regards life, or the society, as a constricted spatial environment with individuals and like-minded groups conceiving of and growing power domains with those individuals who use them becoming consumer objects. These domains of power range include government, multinational companies, defense, education, prisons, medical, and science. There are others of lesser scale in terms of influence and spatial coverage, but still following the same basic constraining feel in their methods of consumer interaction. Indeed at the "lowest" spatial scale, the family or caregiving unit down to one-to-one relationships between friends or partners, the individual subjective aspect will be constrained by the objective subjective gaze of the other during the interactive process, just as the individual would do at the domain scale.

For domains to achieve effective power, the procedure is made easier by objectifying the users of their product. This removes their identity as individual persons; their aspirations, hopes, ways of thinking, likes and dislikes are neutralized; and they become nonperson and, thus, "treatable." In this manner, the objectification subsumes and consumes subjectivity, and the factory of mass objective production hums along. Accordingly, Foucault's archaeological research on madness, human sciences, and medicine looked at how a subject (individual) is represented as a possible object of knowledge (Smart 2002, 17), by a

> genealogy of the present scientifico-legal complex from which the power to punish derives its bases, justifications, and rules in order to understand how "a specific mode of subjection was able to give birth to man as an object of knowledge for a discourse with a scientific status." (Foucault 1977a, 23–24)

In the medical domain, introducing the individual as body laid the anthropologic groundwork for the human sciences to smooth the progress of their conditions of possibility, i.e., the constitution of man as an object of positive knowledge (Foucault 1975). In the government domain, the art of governing faces the challenge of population, or to be more accurate, the manner that the science of government and the re-centering of economy away from the family and population are linked (Foucault 1979c). Essentially by the objectification of the masses through the science of the state of statistics, this became and is a major part of government technology (Smart 2002). For example, the government of a state associates to "a form of surveillance, of control which is as watchful as that of the head of a family over his household and his goods" (Foucault 1979c, 10). Just in the same way, modernity and its science project exert objectifying constraints over the subjective population. This power, this disciplinary power, has been viewed as a "fundamental instrument in the constitution of industrial capitalism and of the type of society that is its accompaniment" (Foucault 1980, Two Lectures, 105). Consequently, the individual has become an object of positive knowledge, with the restraints positivism brings, and the human is both subject and object, i.e., an objectifying subject.

Disempowering the Body

An extremely personal invasion of power procedures of the human regarded as both subject and object is through one's body. For instance, the forces that drive our history do not so much operate on our thoughts, our social institutions, or even our environment as on our individual bodies (Gutting 2005, 47), e.g.,

> Genealogical analysis reveals the body as an object of knowledge and as a target for the exercise of power. The body is shown to be located in a political field, invested with power relations which render it docile and productive, and thus politically and economically useful. Such a subjection of the body and its forces is achieved through a political technology which constitutes, a "knowledge" of the body that is not exactly the science of its functioning, and a mastery of its forces that is more than the ability to conquer them. (Foucault 1977a, 26)

So, a "political anatomy," a mechanics of power, classifies how other bodies are exploited, producing subjected and practiced bodies, "docile" bodies, and, as a result, discipline increases body economic value, and reduces the body capacity to be itself, in relation to political obedience (Sheridan-Smith [1975] 1977, 137–138). Essentially, when disciplining the body it

> dissociates power from the body; on the one hand, it turns it into an "aptitude," a "capacity," which it seeks to increase; on the other hand, it reverses the course of the energy, the power that might result from it, and turns it into a relation of strict subjection. If economic exploitation separates the force and the product of labour, let us say that disciplinary coercion establishes in the body the constricting link between an increased aptitude and increased domination. (Foucault 1979b, 137–138)

Additionally, the ultimate control over the subjective body by the objective domains is for the individual subjects to perform an objective gaze over themselves.

Therefore, this speaks of a form of self-policing reflecting the disciplined statements of society and the desire to be seen and feel comfortable as one of the
(crowd)ed individuals in one's sociocultural living space. Foucault looked at
the "societal mirrored self"—the subject and "the forms and methods...of the
relationship to self by which the individual is formed and recognises himself as a
subject" (Foucault 1984)—and it is this recognition as a subject in the objective
society that is important for self-identity and a sense of belonging. The suggested
insecurity to find one's identity can be taken advantage of to the benefit of the
domain makers and breakers, as they create and sustain their powered history.
Thus, in this manner, "the human body itself is conceived to be subject to history,
to be 'broken-down by the rhythms of work, rest, and holidays...poisoned by
food or values, through eating habits or moral laws'" (Nietzsche 1969, 153).

Methods by which individuals affect their bodies and the attendant thoughts,
souls, and behavior are techniques of the self (Smart 2002). Techniques intimately connected with specific "obligations of truth," since "the more we want
to renounce ourselves, the more we need to bring to light the reality of ourselves"
(Foucault and Sennett 1982, 11). So, a subjective power struggle is occurring
within the individual between relinquishing, rejecting, surrendering, and handing
over oneself, and discovering or rediscovering the potential power of oneself, i.e.,
one's untainted essence. This characterizes modern societies in which people have
directed, governed, and conducted themselves and others according to "regimes
of 'jurisdiction' (authority/power/control) and 'veridiction'" (Smart 2002, 28).
To illustrate, a Foucauldian veridiction is a statement that is true according to
the worldview of a particular subject, rather than objectively true.

Knowledge of Power

The knowing of power and knowing how to apply it or, if not possessing it, how to
avoid it or minimize its effects and affects on oneself offer a knowable advantage
of how to navigate through its potency. The familiar "knowledge is power" is
prevalent here, which can be extended to "knowledge of power," as awareness
of how power works and ac(knowledge)ment that it is power processes that are
impeding or assisting one's life performances are useful tools to get oneself
through life. Hopefully, it is a life of some quality and quantity of goodness, for
whatever that is and means to the individual. Thus, having access to knowledge
of power allows the imaginations of the brain to work on this thing called power
and what else can be done with it from its current state of potentiality. In effect,

this powered consideration produces further knowledge of power potential and actuality, creating a mutual partnership of enhancement:

> Power produces knowledge (and not simply by encouraging it because it serves power or by applying it because it is useful); that power and knowledge directly imply one another; that there is no power relation without the correlative constitution of a field of knowledge, nor any knowledge that does not presuppose and constitute at the same time power relations. (Foucault 1977a, 27)

So, along these lines, knowledge also produces power.

For instance, knowledge vocalizes discursive practice, also the subject's position, and the field of coordination and subordination of statements (Barker 1998). In other words, it is the information and behavioral intention system that power speaks through in its action and reaction, for both action and reaction to the powered action are required for power to have power. If there was no reaction, the powered action would be powerless, but knowledge of statements assists in ensuring that the reaction occurs, as individuals of the population are "trained" in the knowledgeable ways of their sociocultural powered space of compliance. However, the apparent absolute partnership of power and knowledge's devotion to each other may not always be so, since knowing is not merely to be power-affected (Gutting 2005). For example, Foucault said of power and knowledge, "the very fact that I pose the question of their relation proves clearly that I do not *identify* them" (Foucault 1988, 43). Therefore, questioning their relationship may cast doubt over their connectivity, or at least encourage shades of grey areas of the levels of influence one sustains over the other, as these levels would depend on the context of the powered action and reaction.

Powering knowledge and knowledge-ing power returns the narrative to positivism and social constructivism, i.e., the limited or exclusive power perspectives of being positive, to the plurality of diverse construction, with the positives perhaps holding the center position of power (the action), and the constructors performing within this space (the reaction); e.g.,

> Western culture has constituted, under the name of man, a being who, by one and the same interplay of reasons must be a positive domain of *knowledge* and cannot be an object of science. (Foucault 1973, 366–367)

Looking at man and women being a positive domain of knowledge can be seen as a powered maneuver, a purposeful intended position to be more malleable for powered behavior from those "on high" in society. Since positivism advocates objectivity, women and man can be objects of science, at least in a socially constructed form, and whether it is knowledge of power or a less intimate relation of knowledge *and* power:

> There are bodies of knowledge that are independent of the sciences (which are neither their historical prototypes, nor their practical by-products), but there is no knowledge without a particular discursive practice; and any discursive practice may be defined by the knowledge that it forms. (Foucault 1977c, 183)

Powering Foucault's Bodily Power Disempowerment

Individuals in society adopt a variety of disguises or acting roles through their life history. These roles will vary in duration, intensity of interaction, and some individuals will have more roles to play than others, depending on life opportunities and what they want out of life. All these roles depend on the power limitations imposed. For example, roles may be students (school age to postgraduate level), employment of whatever type and "status," bouts of illness and subjected to the health domain, consumers of products, and prisoners of penal institutions and of society (beyond the prison walls, but still residing in the wider societal "prison of life"). However, regardless of if one is within the narrow space of the prison or the wider prison of life, all individuals are subjected to the variations of modern power, but since there are variations, there is no one all-encompassing power source, but a mass of microcenters. In essence, modern power is the chance outcome, in genealogical terms, of numerous small, uncoordinated causes (Gutting 2005).

So, the consideration emerges of not "when does social control end and socialisation begin?" (Stone 1983, 44), but the way humans become subjects and objects in their place within a network of positive and productive power/knowledge associations (Smart 2002). Therefore, one's place within their particular network map creates confrontations and battles, as discourse interactions attack and defend their versions of power and knowledge (Foucault 1978b). This power exorcism or exercise is a movement away from domination, the predominance of sovereignty, law, repression, to economic forms of power over individuals and populations (Smart 2002, 124), essentially techniques of the self (Smart 2002, 69):

> We are all subjects of power in the sense that we both simultaneously exercise it even as we experience its effects, and in so doing constitute even such

fundamental relations with ourselves as our sense of individuality. Indeed, the
individual is one of the effects of power, an articulation of power. (Foucault
1980, Two Lectures, 97–98)

So, each individual is a mini domain of power of the wider domains of power
that make up the societal network, namely the larger societal power domain that
all live within. These scales of power production produce

> a total structure of actions brought to bear upon possible actions; it incites, it
> induces, it seduces, it makes easier or more difficult; in the extreme it constrains
> or forbids absolutely; it is nevertheless always a way of acting upon an acting
> subject or acting subjects by virtue of their acting or being capable of action.
> (Dreyfus and Rabinow 1982, 220)

The actuality of acting and action from the potential possibilities brought on by
self-techniques pressured by the heart of the power matter are the defiance of
the will and the unyieldingness of freedom. However, instead of talking up an
essential freedom from power, it is preferable to "speak of an 'agonism'—of a
relationship which is at the same time reciprocal incitation and struggle; less of
face-to-face confrontation which paralyzes both sides than a permanent provo-
cation" (Dreyfus and Rabinow 1982, 221–222).

It is these subjective ongoing resistances or errors that Foucault views as
unifying in the power relationship, since power requires resistance to acknowledge its existence. Fundamentally, human history flows through with combative
resistance, as it is integral to power relations and should be scrutinized in accord
with intelligibility of struggles and of strategies and tactics (Foucault 1980). Thus,
power relations are concerned with forms of resistance and attempts to dissociate
these relations (Dreyfus and Rabinow 1982). Since the resistance performance
is a close-quarters practice, as are life experiences in general, understanding
and doing and being done by power are at the capillary, micro level of what is
nearest to the individual. To illustrate, nearest to the individual is themselves—
one's mind, spirit, soul, and body—which grants a specific gaze of how specific
mechanisms of power are invested in bodies as they are colonized, utilized,
involuted, displaced, extended, and so on and how particular local mechanisms
of power congeal into forms of "global domination" (Barker 1998, 29). Foucault
sees this as "an *ascending* analysis of power" (Foucault 1980, Two Lectures,
99), and associated with the ascending, is descending. Descending separates,

fragments, and traces differences even in the body of the individual (Barker 1998, 21), and it searches for the subtle, singular, and sub-individual marks that might possibly intersect in them (the individual) to form a network that is difficult to unravel (Foucault 1977b, 145). This view suggests that the body is not an inert substantial material, but is synthetic and susceptible to change (Barker 1998). So, within the spaces of the one body, power processes can be worked on to perhaps produce a body aggregate of that power integration. In other words, a bodily layered powered place of dynamism.

Foucault's' Power Summation

Foucault' power is neither an institution or structure, since he sees it as a

> "complex strategical situation," as a "multiplicity of force relations," as simul-
> taneously "intentional" yet "nonsubjective." "Where there is power, there is
> resistance," that power depends for its existence on the presence of a "multiplicity
> of points of resistance" and that the plurality of resistances should not be reduced
> to a single locus of revolt or rebellion. (Foucault 1979d, 92–97)

Also, relations of power are not considered to be secondary to other relationships "(economic processes, knowledge relationships, sexual relations) but are
immanent (existing within or inherent) in the latter" (Foucault 1979d, 94); e.g.,

> power is not a thing, an institution, an aptitude or an object. Power describes rela-
> tions of force, and as such it is a nominal concept: "One needs to be nominalistic,
> no doubt: power is not an institution, and not a structure; neither is it a certain
> strength we are endowed with; it is the name that one attributes to a complex
> strategical situation in a particular society". (Foucault 1979d, 93)

As a consequence, these complex, strategically placed circumstances show that

- power is coextensive with the social body
- relations of power are interwoven with other kinds of relations: production, kinship, family, sexuality
- power does not take the sole form of prohibition and punishment but is multiple in form

- interconnections of power delineate general conditions of domination organized in a more or less coherent and unitary strategy
- power relations serve because they are capable of being utilized in a wide range of strategies
- there are no relations of power without possible resistances

(Foucault 1980, 142).

CHAPTER 5

Bourdieu

Speaking

Voicing one's position on things and anything(s) is an overt declaration of opinion, a stated belief, and others who hear this vocal comparison point to their subjective vantage points and decide on whether to accept or not, or somewhere in between, what was declared. The decisions reached are not necessarily based on a cold, impersonal measurement of the vocal content uttered, as who is doing the speaking and who are doing the listening are key to the communication process. Therefore, awarded status as seen by others and where one resides in the societal structure can be just as important, if not more so, than what is being said, to get the message across.

Also, where the listeners are in the structure of society may determine how much is listened to, accepted, rejected, or not understood. Additionally, for those detached somewhat from the communicated status levels of society, in terms of being involved in decision-making due to lack of any meaningful power to get involved and have a say, senses of apathy and rejection (as these individuals are in turn rejected by society) may result. As a result, their covert opinions and beliefs are not heard, and maybe there is not even an audience for them, even if the covert becomes overt. Consequently, there is a lack of duty of care at both the subjective and objective society spaces.

Duty of care at one's subjective level of self-preservation involves keeping to oneself various aspects of opinion and belief, and practicing this covertness of voice produces protection. The protective reasons, perhaps at all individual levels in the social hierarchy, shields one's "true" perspectives, since fear of others having access to one's inner being (conscious and unconscious states and their combined capacity) leads one to vulnerabilities that may not be acceptable to the self. Indeed, also to others who probe one's inner being, for they may discover ideology and attendant motivation that is unpalatable to their ideologies, both overt and covert. All individuals carry this beast of burden of what can be voiced and what must remain unvoiced, and this cautious performance is necessary as it also protects the running of society, allowing it to function.

It is individuals who voice society, as their individual voices add up to what society is and how it is practiced and expressed within its totality of existence. Society too will have its hidden and surface aspects, its linguistic expression demonstrated through its physical geography of historical legacy up to the now, and speculative planned building for the future. So, the built physical geography is a concrete expression of power, articulated by the voiced expression of individuals whose sounds power the process. Consequently, individuals are the source of power in how society is shaped and reshaped over time and space, with the powered sound as one aspect of power that Bourdieu engages with. Thus, the chapter will begin Bourdieu's power journey with the articulate expressive voice.

Articulating Language

Language requires a sense of independence, self-rule, and sovereignty, for its expressive powers to permeate all levels of society at effective levels of engagement. So, one must take into account the

> autonomy of language, its specific logic, and its particular rules of operation. In particular, one cannot understand the symbolic effects of language without making allowance for the fact, frequently attested, that language is the exemplary formal mechanism whose generative capacities are without limits. There is nothing that cannot be said and it is possible to say nothing. (Bourdieu 1991, 41)

Therefore, the pliable power of language is the medium through which all that is seen, experienced, lived through and within, both through material and immaterial forms, is mediated and, by means of its independent autonomy, the rules of the game of society are wrought. Also, how words are formed into sentences, what words are selected, and what new words are invented and older ones discarded shape behavioral patterns that limit the game for many in society and enhance the game of those setting the rules of the said game.

From these gamed performances, the "independence" and "autonomy" of language conceal descriptions of the lack of independence and autonomy that drives the language process and practice. So alternatively, language construction can be thought of as a limited form of independence and autonomy, with those driving the language process generally at the center of society, particularly the economic and cultural center, and operate within a space of self-government and self-determination to guide the rest in society to their ways of thinking and doing, via language; its vocalized and accompanying written form. Subsequently, the few limit the many of their potentiality and actuality of expression, with the former retaining and increasing their own potentiality and actuality capacities. Thus, limiting power and its control to the few and consequently limiting the many of their life choices, even if the latter actually recognize they may have had other choices among the prevalent dominant language thoughts that are articulated.

For instance, if one's thought and imagination potential can only be expressed and considered through a predetermined array of words and the structured formations of these words with various groupings and arrangements, the resultant output may not reach beyond the space of the language; i.e., one's potential and actuality is confined to the limits of the language on offer. However, Bourdieu does state that the generative capacities of language are without limits, which is demonstrated by the longevity of languages that constantly evolve due to the vibrancy of societal survivability shown by technological and cultural fluidity; nevertheless, these endless generative capacities may still only operate within the offered language ways of being. For instance, word enhancements are still part of the "being" sphere of influence, still driving the economic and cultural process. Additionally, localized languages scattered across all places in society, with their accompanying slang and informality of expression, would partially still exist, but becoming "part of a political and linguistic unit in which their traditional competence was subordinated and devalued" (Bourdieu 1991, 6). An irony is one of these local languages would have become the dominant language, with its local eventually becoming the regional and national speak. Anyway, an independent and autonomous language (a language of "neutrality") is an inevitable evolvement and involvement, if those controlling and navigating society "advocate" for it; e.g.,

> Recourse to a neutralized language is obligatory whenever it is a matter of establishing a practical consensus between agents or groups of agents having partially or totally different interests. This is the case, of course, first and foremost in the field of legitimate political struggle, but also in the transactions and interactions of everyday life. (Bourdieu 1991, 40)

Both articulating and, in turn, ensuring that the words are powerful, fluent, elo-
quent, and lucid are essential practices. This is because it is the way that words are
uttered as well as what the words mean, within their numerous interpretations as
every individual comprehends the world in subtly diverse ways and perhaps not
so subtle, which are just as important for efficient communication. Consequently,
convincing one's other to do as one would wish, particularly when connecting the
abstraction of words to the concrete of practical implication, is "tacitly adjusted
to the relations of power between speakers and hearers. Their practical competence involves not only the capacity to produce grammatical utterances, but also
the capacity to make oneself heard, believed, obeyed" (Bourdieu 1991, 7–8).
Furthermore, effectiveness of articulation is enhanced when taking advantage
of the social conditions on offer in whatever time and space one happens to live
within (Moraru 2016, 35), i.e., one's essential or inherent place or Bourdieu's
"intrinsic historicity" (Blommaert 1999, 6–7).

So, if one's voice is powerful enough, their intrinsic time period and its processes can be altered by their articulation as this creates new power spaces and
networks. Or it raises the power levels of current domains or institutions toward
greater spaces of power and associated sets of connections with others who benefit
or consume within the powered discourse. To illustrate,

> use of language, the manner as much as the substance of discourse, depends
> on the social position of the speaker, which governs the access he can have
> to the language of the institution, that is, to the official, orthodox and legiti-
> mate speech. It is the access to the legitimate instruments of expression, and
> therefore the participation in the authority of the institution, which makes all
> the difference irreducible to discourse as such—between the straightforward
> imposture of masqueraders. who disguise a performative utterance as a descrip-
> tive or constative statement (Austin 1962, 4), and the authorized imposture
> of those who do the same thing with the authorization and the authority of an
> institution. (Bourdieu 1991, 109)

Emblematic

The purpose of language in its verbal and scribed formats is to symbolize, and
what the symbolism refers to is how power is intended to play out or is tentatively
played out. Tentatively in relation to offering a set of words and phrases to see
how others react to it and how much acceptance, resistance, or indifference is

shown. For instance, when one speaks, the reaction to what is offered is just as vital when contributing to the effective communication as is the role of the listener or reader of words, when determining the powered result. Thus, all speaking and writing symbolize power in action, regardless of whether it is the whispers of seduction between intimate partners, or want-to-be partners, the work environment, sport and leisure, diplomatic relations between countries, families and caregivers, domains, institutions, and government. Or the symbolized power of saying and writing nothing, since the act of nothingness can symbolize effective power sometimes more so than effecting power.

The emblematic nature of symbolism is fundamentally a nature of interaction or contact between people. Consequently, Bourdieu asserts primacy of relations, "against all forms of methodological monism that purport to assert the ontological priority of structure *or* agent, system *or* actor, the collective *or* the individual" (Wacquant 2014, 15). Monism is a reductive process offering that reality is a unified whole and is grounded in a single basic substance or principle, but perhaps the answer lies somewhere in between, that the aggregate numerous, almost infinite, relation encounters and processes add up to a "more than" monistic space, but still connect to it. For instance, in the monistic space of society with its emblemized practices, this may equate to economic, cultural, and political dominance. So,

> the clashes between the visions and previsions of specifically political struggles—imply a certain claim to symbolic authority as the socially recognized power to impose a certain vision of the social world, i.e., of the divisions of the social world. (Bourdieu 1991, 106)

To successfully divide the social world, when utilizing the emblemized symbolism, is to disguise the true meaning and potential actuality behind a veneer of niceness. This is because it would not do to clearly articulate the coldness of exploitation and manipulation that are the real of rationality behind public relations and attracting the public consumer, as power maneuverability and acquisition would be seriously curtailed, at least one would tentatively conclude. Tentative, as some sales pitching of one's power is not necessarily symbolic. For example, the representational aspect of the pitch as an image of the original, not the original, i.e., as not an accurate true picture of the original but a watered-down version, is bypassed to allow the true powered motivation behind the symbolism to actually be the symbolism, i.e., in actuality, rendering the symbolism mute, as the real takes over. The point is the public, or at least some of them, can be persuaded to courses of action by powerbrokers being up front with what they want, particularly if it appeals to the consumer appetite of this public membership.

Emblematic Violence

Violence can be said to be done when the emblematic performance goes through its powered progression. For instance, when questioning authority and legitimation, power has a fundamental role in a polity more generally, or, more specifically, in its underlying organization of collective violence (Guzzini 2006). With physical violence, power and violence exclude each other, since an authority that continuously needs to rely on violence is one whose power is eroding or has eroded (Arendt 1969). However, for the performance to be effective and remain effective, the violent aspect should not be detected, and detection is avoided if the violence is nonphysical. Nonphysical violence is termed *symbolic violence*, and this type of violence can be "more powerful than physical violence, since it is incorporated even in modes of action and knowledge structures of individuals, and imposes the legitimacy spectrum of social order" (Nicolaescu 2010, 6). Consequently, knowledge and performance of this violence as an acceptable normal societal behavioral pattern not recognized as violent, or violence of ideology and practices being done to the self, can be and are ingrained onto one's consciousness and unconsciousness.

As symbolic violence is symbolic, it is difficult to detect, since it is precisely the attached implication of the symbolism component that allows for the forceful aspect to remain cloaked in a thin covering of generated respectability. The covering is slender and delicate because the general public, unless their critical thinking skills and awareness is minimal and/or have been sold the complete package of the violent symbolism, would be aware that will of movement and decision-making is tainted by unseen but felt limitations. Essentially, everyday practice and performance are mainly governed by structured space that tries to ensure people follow predetermined pathways of behavior. Also, the fact that the space is structured indicates that flexibility of what one can do is quite inflexible, since the structure dictates that one can only operate within its immovable rules and regulations.

In this way, if one has inspirational ideas beyond the structure and achieving a post-structural or unstructured state of being and doing, penalties will ensure. These penalties may range from prison time, loss of employment, and loss of status (within the societal measurements of that), and other material risks, to loss of one's acceptance as a productive member of society; i.e., one is demonized, regarded as nonconformist, and does not quite belong anymore. Therefore, the symbolic violence at this point in time and space reveals more of itself, with the implication being that the symbolic aspect supposedly lessens, and the violent aspect increases, exposing more of itself. "Supposedly," because paradoxically in a sense the symbolic also intensifies, since it is utilized to make the reactive violent aspect more powerful to keep the "criminal, corrupted, miscreant, immoral person" under control, or even better, return them back to the space of the straight and narrow.

Symbolic violence symbolizes how control is manufactured through a generally acceptable form for the general public; i.e., it is authenticated and underwritten and, hence, appears legit. This process creates relations of meaning that are misrecognizable (displacement) (Bourdieu 1991), yet retaining the viscosity to enforce and encourage particular realities and to maintain association and separation (Bourdieu 1987). Thus, this instrument of coming together as a cohesive unit or criminalizing protects one group or class over others and maintains dominance (Bourdieu 1991), i.e., the actuality of the dominated becoming and having (Weber 1985). Domesticated implies taming, breaking, bringing under control, being house-trained, and the "societal house" has its functional rooms—politics, economy, cultural, and the social—and the subset cupboards of societal performances that make up the networks of these four usual suspects.

Bourdieu's primacy of relations, just like language usage, is central to symbolic violence. This is not surprising since language formulates and drives the symbolism. The primacy of relations is defined in and through a given relation between those who exercise power and those who submit to it, i.e., in the very structure of the field in which *belief* is produced and reproduced (Bourdieu 1991). So, from those who exercise power, to the submitters, the immediacy of relations for the general public includes all of the public. All is emphasized as all in society are involved, e.g., from those who make the rules and set the benchmark of how to do society to those who go along. Even those individuals in the highest societal circles are trapped and caught up in the process; perhaps actually more so, as they cannot diverge from their established place in society or at least not get found out and caught, although these performances apply to all. For instance, everyone plays the symbolic game to varying degrees of conformity and nonconformity, where this symbolic political game (as everything in life has a political aspect) performs as structured and structuring instruments of communication (Bourdieu 1991). This is where the unstructured spaces of the structured place perform, and this game extends to the global within the symbolic power of world-making (Goodman 1978), i.e., incorporating the global playing (field) and the local playing (fields), and capable of producing real effects without any apparent expenditure of energy (Bourdieu 1991, 170).

Provinces of Power

As emblematic power and language power operates within a structuring framework, this framework would retain support nodes that create cohesion and strength for the structure. To illustrate, the framework can be thought of as society within its whole space, as the essential (P)rovince or (F)ield that the nodes or lesser provinces or fields function within. For example, society as a whole forms a field that is structured according to relations of domination, but society also contains a range of fields in which society should be seen as the paramount field, from which other fields are never fully separated (Peillon 1998). Fields are described in a number of ways and means by Rawolle (2005, 708), guided by Bourdieu (1993):

> structured arrangements; structured power relations at a certain moment in time; practices are governed by "legitimate" laws steering the primacy of relations; strategically distinctive designs retained by dissimilar agents whose nature of performance depends upon position and direction adopted; functionality of the field is perceived as a game; agents are conversant with the risks of the social field and therefore the importance of its sustainability, ensuring one's socialised body retains habitus (looked at later in the chapter); the types of capital applied and how these are possessed through social tussle, and the accompanying measuring and assessment comparisons with diverse capital forms.

Therefore, the field is saturated with power and corresponding power plays. Also, fields are purposely structured to achieve certain results, hence the playing field is not level and skewed to the advantage of those setting the rules, and subsequently those using the fields are limited from what they wish to get out of the encounter; i.e., the dice is loaded. The users are the most essential stakeholders in the fields they enter, but paradoxically the most expendable as they are consumers who are consumed by the game played. Thus, fields would not exist without them, but due to the propaganda of symbolic violence powered by the "common" language and how the field of society is structured, they cannot exist without the presence of the fields. This existence is according to society during its present form, although transforming and transformed society would just construct new fields to engage with.

Although the dice is loaded when fielding, the science of fielding is not exact. For instance, as with all science products, the expected results from the stated hypothesis do not always turn out as assumed or predicted, since there would be a range of resulting powered deals between the field user and the field agent. Even though the "field of difference" in terms of outcome would be marginal with the vast majority of field users, as the agenda is prearranged, it is diverse nonetheless. Diversity occurs as fields retain characters that are disseminated by varied power currencies, and by logic that is necessarily specific to fields, and cannot be reduced to other fields' logic (Jackson 2008). Differences would also occur due to the workable aspect of the field in its interaction, i.e., primacy of relations. Since fields exist in their actuality only during the length of the inter-action encounter, the powered experience can be brief and sometimes intensive. This is a temporary state of power relations or structure of power relations, producing a place of contest between involved stakeholders holding diverse resources essential to secure and protect an escalating posture within that field place (Mustafa and Johnson 2008).

The encounter intensity in that place would depend on results and how the stakeholders in the process felt about it. It is these that determine difference within the common sameness of field encounters, as the common identicalness indicated adheres to the millions of field encounters that occur every day. Even though field is networked, structured, or encompasses relationship sets that may be cultural, religious, educational, intellectual, among other examples (Navarro 2006), these other examples would include the everyday interactions, i.e., with friends, family, nodding or making fleeting eye contact with passing strangers, or asking directions from strangers, as all retain the field capacity for powered actions and reactions. Also, Facebook, face time, texting, paying bills, ordering taxis or food, since these online encounters are field encounters. Hence, every encounter is a potential and actual field encounter. In other words, a multiple measured positional space, of which all positions are understood within a mul-tiple measured structure of coordinates whose values equate to the values of the diverse applicable variables (Bourdieu 1985).

The self would also possess the capacity to have field encounters with the self on a regular basis, and perhaps more than regularly, since the oneself does reside within an ongoing constant process. For example, a power struggle of the self of what to decide, what are the decision limits, how does one feel about it, the extent of acceptance and comfortableness, moral dilemma, compromising principles, and feelings of powerlessness. Thus, from this never-ending process, the self-field may potentially and actually be the most powerful field of all the fields, and the one Field that is society. In this way, the recognition that people often experience power differently, influenced by the field they happen to be immersed in at a particular moment (Gaventa 2003), is testament to how their self-field is operating within that moment or set of associated moments. Power appreciation along this encountered time/space/place of structured production will create unstructured results, constantly updated, as the relations of power dual for ascendency and cope with moments of descendance.

The conclusion to the field negotiation will see the ended field position between the stakeholders, but the self-field afterward may still be reliving the result to reach a self-agreement of acceptance; i.e., a sense of peace of mind must be reached to allow life to continue and the self-field to continue. Bourdieu does say that fields are outlined by compositions of power relations between actors partaking in common aims or interests, but also competing over resources or how supply and need are demarcated (Martin 2003). Therefore, the self-field is also a site of how supply and need are identified. The self-field is of a permanent nature, as one cannot escape from their self, their constant self-reflection and reflexivity. Whereas, all other fields are of a fleeting disposition for users, some occasionally or regularly returned to, but the time and space of them do not incessantly remain. Even field agents, who are exposed to their specialized field for numerous moments of the day within numerous diverse but same encounters, will get away, be it temporarily until the next working day. However, their self-field will be with them in all their time and space.

Biased Field Power

To be in a field is to take sides, be opinionated, and biased. For instance, field produces spaces of self and other, with the gradation and digresses of inclusion and exclusion that follows. Depending on the type of field, the exclusivity of inclusion will control and dictate the performance on offer. For example, agent(s) who work for that field, work for the paymasters of that field, and so work for the latter's agenda. Thus, they are the middlemen/women, placed as the conduit passing on the "wishes" of these master(s) to those who enter the field. This process purposefully is a tiered relationship of power, layered from top to bottom with mini power relationships that maintain field healthiness. *All* involved in the field capitalize on their need to be part of the field, so its levels of healthiness are their accrued aggregate individual health acquisitions and benefits. To illustrate, the health capitalization within this context could imply health from a medicinal perspective, but the heart of the matter here is power health, since in terms of power hierarchy, for those who want as much power as they can get, power means health. This is a self-absorbed feeling of well-being that does these particular individuals good. As indicated, "All" may actually mean All since they all want something out of the field to receive a bit of good.

Capitalization

This bit of good relates to being capitalized, i.e., how much capital one has already in the field and how much more can be obtained. Bourdieu regards the Capital of capital as involving four streams of capital; economic, cultural, symbolic, and social (Peillon 1998). Economic capital is the amount of material wealth one can draw on. Cultural capital is one's level of educational attainment and cultural acquisition. Capital of the symbolic incorporates all the capital forms and seen as lawful, rightful. Lastly, social capital is one's network development with others of like-minded social status. The four are not mutually exclusive, preserving spaces of the others and exchanging spaces according to Bourdieu's interconvertibility theory (Casey 2005). Thus, all four combine within the individual in a field and reflect where one is in the field, i.e., how much power one has there, and how much bias of political capacity over others in the field can be applied.

Political

Since the political performance permeates everyone and everything in society, it correspondingly involves activities from the government right down (if one regards government as the pinnacle of society) to individuals. The performance and prac-ticalities of politics in the field(s) of government, especially related to governing, involves the acquisition of the executive, legislator, and judiciary; e.g., the existence of these three is a prime example of symbolic capital, but the other three capitals are very much in the frame, as at this level of the political environment all four mingle for particular political markets (Casey 2005). Political capital is a fluid capital with its surface and concealed motivations and, therefore, subsequently difficult to pin down what is going on helps its "legitimacy," prejudiced or biased by media reporting and politicians (Kennicott 2004; Suellentrop 2004).

At the individual level, governmental individuals included, the political power interactions among them involving people, groups, or organizations, create uneven influence that in turn creates uneven conflict. Thus, political capital using social capital status is the basis for noticeable differences in configurations of lifestyles and consumers practices (Bourdieu 2002). As a result, possibly political capital is the most forceful capital form, since in this field the agents produce their translation of the world, hence transforming it into their rendition (Thompson, editor's Introduction in Bourdieu 1991). Consequently, the "markets of political capital are repeatedly connected with control over and among actors, especially coercive power of any institution" (Casey 2005, 6–7), and those who have access to capital resources, including political, hold capacity to enter the field struggles (Peillon 1998, 216).

Professional

Accessing capital resources is easier if one is a professional, and also easier to instill one's perspective over others of "lesser" educational or cultural capital attainment, which is assisted by a professional agent regarded as being legitimate, so retaining symbolic capital. Additionally, since a professional agent, such as a lawyer, barrister, solicitor, health worker (doctor, nurse, allied), university lecturer, high school and primary school teacher, accountant, businessman/woman and so on, form such an integral part of the social and economic system of the One Field of society, social and economic capital are central in their performances. Essentially, the power of society cannot function without the power of the professional, and this power is nonneutral, i.e., a power of bias. Hence, the profession label as an acceptance of belief is "dangerous," since it produces an "appearance of neutrality" (Bourdieu and Wacquant 1992, 242). For instance, profession is the "social product of a historical work of construction of a group and of a *representation* of groups that has surreptitiously slipped into the science of this group" (Bourdieu and Wacquant 1992, 242–243).

Doxa

Offering oneself and one's materiality into a field is doxa (Schinkela and Noordegraaf 2011, 78), and the assumptions of a field are outlined by doxa (Bourdieu 1990, 66). Accordingly, the action of doxa is "to appear," "to seem," "to think," and "to accept" (Liddell and Scott 1940) and implies common opinion and belief, i.e., what is taken for granted in any particular society (Bourdieu 1977). From this, the social and natural world is perceived as self-evident (Bourdieu 1977, 164). Therefore, doxa carries symbolic capital so it is accepted and acceptable, resulting in individuals becoming voluntary subjects of those incorporated mental structures that deprive them of more deliberate consumption (Bourdieu 1979). Additionally, doxa is part of the primacy of relations and of the legitimized language package and is utilized to put into words arguments and put into words by arguments. As a result, doxa protects those in power by only engaging with things that do not adversely affect the powered status quo. Thus, the hidden remains hidden and so cannot be debated and is 'conveniently' "relegated to the state of doxa, accepted tacitly without discussion" (Bourdieu 1991, 132).

Class or Classless

Political field control of actors by institutions may assume the existence of classes and their structural differentiation along Marxist lines of societal inquiry, e.g., clearly demarked lines of sociality influenced by all four capitals. However, Bourdieu regards this grouping as simplistic since social spaces are far more complex, as he recognizes the importance of economics to determine social structuring, so regarding economic capital as reducing in rank all other capital forms to disinterested states (Bourdieu 1986b). For instance, pressure of the market structures the formation of capital (Casey 2005), and the application of bias potential and actuality is heavily influenced by how much economic capital one can utilize. Therefore, Bourdieu (1987, 8) surmises that classes or groups do not materialize out of thin air; they are the end result of a complicated work of historical construction; i.e., essentially, "do classes exist or do they not" (Bourdieu 1987, 2). This is a loaded political speculation drawing on social world objectivity and its attendant social tensions.

Civilization

To be civil is to be social, and to be social incorporates the national, the public, the communal, the general, and the common, hence to bring all in society within the "same" attitudes or needs, wants, and desires (Shurmer-Smith and

Hannam 1994). To bring all within the sameness paradoxically requires differ-
entness, as it is within this diversity that power can be allowed to perform. For
instance, if all in society were the same and expected to be the same, power
potential and its actuality would be powerless, or power-neutral, since there
would no need, want, and desire to power up power, e.g., a dormant concept.
However, if this was the case, society would stall, stagnant, and diminish
and would not be in its past and present forms and perhaps would not be. For
example, people would be restless, frustrated, bored, and that is when trouble
occurs, trouble in the form of the breakdown of society and the social order
becoming disordered.

   This is where civilization comes in, as it allows people to get on with each
other and to compete in a controlled manner. For example, rules, regulations,
and expectations are put in place in a "civilized" way for people to challenge
each other, without the whole thing falling over. The falling over is in the interest
of no one, and people are interested in getting ahead, getting power to improve
themselves, if that is their calling of putting themselves forward, rather than
stagnating and going backward. Forward implies development, evolution, progression, cultivation, refinement, and sophistication. Forward also implies an
inevitable diversity of measured capacity to play the societal game effectively,
since more capacity ensures greater civilization and less capacity favors the
"uncivilized," the less cultivated, refined, and sophisticated members of society.
Consequently, a social structure is formed producing stratification, and one that
creates the indefinable defined class system.

Class(less)

As indicated, diversity feeds the power beast as it produces fertile space for
those who want power, lots of it. For instance, these individuals or "elites"
want a class structure to operate within or to operate from above to sustain and
further their authoritative position(s). Also, it is of little consequence to them
that classes are defined as distinct layers, adopting Marxist terminology, or to
"deny the existence of classes as homogeneous sets of economically and socially
differentiated individuals objectively constituted into groups" (Bourdieu 1987, 3),
for as long as there is difference, it can be exploited. Bourdieu stresses a space
of differences underwritten by social and economic differentiation (Bourdieu
1987) when thinking about the class concept, so he does not dismiss class as a
difference label when attempting to define distinct groups in society. To illustrate,

when stating "difference," there are not only different classes but also differences within each class structure, e.g., when regarding a particular class:

> No two members of the same class will have had the same experiences in the same order, but it is certain that each member of the same class is more likely than any member of another class to have been confronted with the situations most frequent for members of that class. (Bourdieu 1990, 60)

So, classes may be formed involuntarily by those who experience a threshold of more "sameness" characteristics with others who too experience and retain these characteristics, even though each still retains subtle uniqueness, i.e., their own identity. For instance, someone, artificially, has labeled these individuals as part of the same group, even though they may have never met or been aware of the other, because the labeling has power purpose. For example, the purpose for class "leads one to pose that the political work aimed at producing classes in the form of objective institutions, at once expressed and constituted by permanent organs of representation, by symbols, acronyms and constituents, has its own specific logic, that of all symbolic production" (Bourdieu 1987, 8). In other words, the production of powered differentiation, resulting in class circumstances that distinguish class from what it is not and especially from everything it is opposed to (Bourdieu 1979).

When producing a societal class representation, one could visualize many layers, rather than the traditional two (owners and workers) to four (upper, middle, lower, underclass). For instance, at the extremity or limit of class differentiation, the layers would equate to how many individuals make up the whole of society and their value to society, i.e., a society of 60 million would have 60 million layers with each possessing individual unique capitals, be that many of these would be infinitesimally different in form. To illustrate, from the capitals of each person, taking measurements (of whatever format that may be or devised, which in itself retains inherent flaws as power plays come into play of who decides how to measure) and extrapolating a numerical figure and resultant societal value or value of that person to society. Hence, constructing a ranking system of how much power, status, and authority each has in society.

Embodied Culture

Intertwined with the civilized classes is the ever-present cultural factor, as one of the big four capitals, cultural capital, guides the classes or individuals along the civil life journey. For example, the cultural and its capital can be an aloof presence, bequeathing upon itself as autonomous, historical, retaining laws, superseding the wills of individuals, and maintaining its space against what agents can get hold of (Bourdieu 1986b, 20), but it only becomes an exploitative power if used by agents and "invested as a weapon and a stake" (Bourdieu 1986b, 20). To illustrate, to be culturally proficient, i.e., an ability to read in an illiterate world, gets a scarcity value from its position in the distribution of cultural capital and yields profits of distinction for its owner (Bourdieu 1986b, 18–19), and adapting "read" and "illiterate," respectively, as metaphors of those in the know and those who are excluded from knowledge implies that the reader owns the power and the illiterate attempts to purchase or rent some of it. This condition of illiterate subsistence is regarded by Bourdieu as agents' space of relativity from material requirement, and the resultant practices implied, with those in society's subordinate levels possessing minimal capital and laid bare to social pressures (Atkinson 2010).

As with Foucault, Bourdieu sees the importance of power disposition in one's body, as much of the cultural capital relates to the body and assumes embodiment (Bourdieu 1986a). For example, it is the way the body is disposed and posed, which signifies distinction, i.e., a difference of appearance, attitude, posture, and position in society. Consequently, elites identify themselves to their fellow selves and their others by body techniques or gestures (Bourdieu 1984), with this personal and personality performance both physically and psychologically showing status. Also, just as important, it shows that others do not have this symbolic status (Bauder 2008) and are not welcomed into the privileged space. This is an ongoing generational elite status positionality, cyclically repeated (Lin 2001). Therefore, embodied cultural capital reflects stratified power of society, and reproduces that reflection seemingly without effort, as it appears so ingrained (Bourdieu 1986a). Hence, the lack of intentional inculcation from the reader to the "illiterate masses," so an unconsciously arrived at power play. Essentially, when building the civilized classes, the concept of civilization equates to culture and society, as it is interchangeable with them and embodies them.

Inhabiting Power—Habitus

To inhabit something is to occupy its space in which senses of lived in are produced, and an affinity is developed creating a sense of connection; e.g., the space is dwelled in and becomes a "dwelling place" (Heidegger 1962). Basically, to simply live, which is not that simple especially when trying to live well beyond the simple, i.e., for one's good, since one's engagement with the societal world around them requires an intimate understanding. For instance, this intimacy can be intimidating when performing on the public stage, as limitations of what one can do and be are curtailed by what others are already doing and being or what they wish to do and be. For example, society is loaded with busy spaces and places all producing their versions of power that one has to negotiate through, and also if not allowed the luxury of negotiation, one grins and bears it as the power process does its work on them. In this manner for both the powered agent, when empowering, and those on the receiving end when interacting in fields, the behavioral patterns demonstrated have already been predetermined. In other words, pre-learned through one's upbringing and adapted throughout life as each new experience alters the thought reactive process of what to do and not what to do in that encounter. Consequently, the updated learning, as well as one's history of learning, is carried forward to the next encounter.

Since each encounter is a power trip, when inhabiting that encounter and guiding oneself through its complexities, Bourdieu offers that the tool that allows one to do so is one's habitus. Each individual carries this within themselves, and it is a reactive adaptable template or blueprint residing in the subconscious that behaves the conscious. Habitus can be thought of as a fluid concept of vagueness, one that cannot be pinned down or emphatically located in terms of understandability, but of a spectral quality that makes it a powerful behavioral tool when reacting to power and applying it to others. Thus, habitus is thought of as

> systems of durable, transposable dispositions, structures predisposed to operate as structuring structures, that is, as principles which generate and organise practices and representations that can be objectively adapted to their outcomes without presupposing a conscious aiming at ends or an express mastery of the operations necessary in order to attain them. (Bourdieu and Passeron 1990, 52)

The nature, character, or temperament of the enduring habitus, enduring since it lasts the lifetime of the individual, is one's civil engineer as it designs the structure that allows one to engage with life. This is a generalized attitude to life that can be applied across many, if not all, encounters without being too concerned of how to achieve a specific outcome. This is not to say that the habitus is indifferent to the process, actually the opposite, for it is within the subconscious act that depths of appreciating situations and the most appropriate course of action to follow for the consciously subjective individual is objectively carried through. For instance, it creates strategic action lines provoking the maximum gain for agents, both symbolically and economically (Bourdieu 1990, 2000; Bourdieu and Wacquant 1992). Thus, habitus can almost be thought of as one's instinctive disposition, when using one's primal survival skills to operate within the modern world and its inherent challenges and dangers. Actually, habitus is inherent, since for each individual it is intrinsic, innate, inbuilt, natural, and inborn, and they are formerly or prior inclined to perform in particular ways, chase certain aims, affirm certain tastes (Bourdieu 1991); e.g., the structure of powered encounter is already preset.

Since the habitus space is not at the conscious level (Atkinson 2010) and outside contemplativeness or manipulation of will (Bourdieu 1984), it retains a place of independence within the individual. This is because since it has power over the will, it is in a sense the "true will" of the person, the center of power of the individual, and, hence, the center of power of society, given that individuals run society. Hence, it is the source of society's power, the "unchosen principle of all choices" (Bourdieu 1990, 61). Therefore, one is being controlled from within and hopefully for the most good that is potentially available to the person, which may equate to semblances of actuality. For example, "dispositions built out of a practical, pre-reflective, corporeal sense of limits and realistic possibilities" (Bourdieu 1977, 77).

Life's real of corpo(real) and its related historical structuring structures due to the habitus performance being overlaid generation after generation do lead to habitus tension. For instance, the power hierarchy of habitus as they vie with each other to achieve the best position possible, shows that one habitus can dominate another partially, to perhaps totally; e.g.,

> Habitus is mutually a system of schemes of production of practices and a system of perception and appreciation of practices, implying a sense of one's place, but also a sense of the place of others. (Bourdieu 1989, 19)

Knowing one's place through the habitus filters of subconscious perception actually allows oneself to know oneself. To illustrate, at the conscious level humans have tremendous difficulty in truly knowing who they are, which implies that their positional decision-making is flawed since they are operating on shifting sands of perception. Consequently, how can one efficiently locate one's other and what they are thinking and doing, and basing reactive and active decisions on that, if one's self-reflexivity is vague. However, it is the unconsciousness of habitus that floods one's self-reflective capacities to maximum potential. This means that their decision-making is the best it can potentially be; i.e., "one has

to escape from the realism of the structure...without falling back into subjectivism, which is incapable of giving an account of the necessity of the social
world" (Bourdieu 1990, 52). So, habitus is an infrastructural space to make the
structures of the social world and to replicate economic, political, and social
structures in society (Jackson 2008). This enables a matching of the subjective
and the objective, what we feel spontaneously disposed to do and what our social
conditions demand of us (Eagleton 1990).

In effect, habitus does not consider the conscious end of a performance but
appears to live in the unconscious improvisation moment. Even though it is
accused of denying the "life of the mind" (Reay 2004, 437; Sayer 2005, 29),
perhaps it is the life of the mind, and to all intents and purposes being the mind's
source of power.

Powered Bourdieu

The powered complexity of existence is faced by all who are born into the
practice termed life. Consequently, generated within this complexity of life is
the unequal primacy of relations opportunities to be faced, as one individual
possesses more capital than another, be it from subtle to significant capacity, to
negotiate for more access to the power experience. Additionally, when negotiating,
more access indicates or promises better life quality and quantity, and within
this competitive environment all have to cope as best they can with their limited
actuality of life encounter capacity. For instance, it can be assumed that those
who hold the advantage of choosing which professional language and emblems
to adopt, through the unequal playing fields and their political bents, apply
these ruthlessly (and probably also ruthlessly cloaked in symbolic violence) to
get desired results. This application can be regarded as fundamental to ensure
power is happening, as these field performances are powerful performances.
To illustrate, the doxa of the masses and divide and rule of the classes produce
the type of civilization and its associated cultural and social form that ensure a
majority degree of success. To elaborate, an embodied demonstration of powered
diversity of access and usage of it, a successful general populous acceptance of
fields, and, more pointedly, how these fields are consumed to maintain power
relations and potentially their future expansion or consolidation to become even
more established and entrenched. However, the assumption of advantage also
requires the extra of habitus. It is this unseen, unlocatable entity of formless

forms of thoughts and survival instincts driving the unconscious conscious or conscious unconscious of how to live for the individual, which may be the key or powered catalyst opening the door to all the encountered practices, i.e., the language, symbolism, fields, and so on through Bourdieu's repartee. Fundamentally, the properties of habitus are not dissimilar to the properties of power as both are unseen, unlocatable, but both can definitely be felt.

CHAPTER 6

Giddens

Putting together structure involves a construction, and the motivation that dictates, drives, and influences the construction is such as to enable the constructor(s) claim to the space of that construction, i.e., having some dominion over it, having some power over it, and exercising that power. The constructive materials cannot be realized from nothing, except in the abstract imaginations of individuals who in that specific time and space of thinking and potential creation do not require material backing. However, to create the ideas of a future structure requires concrete raw materials to work with, and the initial rawness can be polished, folded, and molded into the mind's visual image of what is "in mind." The "rawness" of nature can and does provide material backing within its structured unstructured-ness, to allow the individual or agent to flow from potential to actual structural creation or change of structures that have been previously thought up and produced. An unstructured structure in the sense that nature, the world around and within all living beings, is a fluid, flowing space of movement, e.g., the structure of ongoing change. It is this interaction, and the tension and compromise between structures and agents that Giddens attempts to formulate a workable space that both parties contribute to. Thus, producing a processed power–induced environment of living place.

This processed power or work in process is centered on how individuals, groups, nations, and the multiculturalist presence that permeates try to function or dysfunction in the "structured" landscapes of their lives, particularly since all are an intimate part of that structure. It would be useful at this juncture to draw out what "structure" may imply. To illustrate, structure as construction, assembly, building, arrangement, organization, form, shape, constitute, and configuration. So, from these labels structure may be a material object that can be touched, gazed on, and used, but structure may also be of a social aspect. For example, Homans (1975) views structure as facets of social behavior that remain over time, which fundamentality grants the structural presence to be more established than other passing features. Additionally, structure is a notional social wholeness made up by interdependent elements; however, structure also infers that the whole is more than the sum of its segments (Baber 1991). Sewell (1992, 19) regards structures as "sets of mutually sustaining schemas and resources that empower and constrain social action and that tend to be reproduced by that social action." Simultaneously however, a structure risk may occur due to its capacity and connection, trans-possibility of schemas, and unpredictable resources in relation to numerous techniques and accumulation (Luo 2017).

Continuing the social of structure, Porpora (1989) highlights four concepts: (1) patterns of aggregate behavior stable over time; (2) law-like regularities that govern the behavior of social facts; (3) systems of human relationships among social positions; and (4) collective rules and resources that structure behavior. However, Porpora see limitations with these; the first cannot incorporate the wider society effectively, also reducing structure as secondary to human behavior. The second is weak because agents and connection between social components are not dictated by law. The third is also weak, since goals cannot be achieved by only focusing on social factors. The fourth cannot conceptualize social structure. In Radcliffe-Brown's formulation, network structuralists are more likely to consider structure as real, observable, and concrete patterns of social relations, as these patterns are "tangible" as opposed to merely "ideal" (Bearman 1997, 1384–1385). Hence, social structure is the "whole network of social relations" (Levi-Strauss 1963, 303; Blau 1974, 615), but with tension between the "concrete" (Radcliffe-Brownian) and the "abstract" (Levi-Straussian) notions of structure (Omar 2010, 655). However, since structures are models of reality they cannot be "dual"; thus, they are neither material nor ideal, neither objective nor subjective (Omar 2010, 658).

It is apparent that structure is not a clear-cut term, process, or performance when seeing how power diffuses through it. It is this structural instability that gives power its potency and is what human must cope with to survive and be creative. For instance, humans live within structure in whatever fluid and temporary static forms it takes and offers, i.e., a post-structural structure, but cannot stand outside of it. Therefore, even when devising new or updated structures, they would see themselves as part of its space of production and destruction, depending on aims and desires of how it is to be utilized. This "dueling" or lack of such between abstract/concrete, objective/subjective, and agent/structure is where Giddens enters the structure space through his structuration concepts.

Structuration

The basic domain of study of the social sciences, according to the theory of structuration, is neither the experience of the individual actor, nor the existence of any form of societal totality, but social practices ordered across space and time. Human social activities, like some self-reproducing items in nature, are recursive. That is to say, they are not brought into being by social actors but continually recreated by them via the very means whereby they express themselves as actors. In and through their activities agents reproduce the conditions that make these activities possible. (Giddens 1984, 2)

It follows from Gidden's claim that human social activities, power activities included, underwriting the whole living process within recognized and unrecognized forms is an ongoing flexible and adaptive performance. Hence, even if motivations behind social acting are not regarded as being associated with power creation or power sustainability and self-actualized growth, they are part of the active or activity process, and not being brought into being by social actors is a key point of structuration. To illustrate, if human social activities are not a result of human invention and intervention, then where do they originate from? Since the spatial stimulus that humans dwell in and upon is the fluidity of structure, it would be partially or wholly attributive to catalyst social activities. The "whole" is championed by functionalist (e.g., Parsons 1949) and structuralist (e.g., Althusser 1965; Blau 1977) ways of seeing, by limiting agent processes operating within seemingly overwhelming structural constraints (Baber 1991, 220). However, the other side of society's coin sees another "whole" in terms of ethnomethodologists' (e.g., Garfinkel 1967) error in regarding society "as the plastic creation of human subjects" (Giddens 1984, 26); e.g.,

> interpretive tradition is based upon an imperialism of the subject while functionalism and structuralism presume an imperialism of the social object. (Giddens 1984, 22)

Colonizing the subject and object as two wholes apparently inconsistent to each other, but nonetheless working alongside each other to produce a whole(sum) total or totality, is too much of a polar opposition to actually and actively achieve an efficiently run societal unstructured structure. Consequently, the agent cannot live outside societal structure, except in a nomadic form with the latter's inherent exclusionary tendency of which the agent becomes beyond society or, at the very least, marginalized from it. Also, the structure of society cannot be without agents' input, since it would dissolve into nothingness beyond the existence of human presence and their motivational needs, wants, and desires, and from this what would remain is a decaying materiality that once represented human structural performances in physical form. As a result, the mental, spiritual, and soulfulness embedded in that materiality would fade in tandem with the physical eventual diminishment and disappearance. Accordingly, human power and its structured symbolisms would be in a state of void.

The non-performances and non-processes of agents are not conducive to structural creation and creativity, since the movement of performance and process is required to power up structure. Essentially, the action of movement in human space is a durée, a continuous flow of conduct, a purposeful action composed of intentions, reasons, and motives, in which "an ontology of time-space as constitutive of social practices is basic to the conception of" structuration which begins from temporality and thus, in one sense, 'history'" (Giddens 1984, 3). Also, as a stratification model of the acting self that involves treating the reflexive monitoring, rationalization and motivation of action as embedded sets of processes (Giddens 1984). This stratification creates communion between structure and agency in whatever proportion each holds at a particular time and space context, but a communion nonetheless, and in essence a duality of structure.

A duality of structure, according to Giddens, assists with the formulative connectivity of structure, agency, and power. Even though the answer to how these "function" resides in comprehending social life as a "dialectic of power and structure, a web of possibilities for agents, whose nature is both active and structured, to make choices and pursue strategies within given limits, which in consequence expand and contract over time" (Lukes 1977, 29), Giddens' structure duality brings in the already-introduced recursive nature of social practices; e.g., "structure is both the medium and outcome of the practices which constitute social systems" (Giddens 1981, 27). Thus, identifying structure solely with constraint is rejected (Giddens 1979), as instead structures are created by human agency and, at the same time, reproducing conditions of human agency. Also, this creative action does not exist in separation from the body, its mediations with the surrounding world, and the coherence of an acting self (Giddens 1984).

Giddens' conceptualization of agency is the emphasis on the actor who "could have acted otherwise" (Baber 1991, 223). Acting otherwise implies power of choice, and the consideration of how many choices are available and the extents of these within societal allowances and restrictions, returning the debate, if it ever left it, to the spatial mix of structure and agency. All structural properties of social systems are enabling as well as constraining (Giddens 1984), and depending on where one resides within the hierarchal socioeconomic space in society, will heavily influence the scope of one's enabling and constraining in terms of active decision of how best to navigate through the life course. A course plagued with pitfalls, traps, compromise, competition, repetition, occasion senses of freedom, but mostly conforming to the unstructured structural system dwelled in. Those at the "higher" end of society would experience more enabling and less constraining, especially since they are more likely to be the enablers.

Agency structural constraints are associated with the knowledgeability of agents tied to historical circumstances (Giddens 1979). Accordingly, the achieved capacity for knowledge to act as a leverage for power is confined by how much one knows in ones accumulated time and space. This capacity is the moments of the now positionality of the agent in society's structure, a position achieved due to one's efforts, but also the legacies left of previous positions gained or lost by one's kin descendants. Consequently, the descendants' performances within their specific societal structured times and spaces may be the more significant influences to determine whatever their current descendant can potentially achieve, and actually achieve, than whatever their current agent decides to do and be. Thus, their aggregate performances may far outweigh their offspring's performance, and so placing their own restrictions and enablers on that unfortunate or fortunate contemporary agent in terms of the socioeconomic legacy left.

This creates further complexity to the agency/structural relationship, since previous structural and agency formations merge and overlay or underlay the next one along in the linear time and space progression that makes up the generational human existence. Therefore, adding to the now of what was before. Giddens (1984, 179) saw that constraint is variable not only in relation to the material and institutional circumstances of activity but "also in relation to the form of knowledgeability that agents possess about these circumstances." Accordingly, these structure/agency indicators of performance of an individual's freedom of movement bring in past structures/agencies that contribute to current material and institutional circumstances and how much knowledge the agent has. Also, just as important is how much of that knowledge can actually manipulate the structural situation the agent is in. For instance,

> To be able to "act otherwise" means being able to intervene in the world, or to refrain from such intervention, with the effect of influencing a specific process or state of affairs. This presumes that to be an agent is to be able to deploy

(chronically, in the flow of daily life) a range of causal powers, including that
of influencing those deployed by others. Action depends upon the capability of
the individual to "make a difference" to a pre-existing state of affairs or course
of events. An agent ceases to be such if he or she loses the capability to "make a
difference," that is, to exercise some sort of power. (Giddens 1984, 14)

Accordingly, actors are knowledgeable agents who act on the basis of both "practical consciousness," tacit knowledge which cannot be formulated discursively,
and "discursive consciousness," which the actors can talk about (Giddens 1982,
31). In this manner, both the spoken and unspoken at the level of consciousness
demonstrate a dynamic relationship between what is possible in concrete terms
and what may be yearned for in abstract terms. Giddens (1982, 32, 73) also
identifies the agent's "unconscious" as limiting action; however, this supposed
state of unawareness, insensibility, or being uninformed, may actually be a
heightened awareness, sensibility, and informed state of being to provide lifeless,
cold assessments of structural encounters. Thus, in a sense standing outside of
the structure to allow for an objective decision process informing the subjective
agent within the structure.

Encountering the structure from without and within may reflect or contribute to
what Giddens (1979) states about structures not existing in time-space, except in
the moments of the constitution of social systems. For instance, if one is without,
one possesses one's own time-space independent of the structure's time-space
properties, and during the moments of engagement as the unconscious without
enters the conscious within, all three time-spaces encounter each other producing
the system product of the social. Hence, the three time-spaces create the one
time-space of visible agency/structure, visible in the context of consciousness,
assisted by the invisible of the unconscious and past agency/structural conscious
unconsciousness. Even though this seen/unseen state of affairs may not exist in
how the duality of agency/structure performs, and is perhaps pure speculation,
nonetheless human performance and motivation are driven by far more than
just the "surface" "rationale." For instance, it is the irrational within humans,
wherever that comes from, perhaps from the unconscious, that is often the more
powerful behavioral determinant. Therefore, a detached agency component
feeding the agent encounter with structure. Even so, social systems "only exist
insofar as they are continually created and recreated in every encounter, as the
active accomplishment of human subjects" (Giddens 1979, 118).

Since *agency* refers to a "continuous flow of conduct" (Giddens 1979, 55), this
incessant, unceasing performance implies that the moments of contact to create

social systems is actually a one moment of unremitting existence. Following on from this, structures continually exist in time-space, perhaps only at the whim of agents, but a permanent existence nonetheless as long as the agents are actively ongoing and action their motivations:

> action or agency (is defined) as the stream of actual or contemplated causal interventions of corporeal beings in the on-going process of events in the world. The notion of agency connects directly with the concept of Praxis. (Giddens 1976, 75)

It is praxis that gives material shape to agency and structure, a visibility of evidence that both exist and encounter each other and encounter agent to agent. Essentially praxis reproduces or changes structure, i.e., acts of production.

Structuration as Limiting

Structuration theory is "intended to demonstrate the complex interrelations of human freedom (or agency) and determination (or structure) where individual choices are seen as partially constrained, but they remain choices nonetheless" (Bratton et al. 2007, 373). Structuration attempts to extend the limits of the structuralism concept, a concept that offers leverage of how identity and value of specific elements in a given social and cultural context derive not from their inherent properties but from their position in an implicit (or "deep") relational system (Benveniste 1971, 80). Also, Douglas (1968, 364) conceives that the structuralist method as "structural analysis does not work by reducing all symbols to one or two of their number; rather, it requires an abstract statement of the patterned relations of all the symbols to one another."

It is the abstraction that is questioned in structuration when applying it to the concrete of living performance, i.e., needless abstraction and detachment from the hard realities of the empirical world (Goldthorpe 2002; Marshall 1997). For example, Bourdieu (1990, 11) rejects the structuralist account as a credible onto-logical or empirical description of the practical models and cognitive structures (schemas) deployed by the social agent; instead, he sees that logical models "...become false as soon as they are treated as the real principles of practices." Also questioned is how agent and structure are structured in Giddens' thought processes as a system of relations between each to the other. For instance, Bryant and Jary (2011, 443) find weakness in this theoretical system:

Missing from Giddens' theory of structuration is concern for the strategic context of action (Stones 1991) or agent's context analysis (Stones 1996). By reworking Giddens' knowledgeability in terms of strategic context, Stones focusses on the agent's strategic terrain…"the social nexus of interdependencies, rights and obligations, asymmetries of power and the social conditions and consequences of action," (Stones 1996, 98), making up the perceived and perceivable possibilities of action and their limitations.

This nonvirtual space of agents' context analysis questions Giddens virtual structure and the structural possessions of social systems and their prominence as actual (pseudo) things (Omar 2010). Also, Giddens seeing them as positioned in the reversible time of Levi-Straussian mechanical models. For instance, Levi-Strauss (1963) extends Saussure's langue and parole to reversible time and nonreversible time in which parole exists in linear time, i.e., one direction, whereas langue, being the structure, has presence in the past, present, and future. So, along these lines, Archer (1982, 461) asks, "why should we accept this particular ontological status for structural properties?" For if structure exists over multiple place and time periods, it may not be virtual. Parole too carries a virtual quality, as it is spoken in the moment, but it also retains a multiplicity of time directions since the content of the words retains a past, present, and future influence. Influenced by what was to what is now, and how that translates into future action and belief and, hence, has structure.

However, there is structure and structure, ranging from the abstract to the concrete, i.e., insubstantiality to substantiality. It is the insubstantiality that has some people struggling with Giddens' abstractions, of structure as representing the actuality of societal fundamental components, of structure being "property" and not a tool of methods (Sewell 2005; Thompson 1989). In addition, the substantial cannot reconcile with the virtual in an easy way, since just as "reversing" time is an insubstantial imagining, so connecting to and being a part of the substantial of structure is problematic. To illustrate, when extending/altering methodological structuralism, Giddens imagined those moments or moment of "virtual existence" of time-space structure, but this results in applying a problematic, quasi-referential notion of structure, selecting a set of problematically defined properties of assumed, supposed, actually existing entities frequenting the social world (Omar 2010, 661). Thus, structure becomes a mystifying quasi-existence both in and out of "time-space" and only exhibits "paradigmatic" properties "as instances" (Archer 1982, 1995; Sewell 2005; Thompson 1989).

Giddens' account of the reproduction of structures can be taken to imply "that the 'structure' and 'systems' concerned are inchoate and evanescent, appearing and disappearing at the behest of specific individuals in specific encounters" (Layder 1985, 143). This emphasizes Giddens' focus of de-emphasizing the dominant conception of structures as constraining agency and action (Baber 1991, 227), hence not constraining social reproduction "as is" in the structure but constraining social production as potentially "could be" to alter the structure. However, "according centrality to the notion of social reproduction does not imply emphasising stability at the expense of radical discontinuities in system organizations" (Giddens 1981, 27), which is what structuration adheres and leads to (Baber 1991, 27).

Being immersed as agents in the many substantial structures on offer or as "made up" in the virtual insubstantial of the moment, a moment that may last a lifetime, recognized as concrete experience or as abstraction, may not be the most significant aspect of the agency/structural encounter, since what the agent does with the experience subsequently, creating a substantial or insubstantial outcome, is more significant. Thus, structuration, as contributing to power decisions, may just be a consultancy, one among many influencers of how power may be, and actualized in practice. Along these lines, Giddens recognized abstractive imaginings as not being the answer, but assisting toward getting closer to the answer:

> There is, of course, no obligation for anyone doing detailed empirical research, in a given localized setting, to take on board an array of abstract notions that would merely clutter up what could otherwise be described with economy and ordinary language. The concepts of structuration theory, as with any competing theoretical perspective, should for many research purposes be regarded as sensitizing devices, and nothing more. (Giddens 1984, 326)

So, thinking in the moment is a virtual abstract process as well as a simultaneous connectivity to the concreteness around. Consequently, the unlimited quality of the virtual space and its abstract nature allow thinking to reach beyond the substantial limits of structure, even if in practice the concrete of structure and other agents realities prevents that unlimited space from being attainable.

Self-Identity

It is important for agents to have virtual capacity to allow room for their self-identity to develop. This room, this space, is a counterweight against the structural limits of society and indeed the agency limits of the agent. For instance, what one dreams about aspiring to is often more than one's capacity to do so, which is not necessarily a self-imposed limitation as ones imposed from others in the structure, and the structure itself is a frequent occurrence. Following on from this, to achieve acceptable self-behavior among power imposition is a minimum state of being that many agents find themselves up against; i.e., "we not only follow lifestyles, but in an important sense we are forced to do so—we have no choice but to choose" (Giddens 1991, 81). Nonetheless, lifestyle choices of how to behave implies individuals do have choices; however, the extent of these and how many the self has power over to indeed make meaningful choices vary between agents.

Skeggs (2004) points out that Giddens' reflexive self-making does not consider resources and ownership by advantaged others in creating an identity of self, but Giddens' wording reveals an awareness of inequality. For instance, lifestyle is "a more or less integrated set of practices which an individual embraces [to] give material form to a particular narrative of self-identity" (Giddens 1991, 81), with these integrated practices partially constructed by the individual but skewed by the spaces these practices reside in. Hence, the particular narrative. Giddens may be talking about the individuality inherent in each agent, but he could also imply the structural inheritance that effects and affects individuals in unique ways. For instance, there will be similarities for those "within" close resource levels to each other, since their choice capacities would have commonality. In addition, lifestyles are "reflexively open to change in light of the mobile nature of self-identity" (Giddens 1991, 81). Even though mobility suggests choice, this may be a result of the choice of others or how the structural system, in terms of its mobility, moves.

The reflexive self is comprehended by the individual in relation to the "individual" biographic narrative, a mobile "ongoing 'story' of the self" (Giddens 1991, 53–54), of which the mobile nature in late modernity is structurally, unstructured. Consequently, there is a performance of biographical "multiple choice" (Giddens 1994a) that is

> reflexively organised in terms of flows of social and psychological infor-
> mation about possible ways of life. Modernity is a post-traditional order, in
> which the question, "How shall I live?" has to be answered in day-to-day
> decisions about how to behave, what to wear and what to eat—and many other
> things—as well as interpreted within the temporal unfolding of self-identity.
> (Giddens 1991, 14)

Many of these multiple choices occur in permissible spaces, permissible in terms of a lack of resistance from the structural system and influential agents of power. This lack would occur because the choices made benefit the structure and those "upper echelon" agents, in economic capacity, maintenance, and sustainability. Accordingly, the "choices" of what to wear and eat are in a sense irrelevant, just as long as they contribute to economic well-being, and one can have as many choices as one can manage as long as they reside within the structural norms and values of society. So, actualizing the self produces "control [over] one's own life circumstances" (Giddens 1991, 202), and "freedom of action" (Giddens 2002, 47), but within an "inherently fragile" narrative of self-identity (Giddens 1991, 185–186).

Class

Societal formats are of three types; tribal, class-divided, and class (Giddens 1984). The tribal performance is verbalizing culture that controls local organizations, tradition, kinship, group punishments, and connectivity of social and system integration. Class-divided also possesses tradition and kinship, but it also involves military and political power, economic interdependence, social and system-integrated differentiation, localized organizational dominance, and synergy of countryside and city. Class is still kinship but of family disposition, state arrangement, again military and political power, surveillance, and economic interdependence (of a greater scale and space than the class-divided) (Giddens 1984). These three types work at different spatial scales of production, wheels within wheels that perform the complexity of society, and perhaps loosely measured as local, regional, and national with all influencing each other, but not necessarily on an equal exchange of power plays flowing back and forth, and also all influenced by the international or supranational of global "society." "Loosely" is tentatively offered as Giddens may not have seen society in this way, but parallels are there to extend the tri-"structural" imagery to relate to the processes and performances within the diverse-sized places and spaces of society, especially if agents recognize a semblance of belonging to particular geographical scales within the societal framework. Indeed, agents may recognize attachment to all three, depending on the contextual encounters of their daily life. For instance, individual attachment to one scale within the moments of their daily time-space, to attachments to two or all three during other moments. In this manner, a virtual to concrete experience occurs along the power trip of the day.

The most dominant type of the three in modern capitalist society, i.e., class, is itself dominated by economics. For Giddens ([1973] 1981), economic classes within his early engagement with the concept were understood through "market capacities," i.e., property, skills, or manual labor power, and all bestowing diverse negotiating strengths in the labor market of capitalism. For example, groups of agents with common market capacities of strength (although for some, perhaps not so much of access to power/strength in terms of available resources on hand and attendant unlimited mobility) created classes in the social of society. The process was called (the already highlighted) structuration (Atkinson 2007), with the focus being labor commodification and contract to capitalism (Giddens 1981).

Regardless of if agents see themselves as part of a coherent group of like-minded and similarly possessed "economic sameness," i.e., the actual existence of class in practical concrete economic terms, capitalism can and does contract and commodify people. Thus, as Giddens ([1981] 1995, chap. 5) observes, when labor is in conflict with capital, exploitation and domination flow into the productive process and are very influential to agents lives. However, the word "class" was omitted from the previous sentence, e.g., "class exploitation…" purposely, as the claim of conflict still stands without it. This is because the reason for questioning "class" as economically determined was part of Giddens' evolving engagement with class conception and what creates it, since he wished to dispute the markedly established antievolutionary and evolutionary theories of class-based Marxism by looking at multidimensional resource-domination theory (Wright 1983, 457) and how class fits into that. For instance, within economic reductionism, capitalism is downgraded to merely one institutional element of modern societies, with others being conversion of industry and/or nature, surveillance, and military power, and all contributing to conflict and politics (Giddens 1985).

If capitalism is downgraded and class enjoys intimacy with capitalism, it follows that class itself as a supposedly concrete entity or agent of society is also downgraded. Accordingly, its potency of explanatory value of power and powered structures in society becomes weak and as an explanatory force what is left if "groups" or "classes" are being deconstructed are individuals or sole agents as representatives of the societal demographic and what they produce as lifestyle. Consequently, lifestyles are increasingly

> becoming structuring features of stratification and social differentiation and can no longer, as is usually the case, be considered merely the "'results' of class

differences in the realm of production." (Giddens 1991, 82, 228, cf. 1994a, 76, 1994b, 143)

Lifestyle choice across agents is inequitable within society's spectrum and may be dependent on life chances and socioeconomic circumstances of particular groups such as occupational (Giddens 1991) and classes (Giddens 1997). Also, the "choice of work and work milieu form a basic element of lifestyle orientations" (1991, 82). In this way, on the one hand Giddens advocates class reductionism and economic reductionism as influential power domains and, on the other, choice of work and class are still present as explanatory devices of an agent's degree of movement. This dichotomy is acknowledged; e.g.,

> though the constraints and opportunities associated with class are still held to exist they have little bearing on the actual social behaviour of individuals (1995, xv), are "thoroughly permeated by the influence of 'biographical decision-making'" (1994c, 188) and, in any case, retain only a "refracted" and transitory influence on life chances given the upsurge of mobility and unemployment at all levels. (1994b, 143–144)

So, the context of individual and class is another way of engaging with agency and the structural and the accompanying complexities of explanation character-izing both or, indeed, agency and the post-structural of class explanations. For instance, post-structural in the sense of the diluted or unstructuredness of class as a "concrete" explanation. However, Giddens as an individual is not separate from class identity, as the idea of class is used by agents when constructing relational difference and individuality, rather than similarity and collectivity (Savage 2000). Also, Laing's (1965) "ontological security" is utilized by Giddens (1979) when constructing the self as individual, since individuals have a fundamental psychological requirement to minimize angst and sustain faith in event ongoing-ness, to feel ontologically secure, which is accomplished through the "routinisation" of social conduct (Giddens 1979, 1984). This ontological structuralism is of an enduring quality with fundamental nature properties and agency capacities involved in social transformation, reproduction, and solidarity (Bryant 1992). Essentially, the power of the individual agent or power of the structure of class or structure of society itself, in whatever configurations these may be to each other, create agent action flowing from a reflexive "filtering [of] all sorts of information relevant to [one's] life situations" (Giddens 1994b, 6). This reduces politics of freedom related to class and life equality and promotes "life politics" (Giddens 1991, 209–231), of "choice, identity and mutuality" (Giddens 1998, 44), and as individuals want to be ontologically secure in their own politics of life, rules assist the process.

Rules

Giddens (1984) suggests that there is a recursive relationship between structure (external forces such as rules, resources, and social systems/macro) and agency (capability to make a difference/micro). For Giddens (1979), structure refers to "rule resource sets" implicated in the chronic temporal reproduction and historical transformations of social systems, and rules are defined as "generalizable procedures" deployed by knowledgeable actors (agents) in their everyday "enactment/ reproduction of social life" (Giddens 1984, 21). As a result, Giddens (1984, 17–18) offers a number of rules for his rules:

1. Rules are often thought of in connection with games, as formalized prescriptions. The rules implicated in the reproduction of social systems are not generally like this. Even those which are codified as laws are characteristically subject to a far greater diversity of contestations than the rules of games.
2. Rules are frequently treated in the singular, as if they could be related to specific instances or pieces of conduct. But this is highly misleading if regarded as analogous to the operation of social life, in which practices are sustained in conjunction with more or less loosely organized sets.
3. Rules cannot be conceptualized apart from resources, which refer to the modes whereby transformative relations are actually incorporated into the production and reproduction of social practices. Structural properties thus express forms of domination and power.
4. Rules imply "methodical procedures" of social interaction. Rules typically intersect with practices in the contextuality of situated encounters.
5. Rules relate on the one hand to the constitution of meaning, and on the other, to the sanctioning of modes of social conduct.

From the reading of these five rules, one can see their spatial delimitations are flexible. This is because there appears to be no hard-and-fast rule to these rules. For example, they are vulnerable to contestation, loosely organized sets, transformative relations, situated encounters, and meaning making, and all these suggest fluidity of performance when "rule doing," i.e., an evolving process depending on how rules are interpreted by the involved stakeholders. There are parallels here of how the legal profession performs in the court of law, such as when the defendant and plaintiff verbalize their objectively subjective take on the Rule of Law from diverse, adaptable perspectives.

Consequently, appreciating what rules actually imply becomes a slippery customer; e.g., attempting to fathom myth from reality, or is it that myth forms reality, thus creating truth from fiction or falsity? Or are both really the same and just labeled differently for convenience of explanation? However whichever way one interprets rule making, the slippery environment of law production can be extended to how rules are produced to cope with the complex strategical situa-tionism that is society and its corresponding loose structure and is an example of a model artificially created to fit the practicalities of societal processes, e.g., artificial within a sensation of misrepresenting the actual by a potential of it. Hence, a sense of the virtual.

Accordingly, when attempting to represent agents' practices and performances, there are always degrees of inaccuracies as the representational process is a virtual process, i.e., a simulation and an ontology. For example, structure "refers to rules and resources instantiated in social systems but having only a 'virtual existence'" (Giddens 1981, 170). So, the virtual of mis(representation) of how agents "see" society and its structures produces distortions of it, in the ways it is seen, by the actual unavoidable and necessary contact between agent and society. To illustrate, if an agent ceases to contact, she or he is an agent no more as there is no need to be an agent—at least in the form and formats currently visualized. As a result, a new agency and structural "model" of reality may be required to explain noncontact and, subsequently, new rules of engagement have to be learned and applied, and so the virtual cycle repeats, be it to a different drum of existence, i.e., a different power relationship, or lack of relationship of agent and structure. These musings can be thought of as the ramblings of virtual imagery and the difficulty of matching rules to such vague and foggy spaces, but the point is that understanding the role of agency and structural connectivity is challenging and perhaps more so when covering the two with blanket(s) of rules and trying to understand power processes within this misty (and mystifying) space.

Rules form social positions that relate to a power differential, according to Porpora (1989), who questions Giddens of awarding precedence to rules and not acknowledging that a social system has causal belongings outside of agency rules. Also, the differential that is caused by domination, since it reconstitutes domination by rule reassertion. However, it is the imprecise nature of the causal social system that causes rules and their interpretations and applications to be of the moment. To illustrate, a moment drawing on the interactional encounters of the now and prior acquisitioning of historically related knowledge, since one really only has the moment one is in to appreciate that one exists and does. Even though that moment is supplied by past legacy and future aspiration, the context of the now cannot be underestimated, for it is filled with thinking, emotion, weariness, culturalness, structure, post-structure, rules, and the instantaneous reforming moment itself. Fundamentally, these are much to deal with in the daily life's "billions of encounters" (Thrift 1999, 302). As Giddens says when defining the practice of practices, of

> the uncertainty and "fuzziness" resulting from the fact that they have as their principle not a set of conscious, constant rules, but practical schemes, opaque to their possessors, varying according to the logic of the situation. (Bourdieu 1990, 12)

So, rules as power signifiers can be overridden by the power of the practical moment, in whatever form that takes and whatever one encounters within that. Also, rules of social life can be visualized as generalized procedures or techniques applied in the enactment and reproduction of social practices (Fuchs 2002, 13), returning the narrative to ontological security:

> The structuring qualities of rules can be studied in respect, first of all, of the forming, sustaining, termination and reforming of encounters. Although a dazzling variety of procedures and tactics are used by agents in the constitution and reconstitution of encounters, probably particularly significant are those involved in the sustaining of ontological security. (Giddens 1984, 23)

Thus, ontological security sustainability is the ongoing maintenance of one's identity of self, essentially to empower oneself within the power disempowerment of societal structure.

Power of Giddens

> Agency refers not to the intentions people have in doing things but to their capability of doing those things in the first place (which is why agency implies

power...the Oxford English Dictionary definition of an agent as "one who exerts power or produces an effect"). (Giddens 1984, 9)

Intentions have connections to potentialities, and capability relates to actuality, and gravitating from potentiality to actuality is not a given since not all potentials can emerge into a concrete state. For example, some potentials remain within the abstract which is their virtual time and space, and other potentials can break through and translate or transform into concrete space and time. Therefore, action is created, and power is created. Action depends on the individual faculty to "make a difference" to a preexisting state of affairs or course of events (Gaventa 2003), and an agent ceases to be such if they lose the capability to "make a difference," that is, to exercise some sort of power (Giddens 1984, 14). For Giddens, "power" is fundamental in the social sciences (Best 2001), so, by default, power is fundamental in the practice of society.

To assist with this fundamentality, seven canons of Giddens' understanding of power are offered by Mcphee (2004, 130–131):

1. Power is weighty but not completely essential to how Giddens constructs abstractions of individuals' connectivity to society.
2. Power as duality of the practice of power in reproducing institutional domination structures.
3. To apply power is to get involved to make a difference. A basis of agency.
4. Exercising power is the substance of material practice in space and time.
5. When exercising power, agents bring into play "dominion over material facilities 'versus' the means of dominion over the activities of human beings themselves. Both sources of power depend to a large degree upon the management of time-space relations" (Giddens 1987, 7).
6. Power as interaction working with norms and meaning. It is produced from communication and value alignment, resulting in ensuring that one's values and meanings have weight in all circumstances.
7. Agents having power over other agents within a dialectic of control. The stronger relies on the weaker to obtain power's profits. Resistance is the consequence.

From these, power permeates society, and as Giddens (1979) points out, the exercise of power does not constitute a discrete act; rather, it is a regular, routine phenomenon, occurring during the course of action.

It would be too simplistic to say power is practiced "on many levels," as that would imply omissions of power presence on certain other levels. Also, societal structure cannot be reduced to a model of levels as that would make it too simplistic since power is not intrinsically tied to the achievements of sectional interests, and the use of power does not characterize specific types of conduct but is implied in all actions (Giddens 1984). The all is essentially the totality of performance of the social. Therefore, social interaction involves the use of power as a necessary implication of the logical connection between human action and its capacity to transform structures (Giddens 1981). This implication or effect of human and structure shows that power retains a virtual character. So, the challenge reappears of matching a virtual model to the space of complex concreteness, in the context of power indefinability.

Social systems equate to power systems, implying they encompass the "institutional mediation of power" (Giddens 1985, 9). In practice, institutions try to control individuals by applying rules that become normalized (Best 2001). It is this perceived normalization that allows power rules to be accepted in conjunction with degrees of resistance, whose extents depend on how the agent reacts to being institutionalized. For example, modern nation-states are "polyarchic" in nature according to Giddens, meaning that they have a set of legal rules that provide individual people with civil and political rights, such as free speech, which gives them status as a "citizen" (Best 2001, 9), hence a status to practice degrees of resistance. Giddens (1984) refers to this resistance as "the 'dialectic of control' in social systems" (16), and one space of "controlled" social systems in modernity is the nation-states. A Nation-state is regarded as

> a political apparatus, recognised to have sovereign rights within the borders of a demarcated territorial area, able to back its claims to sovereignty by control of military power, many of whose citizens have positive feelings of commitment to its national identity. (Giddens 1989, 303)

So, positive feelings of commitment help the structure of society to have structure or a sense of structure, since perception of reality can be more real than the actual reality, for it *is* reality to the agency gaze. For instance, Giddens utilizes an ontological over epistemological "reading" of how social systems through agency and structural duality tell their story of interaction. Returning to structure, if a social system has many resources to power its institutions, simultaneously these resources retain and maintain much power. To illustrate,

Resources are the media whereby transformative capacity is employed as power in the routine course of social interaction; but they are at the same time structural elements of social systems as systems, reconstituted through their utilization in social interaction. (Giddens 1979, 92)

Additionally, constructing resources requires knowledge of who the population is and what they are doing, since their types of performance and the extent of performance have to be measured. To do this, Giddens regards surveillance as the means to absorb the demographic practices to sustain, retain, and maintain power for social systems; i.e., "all states involve the reflexive monitoring of aspects of the reproduction of the social systems subject to their rule" (1985, 17). So, as Fuchs (2002) says, the nation-state and surveillance in the modern capitalist society is the fundamental mechanism of integration; e.g.,

Surveillance as the mobilising of administrative power—through the storage and control of information—is the primary means of the concentration of authorative resources involved in the formation of the nation-state. (Giddens 1985, 181)

Giddens (1979, 91) views power "both as transformative capacity (the characteristic view held by those treating power in terms of the conduct of agents), and as domination (the main focus of those concentrating on power as a structural quality)." *Transformative capacity* refers to the power of an individual to "intervene causally in a series of events" (Baert 1998, 101), and in this sense all actions depend on exercising power. Ultimately, power can be conceptualized as "relations of autonomy and dependence between actors in which these actors draw on and reproduce structural properties of domination" (Giddens 1981, 28).

The primary problem that the theory of structuration was designed to solve was not methodological or epistemological but ontological (Omar 2010). As Giddens (1984) notes, while the former concerns are important, "concentration upon epistemological issues draws attention away from the more 'ontological' concerns of social theory, and it is these upon which structuration theory primarily concentrates" (xx). Accordingly, the ontological can mix quite well with the virtual and concrete of perception, performance, and practice of self-identity, class, and rules—when doing power.

CHAPTER 7

Marx

The history of all hitherto existing society is the history of class struggles. Freeman and slave, patrician and plebeian, lord and serf, guild-master and journeyman, in a word, oppressor and oppressed, stood in constant opposition to one another, carried on uninterrupted, now hidden, now open fight, a fight that each time ended, either in a revolutionary reconstitution of society at large, or in the common ruin of the contending classes. (Engels Communist Manifesto, Chap. 1, (Marx and Engels 1848))

Engels reveals the Marxist power process as a practice based on, and in, tension between competing parties, groups, and classes. From this, there is an assumption that the individual does not count for much; i.e., "Society does not consist of individuals, but expresses the sum of interrelations, the relations within which these individuals stand" (Marx and Nicolaus [1858] 1993, 265). However, relations are relative, relative to who one associates with and who one's contacts are, to allow states of affairs to be. For instance, associations can be who one does trade with in terms of buying and selling, set within a space of mutual profitable benefit, in which differentiation of power capacity is not too marked. Even though the difference in power acquisition and application may be unequal between the trading individuals and who they represent, the inequality is negligible when compared to those who work for them. This is because these workers do not retain enough power to significantly challenge the decision-making of their employers and only retain power in the working space by what is "awarded" to them. Awarded in the sense of promotion within the hierarchical structure, set up in and as the workplace. Additionally, even within this power differential at the working level, i.e., nonowners, the influence and exercise of power are not too marked between the "lowest" and "highest" workers in terms of their status in the company, as compared to between the owners/employers and employees.

It is the living performance gap concerning employees and employers that produces disparity in terms of economics, cultural positioning, social attitude, political perspective, and how one "side" views and treats the other. These result in those of similar living performances gravitating toward each other and forming an exclusive club for protection for what they have got, or indeed for what they have not got, e.g., the clubs of the "haves" and the "have-nots," with each suspicious of the other, as the "haves" attempt to control the "have-nots," but still feeling slightly uncomfortable in doing so due to potential resistance of the latter. In turn, the latter or "have-nots" also feel uncomfortable, since feeling and being "powerless" is uncomfortable, but the potential is there to react, to threaten the well-being of the "haves." Thus, the economic form creates inclusive and exclusive players or different classes of players. Whether or not "classes" as an apt label or term to define the individuals who play the game of economics in differentiating the haves and have-nots is appropriate, as the Marxist power journey is traveled through, it is at least a "rough and ready" Marxist trademark to commence with.

Class

Class ascendency in societies that are capitalist in form and practice underwrite Marxist considerations of power. Thus, power relations as expressions or indicators of a specific arrangement of class domination, rather than from individual to individual who lack a more in-depth presence in the social structure (Jessop 2012). Consequently, the former may be the more "permanent" structure, as opposed to the more "temporary" presence of individuals operating in that structure, that holds sway as to power retention and intention. For example, Marx's definition of class relates to property ownership, and this ownership is of an exclusionary disposition that advantages the owner (Dahrendorf 1959, chap. 1). From this exclusory space, nonowners cannot access the advantages the property potentially and actually offers, and over time, dating from the origin of the property acquisition, the gap between owner and nonowners in terms of income and status expands. It is this gap that encourages identity separation into different groups.

Power capacity simultaneously widens within this ownership space, and individuals are labeled accordingly to where they are perceived to perform within the societal structured economic hierarchy or order. Within this labeling performance and for ease of (class)ification, individuals are placed in classes reflecting their powers of ownership. However, these class categories may not respect individual differences of those who find themselves, probably unwillingly, as part of a class. For instance, many may be unaware of being placed in this abstractive imaginary exercise called class, as they continue in their daily lives. Therefore, defining class and differences between classes is literally a blanket process, since a metaphoric blanket is thrown over those deemed to retain a similar level of ownership, and the blanket obscures difference. As a result, the aforementioned ease of classification allows theories of economic ownership to be constructed from the unstable (class)ified infrastructure. To illustrate, "Society does not consist of individuals, but expresses the sum of interrelations, the relations within which these individuals stand" (Marx and Nicolaus [1858] 1993).

According to Marxist theory, all in society retain property ownership; however, this ownership depends on what is owned. Even though all individuals "own" their own embodied selves in terms of movement, knowledge, experience levels, and thinking, beyond this very personal ownership the "own" aspect comes under pressure from the ownership potential of others. In other words, one's "own" begins to be compromised, resulting in a loss of control of that ownership since one is owned by another individual, expanding the ownership potential of the latter, and consequently reducing the ownership potential of the former. Essentially, the former becomes the property of the latter. Property, in Marxist terminology, produces three classes (Rummel 1977). Firstly, the bourgeoisie who owns the means (factory buildings and machinery) of production, making money from profit. Secondly, landowners making money from rent. Lastly, the proletariat who own their embodied selves and sell it for a salary.

One of the methods to maximize profit is to pay as minimum a salary as possible from the bourgeoisie to the proletariat. Also, maximizing profit from maximizing rent levels, which may be applied from the landowner to the bourgeoisie (who may be one and the same) or from the landowner to the proletariat. Either way, or in combination, the salaried worker faces an ongoing struggle against the economically disadvantaged situation found within, as they are dominated by the economic system in place and those who conduct its capitalistic tune, and this conduct transmits "down the hierarchy" of economic control, supported by societal ideology.

Marx does not define ideology but uses the concept to indicate an image production of social reality (McCarney 2005):

> ideology is a process accomplished by the so-called thinker consciously, it is true, but with a false consciousness. The real motive forces impelling him remain

unknown to him; otherwise it simply would not be an ideological process. Hence
he imagines false or seeming motive forces. (Engels [1893] 1968)

However, the unknown aspect of motivation behind the ideology is questionable,
since those of considerable ownership property status would retain a fair idea
of why they promote a particular capital structure, as it is in their self-interest
to do so. Accordingly, it depends on how false the false consciousness is in
impeding or enhancing the capitalist space of production and sustainability for
those who own it:

> The ideas of the ruling class are in every epoch the ruling ideas, i.e., the class which
> is the ruling material force of society, is at the same time its ruling intellectual
> force. The class which has the means of material production at its disposal, has
> control at the same time over the means of mental production, so that thereby,
> generally speaking, the ideas of those who lack the means of mental production
> are subject to it. The ruling ideas are nothing more than the ideal expression of
> the dominant material relationships, the dominant material relationships grasped
> as ideas. (Marx and Engels, *The German Ideology* 1998, 67)

Also, the self-gauging of the false consciousness of those labeled *proletariat*
should be considered, since if there is a recognition of falsity behind the surface
ideological facade of the bourgeoisie, some or many in the proletariat may
chose paths of resistance; hence, a class struggle. For instance, *The Communist
Manifesto* (1988) demonstrates Marx's revolution theory centered on economic
class struggle (Scott, n.d.), with communism opposing oppressive power as
class differentiation causes oppression. In effect, all history is underwritten by
this class existence and subsequent societal tension, according to Marx, and the
history of class warfare has caused the modern bourgeois society, of which its
origins are traced to the prior feudalism:

> The modern bourgeois society that has sprouted from the ruins of feudal society,
> has not done away with class antagonisms. It has but established new classes,
> new conditions of oppression, new forms of struggle in place of the old ones.
> (Marx 1988, 56)

The clash of these two historical forces reveals the oppositional nature (De
Angelis 1999) of the "present form of production relations" which "gives signs

of its becoming—foreshadowing of the future" (Marx [1858] 1974, 461). To illustrate, the oppositional nature of

> Freeman and slave, patrician and plebeian, lord and serf, guildmaster and jour-
> neyman, in a word, oppressor and oppressed, stood in constant opposition to
> one another, carried on an uninterrupted, now hidden, now open fight, that each
> time ended, either in the revolutionary reconstitution of society at large, or in
> the common ruin of the contending classes. (Marx, 1988, 55)

The foreshadowing of the future is created in the present and past and is not a predetermined future. For instance, Marx envisioned a future of power parity where the class distinction would eventually disappear, and in a sense one class would be left to run society as a uniform, group effort; i.e., society would be the class or society simply an egalitarian endeavor of ownership, so "when division of labor and private property are abolished by communal ownership, individuals are free to pursue their own interests" (Marx and Engels 1998, 86).

However, to move from the potential to actual "equality," the capitalistic structure must be overcome, which is perhaps an insurmountable obstacle. For instance, there will be significant numbers of individuals in both classes, assuming individuals see themselves as being in classes and not as agents endeavoring to move within the societal system as best they can, who do not wish for equality. This is because powers of motivation to gain greater power are important for some or many or all. Basically, it is difficult to ascertain the societal percentage since some individuals may not see the process as to do with power but to do with senses of well-being, fulfillment, and contentment.

If classes do exist in society or at least in the form of loose "like-minded" groups, to which Dahrendorf extended Marx's ideas post-Marx (Holmes, Hughes, and Julian 2007), the extension generally focused on Marx's deep structures of unseen power residing in the capitalist system (Booth 2015). For example, three areas were focused on: (1) classes that exist in society, (2) societal inequalities, and (3) functionality of society to favor the powerful class, all of which results in conflict (Haralambos and Holborn 1991; Holmes, Hughes, and Julian 2007). So, not really stepping outside Marx's concepts but perhaps adding to it, which in and of itself is telling in how capitalism operates. Essentially, Marx attempted to create a political theory substantiated by the working-class space. A theory associated with structural contradictions and class conflict (Jessop and Wheatley 1999).

Political State

> The oppressed are allowed once every few years to decide which particular representatives of the oppressing class are to represent and repress them—Marx. (Lenin 1917, chap. 5)

Within this "repressive" environment, supply and circulation of political power are dictated by production power or capital that the bourgeoisie utilize to insulate their property, making them acceptable, thus normalizing their version of social relations (Rummel 1977). As with all communication between two parties, in this case the bourgeoisie and the proletariat, political space hovers in the background to "guide" the narrative or discourse, and leading the discourse of power performance is the bourgeoisie, who effectively represent and practice the state business. However, to what extent the state favors this process to the detriment of the proletariat is a matter of perspective, of which Marxist doctrine advocates three types—instrumentalist, structuralist, and "strategic-relational" (Jessop 2012).

Instrumentalists advocate the state as neutral, neutral in the sense that whoever is driving the state process at the time reflects their well-being. To illustrate, well-being in this context is the control of and over society:

> the "ruling class" of capitalist society is that class which owns and controls the means of production and which is able, by virtue of the economic power thus conferred upon it, to use the state as an instrument for the domination of society. (Miliband 1969, 22)

Paradoxically, this process implies the state is biased, with the bias originating from those possessing it. Or the space of state within its abstract and concrete forms is vulnerable to exclusory interests, who, through the perceived "neutrality" of the state as the key instrument of societal welfare and general well-being, are accepted as legitimate. Therefore, as with any design and construction, there is inbuilt prejudice and partiality at the outset, reinforced and adapted when necessary to maintain the state structure. Also, this maintenance simultaneously maintains the state users, the ones controlling the state during particular times and spaces.

This inbuilt prejudice and partiality reflect the structuralist perspective, which maintains that since the state has been designed to favor capitalism and disfavor the demographic population who are regarded as being socially, politically, and geographically excluded from the hierarchical power of society, who "controls" the state is immaterial. For example, the control may be immaterial to those who actually control, since it benefits them, but is materially significant for the excluded. Since structuralists maintain that the modern state structure systematizes capital and dislocates the working class, the state's "independence" from explicit management over production means, i.e., being privatized, creates a dependence on a healthy private sector (Offe 1984). Hence, looking after the private profiteers means the state retains a vested interest in looking after itself, as profitability of capital must be maintained. However, a sense of equilibrium is also present to ensure state legitimation, as the economically dominant class cannot formally envelope political power, so plays the powered game through the Rule of Law. Of course, if aspects of the Rule of Law encourage the capitalistic process, all to the good for the dominant class. As part of this controlling process, subordinate classes are constrained materially within this capitalistic space, being offered concessions, but if profit is endangered these concessions become vulnerable (Jessop 2012).

Agencies of state, both within economically dominant and subordinate classes, are obliged to operate as if capitalism is the only course of action available. Of course—it probably is!—as agents, in and out of state power, have experienced capitalist processes over the course of their lives since it is the predominate influencer of behavior, needs, desires, and wants, and subsequently there is an inevitability of naturalization of the capitalist program. For instance, how else would a capitalist agent conduct the business of business in the political sphere, if not by encouraging the machinery and materiality of capitalism, or at the least by reacting to it in decision-making since that is what the agent is familiar with?

Strategic-relational theorists suggest the state performs due to the wider social relations in which it is embedded, particularly due to the equilibrium of social forces, and within the state's geographic, historical, and experienced events, it adopts various forms to perform accordingly. These selective forms or what Jessop (1990, 367) terms *structural selectivity* see state structures that "offer unequal chances to different forces within and outside that state to act for different political purposes." Within this "state of affairs," structures of the state produce variant outcomes in an assortment of economic and political approaches, creating inequality as to who or who does not receive benefit. Like so, the connectivity of these approaches demonstrates exertions of state power, and this strategic-relational mode of political operation augments Marx's capital not as an entity but as a social relation.

The state is also a social relation, according to Poulantzas (1978), who argued that yes, the modern state retains certain biases, but these are not powerful enough to sustain capitalist rule. To elucidate, the state actually reproduces class tension and state contradictions, so state power's effectiveness relies significantly on the fluctuating equilibrium of forces in combination with tactics and strategies chased by class and nonclass forces correspondingly. The reliance is there because the state does not exist except in the minds of its practitioners, and it is they who award it the status of power; i.e., of itself it has no power and therefore cannot apply it. So, as a result, the practitioners in the shape of state officials, civil servants, and politicians who populate various parts of the state structure in conjectural roles, all who are replaceable over time, are the agents who "power" the state (Jessop 2012). Consequently, a state of social relationships, and social relationships, even the best and most intimate of them, can experience breakdowns in lines of communication. Also, the state as an ongoing human project has a porous sense of power within its apparent impermeable nature, and it is this porosity that allows power bases from the "inside" and "outside" to influence it, transform it, and shape policy, since the social is saturated with unlike-minded agents as well as like-minded.

Marx viewed the state in its modern form as serving the interests of the ruling economic class through oppressing the proletariat collective (Scott, n.d.). Therefore, to neutralize this affair of state, "communal control of the means of production that offers freedom from the tyranny of the common interest of the state, with its imposed division of labour and privatization of property," (Marx and Engels 1998, 52), was proposed as a solution to this inequality of power. Also, proposing along similar lines, the "only solution is a revolution in which the dominant modes of production are abolished altogether" (Marx and Engels 1998, 61).

Marx regarded the state as distant from civil society, essentially opposed to it (Adam 2010). For example, "The modern bourgeois state is embodied in two great organs, parliament and the government [the executive]" (Marx and Engels 1971, 196). In this manner, parliamentarism is not distinguished by effectual influence from the "lesser" class(s), but with professional politicians not strictly responsible to the public. Additionally, this autonomy or detachment from the general populous extends to other "public servants":

> The "police," the "judiciary," and the "administration" are not the representatives of a civil society which administers its own universal interests in them and through them; they are the representatives of the state and their task is to administer the state against civil society. (Marx 1975, 111)

Consequently, the state as an insulated space becomes a state within its state creation and takes on a life of its own. Essentially, the "inner state" has ownership over the state and, hence, has ownership over society and the civil. This relates to Marx's property ownership, which is the means to produce the state for individual agency aims; i.e., "as for the individual bureaucrat, the purpose of the state becomes his private purpose, a hunt for promotion, careerism" (Marx 1975, 108). As the members who work within the state are also members of civil society, and its associated class distinctions (apparent or real), the "*class distinctions* of civil society thus become established as political distinctions" (Marx 1975, 136). What Marx is adhering to is that the state and its agents (deputies), in terms of a representative democracy, hold the monopoly on power, rather than the demographic as a whole:

> The separation of the political state from civil society takes the form of a sep-aration of the deputies from their electors. Society simply deputes elements of itself to become its political existence. There is a twofold contradiction: (1) A formal contradiction. The deputies of civil society are a society which is not connected to its electors by any "instruction" or commission. They have a formal authorization but as soon as this becomes real they cease to be authorized. They should be deputies but they are not. (2) A material contradiction. In respect to actual interests...Here we find the converse. They have authority as represen-tatives of public affairs, whereas in reality they represent particular interests. (Marx 1975, 193–194)

To create an equilibrium of power, in which all in society, i.e., civil society, have a voice and practical input and receive output from societal resources, is challenging in practice. For instance, politics gets in the way to protect against equal opportunity, and for all agents in society to get meaningfully involved in the political power process would inversely proportion the effective extent of how the society would function in practice. Thus, the political state would become the civil state with power so dissolved among the masses that it would tend toward powerlessness. Accordingly, there is some practical sense in the parliament being "removed" from the mass population to allow decisions to be implemented reasonably quickly and effectively, since the alternative is a stifling of power as too many individuals want their interests to be taken into consideration, as opposed to the current state "status quo" of minority interests sold as majority interests. Marx summarizes:

> The efforts of civil society to transform itself into a political society, or to make the political society into the real one, manifest themselves in the attempt to achieve as general a participation as possible in the legislature...The political state leads

an existence divorced from civil society. For its part, civil society would cease to exist if everyone became a legislator. (Marx 1975, 188–189)

Alienation/Alien Nation

The less you eat, drink and read books; the less you go to the theatre, the dance hall, the public house; the less you think, love, theorize, sing, paint, fence, etc., the more you save—the greater becomes your treasure which neither moths nor dust will devour—your capital. The less you are, the more you have; the less you express your own life, the greater is your alienated life—the greater is the store of your estranged being. (Marx 1844)

Thus, when considering the extent of one's alienation, the space of power as a space of production is a vital influential factor. For example, in the economic context, material goods are produced, immaterial goods are produced in the form of information and communication, ownership profit is produced, and wages for workers are produced. What is also produced is disparity of living quality, leading to a loss of the self for many of society's agents. To illustrate, a loss of the self from loss of one's time and space as a subjective choice, as the political economic environment overrides to a great extent how one utilizes their time of living and where the spaces of that living is to take place. In relation to time and space control, there is a loss of one's creativity, critical thinking, and actually a loss of building something that is a part of oneself, reflecting one's creative potential.

Fundamentally, a loss of oneself as an individual human being, and instead becoming, and have already become, a commodity in the state's aim for profit, i.e., just regarded as a commodity by the state owners as a part of the productive machinery of profit, a mere cog. For instance, as capital introduces machinery, "the most powerful weapon for suppressing strikes, those periodic revolts of the working class against the autocracy of capital" (Marx [1867] 1976, 562), what better way to control workers as to make them part of the machine. Additionally, the losing of oneself when playing the game of commodity, as being a customer of commodity, e.g., by purchasing and using the manufactured materials and immaterials offered, so becoming an alien in one's own nation and experiencing alienation, as power performs its potent dance.

Consequently, Marx's analysis of alienation is centered on the idea that capitalism is a sort of disenchanted "religion," where commodities replace divinity (Löwy 2002):

The more the worker estranges himself in his labour, the more the estranged, objective world he has created becomes powerful, while he becomes impoverished...The same happens in religion. The more man puts things in God, the less he keeps in himself. (Marx 1844, 1962, 57–58)

That is what power can do, since the more influence it exerts over an agent, the less is the self-power the agent retains. The reverse is also applicable, as the more an agent keeps of possessing a controlling influence of power, the more the agent's self-power is utilized. However, the "kept" is in the space of power flows, not necessarily in how Marx views it, i.e., a view that regards the individual as giving away self-potentiality, consciously and unconsciously, of what they may be capable of but for the influence of power in the capitalist interest framework. As Marx points out, "the *practical* struggle of these particular interests, which *actually* constantly run counter to the common and illusory common interests, necessitates *practical* intervention and restraint by the illusory 'general' interest in the form of the state" (Marx and Engels 1998). So, to create space of freedom or emancipation above and beyond the capitalist power, human behavioral limitation will happen

only when real, individual man resumes the abstract citizen into himself and as an individual man has become a species-being in his empirical life, his individual work and his individual relationships, only when man has recognized and organized his forces propres [own forces] as social forces so that social force is no longer separated from him in the form of political force, only then will human emancipation be completed. (Marx 1975, 234)

Consequently, power's capitalist Marx alienation of the individual effects the social of society, e.g.,

When real individuals are fragmented from one another and become estranged then their mediating function must in turn become independent of them: that is, their social relationships, the nexus of reciprocity which binds them together. Thus, there is an evident parallelism between the hypostasis of the state, of God, and of money. (Colletti 1975, 54)

For instance, the underlying reality of money and the power that is gained from it, utilized through the state apparatus, supported by human interpretations of how a "God-like" presence would recommend "appropriate" courses of action to give the performance further legitimacy, weight upon and affect the majority of human behavioral patterns and choices. So, a profound degradation of social relations and an ethical regression with respect to pre-capitalist societies (Löwy 2003), where everything has a price:

> At last, the time has come in which all that human beings had considered as in-alienable has become the object of exchange, of traffic, and may be alienated. It is a time when the very things which before were conveyed, but never bartered; given, but never sold; conquered, but never purchased—virtue, love, opinion, science, conscience etc.—when, in short, everything has finally become tradable. It is a time of generalized corruption, universal venality or, to speak in terms of political economy, the time when anything, moral or physical, receives a venal value, and may be taken to market to be appraised for its appropriate value. (Marx 1947, 33)

In this way, the agent's value to the state is perceived as a monetary value, as a level of contribution toward the state's well-being and a collective of agents' labors reflecting an economic "one class" of and as society. In a sense Marx achieved the dream of everyone belonging together, except the one class is an alienated class and as such living labor and the labor of living is that

> the material on which it works is alien material; the instrument is likewise an alien instrument; its labour appears as a mere accessory to their substance and hence objectifies itself in things not belonging to it. Indeed, living labour itself appears as alien vis-à-vis living labour capacity, whose labour it is, whose own life's expression it is, for it has been surrendered to capital in exchange for objectified labour, for the product of labour itself. (Marx [1858] 1974, 462)

Therefore, the alien nation has been constructed and "working" well; however, there is uncertainty concerning the "being" part of well as that is a matter of powered opinion!

Capitalism and Attendant Economy

Economy is the focus of Marx's sociological theories, with society being the consequence of an economic base driving religion, ideology, politics, and social superstructure (Scott, n.d.). So, social and political structures are derived from the economic means of production (Marx and Engels 1998), and the economic aspect involves labor division, a division harboring conflict between common and individual interests (Marx and Engels 1998). The economic means of production such as factories, machines, and raw materials sits within the Marxist-termed mode of production. This is a mode that refers to the way society is prearranged, structured, and ordered, in an economic production of goods and services. Labor power is integral to this and how that power is manipulated, and a highly influential mode of production in society is capitalism. This is fundamentally a mode of private ownership of productive means, that

> the capitalist mode of appropriation in which the product enslaves first the producer, and then appropriator, is replaced by the mode of appropriation of the product that is based upon the nature of the modern means of production; upon the one hand, direct social appropriation, as means to the maintenance and extension of production on the other, direct individual appropriation, as means of subsistence and of enjoyment. (Engels 1882, chap. 3)

To reach these levels of appropriation is the process and performances of history. History is "dependent on the existence of human beings, who produce their own means of subsistence, and the resulting means of production determines their way of life" (Marx and Engels 1998, 37), in which the legacies of prior histories power the present one, and the capitalist project is no different according to Marx, when considering primitive accumulation.

Embryonic Capitalism

Time eras practice accumulation, and to ensure this practice has a sound grounding to make it effective, the accumulation process presumes aspects of prior pre-accumulated capital assists the production process (De Angelis 1999). This practice Marx terms *primitive accumulation*, which is based on class relations:

> The capital-relation presupposes a complete separation between the workers and the ownership of the conditions for the realisation of their labour [and] the process…which creates the capital-relation can be nothing other than the process which divorces the worker from the ownership of the conditions of his own labour; it is a process which operates two transformations, whereby the social means of subsistence and production are turned into capital, and the immediate producers are turned into wage-labourers. Primitive accumulation…is nothing else than

the historical process of divorcing the producer from the means of production. (Marx [1867] 1976, 874–875)

A divorcing "separation anxiety" that overtime increases, as accumulation "reproduces the separation and the independent existence of material wealth as against labour on an ever-increasing scale" (Marx 1971, 315) and "as a continuous process since what is in primitive accumulation appears as a distinct historical process" (Marx 1971, 271, 311–312). "Once this separation is given, the production process can only produce it anew, reproduce it, and reproduce it on an expanded scale" (Marx [1858] 1974, 462). Essentially, what "may be called primitive accumulation…is the historical basis, instead of the historical result, of specifically capitalist production" (Marx [1867] 1976, 775). Along these lines, the primitive nature of humans is a process of possession, of retaining power over something, someone, some space, some place, and of setting up inclusory and exclusory performance.

Maturing the Embryonic

Capital is wealth, money principal, investment, assets, resources, funds, a center, hub, and headquarters. It reflects the identity of and empowers those agents who retain possession of capital and simultaneously reflects the identity and disempowerment of those agents who have minimal or no possession capacity. Thus, all in society reside somewhere along the empowerment to disempowerment continuum, the shape of which with the number of agents measured against the "Y Axis" (going upward from zero to maximum number of agents in society), against, moving from left to right along the "X Axis" depicting correspondingly, empowered to disempowered, would show a $\nearrow$. Also, the "X Axis" explanation could just as easily read means of production to no means of production (left to right), as well as the "Y Axis" legend being replaced or added to by accumulation and concentration of capital (i.e., the greatest value at the base and becoming lessor and eventually to nothing, as one travels up the axis).

Hence, the capitalist process and performance are a purposeful separation between those who have and those who do not have. It is a

divorce between the conditions of labour on the one hand and the producers on the other that forms the concept of capital, as this arises with primitive accumulation…subsequently appearing as a constant process in the accumulation and concentration of capital, before it is finally expressed here as the centralization of capitals already existing in few hands, and the decapitalization of many. (Marx [1894] 1981, 354–355)

"Once developed historically, capital itself creates the conditions of its existence (not as conditions for its arising, but as results of its being)" (Marx [1858] 1974, 459). Its being or actuality constantly replenishes to accumulate its sense of being, assuming the social environment maintains a healthy state of affairs; i.e., the agents themselves do not begin to literally die off as an endemic or pandemic virus flows through the globalized societal network of integration making the economic structure dysfunction. For instance, it is the individual level of health that, if becoming an ill collective, e.g., involving a significant number of dysfunctional economic agents, that can become more powerful than capital as it can temporarily or permanently bring it down. To illustrate, even though accumulation relies *primarily* on "the silent compulsion of economic relations [which] sets the seal on the domination of the capitalist over the worker," …in the case of primitive accumulation the separation is imposed *primarily* through "direct extra-economic force" (Marx [1867] 1976, 899–900).

This extra force, to enhance the already-present economic force, is sourced and constructed from public debt, international credit systems, and taxes (De Angelis 1999). For example, public debt

> becomes one of the most powerful levers of primitive accumulation. As with the stroke of an enchanter's wand, it endows unproductive money with the power of creation and thus turns it into capital, without forcing it to expose itself to the troubles and risks inseparable from its employment in industry or even in usury. (Marx [1867] 1976, 919)

Complementary to public debt is the modern fiscal system,

> whose pivot is formed by taxes on the most necessary means of subsistence (and therefore by increases in their prices), thus contains within itself the germ of automatic progression. Over-taxation is not an accidental occurrence, but rather a principle. (Marx [1867] 1976, 921)

Finally, the international credit system

> often conceals one of the sources of primitive accumulation in this or that people…A great deal of capital, which appears today in the United States without

> any birth-certificate, was yesterday, in England, the capitalised blood of children. (Marx 1867 [1976], 920)

Capitalized blood is in constant spillage, metaphorically speaking, through the consequences of its endeavor, as the victims and perpetrators of capitalism all experience bloodletting through its paradoxical accumulation of wealth and accumulation of alienation of the self from the self, production, and freedom of choice(s). Thus, the produced economic system can be all-encompassing on people's sense of being, being subsumed under the economic (B)eing, since

> direct extra-economic force is still of course used, but only in exceptional cases. In the ordinary run of things, the worker can be left to the "natural laws of pro- duction," i.e., it is possible to rely on his dependence on capital, which springs from the conditions of production themselves, and is guaranteed in perpetuity by them. (Marx [1867] 1976, 899–900)

Timing and Spacing Capital

The state of existing within or having some relationship with time and space when accumulating capital is a vital part of economic domination and profoundly affects political and sociocultural relations (Jessop 2012). For example, the historical of primitive accumulation is one state of existing, and there are others, e.g., labor time, absolute surplus value, socially necessary labor time, relative surplus value, machine time, circulation time, turnover time, turnover cycle, socially necessary turnover time, interest-bearing capital, and expanded reproduction (cf. Grossman 2007). Marx positions these to demonstrate ways the concrete temporalities of specific processes relate to the ongoing rebasing of abstract labor time, as the driver behind the enduring toil of competition from which neither capital nor workers can break out (Postone 1993). Hence, not only is history changed by rebasing, the state of nature is also changed, as it is the fundamental product that drives economics.

Accordingly, nature-society relations form the core of Marx's materialist explanation for society, with materialism implying whatever exists relies on matter. Therefore, Marx's First Nature underwrites society; producing food, shelter, and clothing, and shadowed by a Second Nature transformed, reshaped, and commodified by society (Aitken and Valentine 2009). Thus, nature is pro- duced by humans, and for Marx, production is always social (Brewer 1990).

Marx believed that those who own the means of "natural" material products also own the means of intellectual production (see the Class section) because it is their ideas that dominate through more "airtime" (Akard 2001). "In other words, workers unwittingly reproduce the power that rules over them" (Holmes, Hughes, and Julian 2007, 37). Hence, reproducing nature-society relations. For instance, nature rules over what materials are available to be "powered up," but it is also ruled over by how the capitalist journey travels through nature and what is picked up or accumulated along the way of human space-time clashing with nature's space-time. However, the duration and relationship of these two may not correspond all that well when measured by geological time, e.g., human capitalism being temporary, and nature's capital or wealth being permanent in whatever form taken through exploitation and adaptation.

Nonetheless, capital in its temporary form retains capacity as "one sole driving force, the drive to valorise itself, to create surplus-value, to make its constant part, the means of production, absorb the greatest possible amount of surplus labour" (Marx [1867] 1976, 342), and within this surplus space of accumulated sociality,

> the capitalist process of production...seen as a total, connected process, i.e., a process of reproduction, produces not only commodities, not only surplus-value, but it also produces and reproduces the capital-relation itself; on the one hand the capitalist, on the other the wage-labourer. (Marx [1867] 1976, 724)

Currencies of Actual and Potential Power

The Marx spaces of social power consideration focus on power as capacities, rather than power actualizing these capacities (Jessop 2012), capacities powered in ongoing social relations of structure over individual agents' desires to grasp some of that capacity. However, if there are actualizations of capacity, these are reliant on particular performances by particular agents in particular situations, thus a lack of universal power, of only specific powers and the aggregate of particular power movements (Jessop 2012). So, within these movements of power, Marxist geography is motivated by concentrating on the geographical conditions, processes, and outcomes of socioeconomic systems, and primarily capitalism, by using the tools of Marxist theory (Gregory et al. 2009).

Marx preferred mass movement or mass sharing of the capacities of power, and the sum of individual power actuality equating to the societal power capacity. For example, a so-called proletarian dictatorship or a proletarian state that replaces the capitalist state, at least within the transitional stage of one becoming the other, i.e., a transition from one power framework to an alternate version. However, Bakunin (2005, 178) was not convinced about the process and period of state transition, since "if there is a state, then there is domination and consequent slavery. A state without slavery, open or camouflaged, is inconceivable—that is why we are enemies of the state. (also) What does it mean, 'the Proletariat raised to a governing class?'" It means that the

> proletariat, instead of fighting in individual instances against the economically privileged classes, has gained sufficient strength and organisation to use general means of coercion in its struggle against them; but it can only make use of such economic means as abolish its own character as wage labourer and hence as a class; when its victory is complete, its rule too is therefore at an end, since its class character will have disappeared. (Marx and Engels 1989, 519)

In this manner, the proletariat in their struggle for equality of power would have alienated their alienation if this process became actualized. Thus, an achievement of performance of individuals in a collective manner to overcome the social relations of structure, and a paradoxical Marxist process of addressing the power issue that pervades human society. Paradoxical in the sense that individual power actualization, a process not specifically of influential concern to Marxists, at least according to Jessop, is the one thing that can challenge the established structural relationship. Another layer of this paradox is that the individual agent is part of the established social structure and will carry the legacy of that into the "newer" form of the social structural relationship—i.e., the older form may merge with the newer form—however much this may be resisted, intentionally or acted, and with the risk that the older form will be reproduced in some form.

Essentially, power is ever present and by its very nature creates a hierarchy based on ownership of property. Property in this case will be in the hands of those "dictating" how the new social system will work in practice, and even though the "system starts with the self-government of the communities" (Marx and Engels 1989, 519), each community would, in actuality, have capacity translated as power. So, not a collective as a whole or single unit, but a set of individual collectives powered by individuals within each collective. However, a distinct possibility would be that power struggles would emerge within each community, and when that is "resolved" with its attendant inclusion and exclusion, a further power struggle would emerge on the greater geographical scale between communities.

For instance, groups of communities may join in a loose union to neutralize other isolated communities or those of lesser group power, eventually ending up as one community that rules over the others and creates a new hierarchical structural relationship, one that echoes the one supposedly extinguished.

Perhaps the Marxists are correct in focusing on structural relations of society, as structural relations do appear to endure over and beyond individual agency, even though these agents are the units of power that drive the "collective" structure. As Marx says of ownership and its gradual limiting centralizing tendency, competition among capitalists would grow so fierce that, eventually, most capitalists would go bankrupt, leaving only a handful of monopolists controlling nearly all production (Prychitko 2002). Also, just as the monopolists may eventually control and perhaps end in a monopolist control of a small minority or one individual, the communities could follow the same monopolist pathway.

Marx saw that the powered relations of the societal structure is a relationship of deception, advocating that the economic capitalist bourgeoisie fosters a falsehood that the interests of the capitalist and those of the worker are one and the same, asserting that the fastest possible growth of productive capital was best not only for the wealthy capitalists but also for the workers because it provided them with employment (Marx 1849). Along these lines, the labels and potential actualities of class, political state, alienation, capitalism, and its temporal quality, all fall under the power of invention and deception, greased by the medium of money:

> THE POWER OF MONEY is one of the most brutal expressions of this capitalist quantification: it distorts all human and natural qualities, by submitting them to the monetary measure: The quantity of money becomes more and more the unique and powerful property of the human being; at the same time that it reduces all being to its abstraction, it reduces itself in its own movement to a quantitative being. (Marx 1844, 1962, 101)

Also,

> If money is the bond binding me to human life, binding society to me, connecting me with nature and man, is not money the bond of all bonds? Can it not dissolve and bind all ties? Is it not, therefore, also the universal agent of separation? (Marx 1844; Marx and Engels 1988)

Engels revealed that the Marxist power process is a practice based on, and in, the tension between competing parties, groups, and classes, and whichever way one wishes to label a gathering of agents, ownership of power *does* create tensions and competition. Consequently, Marx's exposé of political economy and the hierarchal nature resulting from its practice and falsehoods, depending on where one sits in the societal structure, encourages a reduced alienation of misunderstanding power. This is particularly focused on the capitalist power structure and process, since after all, equities are not exactly equalities.

CHAPTER 8

Gramsci

Ideology, Consciousness, Individual, and Mass

The individual is the smallest or unitary component of power imaginings and creations. An individual who possesses potentials that may turn into actuals or, at the very least or most, actuals as diluted forms of the potentials envisaged. Diluted forms are highlighted as the individual faces off against the structural integrity of society, which has already been immersed in countless numerable and immemorial forms of individual unity of how power should be and is played out. Paradoxically, even though the individual is the unitary power creator, this apparent humble beginning can, and has, transformed society and indeed fashioned these things called society. Hence, one's individuality is key to driving the process, for that is how power exists and is driven, and how effectively the power is used and the meaning of the term *effective* are open to individual interpretation, i.e., how the individual regards themselves, i.e., one's self-critical appraisal:

> The starting point of critical elaboration is the consciousness of what one really is, and "knowing thyself" as a product of the historical process to date, which has deposited in you an infinity of traces, without leaving an inventory…therefore it is imperative at the outset to compile such an inventory. (Gramsci 1971, 324)

To know thyself is a challenging prospect, and the ability to critique from a workable platform of one's sense of self adds to that challenge. Another layer adding to the uncertainty of self-realization is being born into one's societal structure and the inventory of control, expectation, oppression, behavioral patterns, normalities, and expectations of conformity that accompanies that agency and structural relationship. The individual knowing, at critical levels of intellectual combat, what the hidden aspects of the structural inventory may actually mean and imply, allows for an intimate experience with power toward its pure form.

Toward, but not actually at, is emphasized, since there would only be a few individuals who would act as if they were responsible for power and its implementation at its purest —pure in the sense of possessing the capacity to influence the lives of many. However, no one individual would equate to pure power, since other individuals, the societal structure, and limited temporality would temper the purity. Also, the critical limits of the self would mitigate power usage within a self-contaminated form. Contaminated in the sense of all individuals possess consciousness of what their one's self really is, and "knowing thyself's" shortfalls; e.g., no one has perfection, whatever that implies.

When mitigating and moderating how things are, "every man contributes to modifying the social environment in which he develops (to modifying certain of its characteristics or to preserving others); in other words, he tends to establish 'norms,' rules of living and of behaviour" (Gramsci 1971, 539). The ability to do this indicates power at work, but also simultaneously indicating a redirectional process of human base behaviors from animal to civilization. Or perhaps a cloaking of animal behaviors within more sophisticated playing environments produced over the courses of history. For instance, an "uninterrupted, often painful and bloody process of subjugating natural (i.e., animal and primitive) instincts to new, more complex and rigid norms and habits of order" (Gramsci 1971, 298, 1975, 2160–2161).

So, a power struggle is occurring within individuals and has been from the moment of human emergence or beginnings, and the original designed embodied intellectual form at its most base animal formation has created a dichotomy with itself. This may be viewed as a struggle to get away from what nature initially provided as material configuration, to best deal with the living environment of that time and space. To illustrate, as individuals multiplied, brain power grew, time traveled, climates and environments changed, and significant rivals of other living beings were "tamed," eliminated, or "naturally" died off, an evolvement, also of natural disposition, as nature to survive is a fluid, flexible performance, created a widening gap from the original. But that is not to say the "primitive" original nature of human being disappears, as it may still control events, actions, and intentions, be it from a subtle, covert, and central place within the human psyche—soul, spirit, and mental spaces. Therefore, it may be the primitive and animal part or whole of the human that generates individual power, and hence the norms and values of behavioral imaginary, translated into practice as much of that power as is allowed by other individuals or societal structure, as practically feasible.

These "norms" and values or habits of order being "self-directed and self-imposed" (Fontana 2002, 163) are labeled second nature by Gramsci (1971, 298, 1975, 2160–2161). This "active norm of conduct," empowered by the propagation of thought within the sociocultural space, is an act of becoming, as it becomes society's practical and everyday way of life (Gramsci 1971, 298, 1975, 1486). Thus, a naturalized dynamic space, but also repressed space of self-direction and self-imposition:

> To know oneself means to be oneself, to be master of oneself, to free oneself from a state of chaos, to exist as an element of order—but of one's own order and one's own discipline in striving for an ideal. (Gramsci 1977, 25)

To strive for an ideal is to become that ideal. Also, in a living space of limitless power for individuals, the ideal becomes the actuality and probably greater than 'the actuality', i.e. the ideal becomes more than the actuality; a limit of no limits. However, there are no limitless spaces of power in society as a whole or within parts of it, and the powered ideal just remains an ideal, e.g., its perfection, epitome, or essence is out of reach. Although knowing oneself is a positive step toward one's ideal, it is toward a place of unattainable consciousness since the consciousness aimed for is false; i.e., for Gramsci, the obstruction with false consciousness was not the conscious aspect, but the falseness (Burawoy 2012). In other words, the individual as part of the workforce saw their ideal version through the filters of capitalist imitation, a version clouded by the "natural" position of domination and subordination. Thus, an ideal space beyond capitalism was not appreciated, except within an embryonic formation requiring intellectual critical considerations. Hence, a duality of consciousness begins to emerge, rather than just remaining false (Burawoy 2012).

However, this conscientious dualism by taking on board intellectual contribution may still encourage false aspiration, as the intellectual's error is believing that one can know without understanding, feeling, and being impassioned (Fontana 2000); i.e., the certain historical situation and correlation with the laws of history that is addressed are required by these three characteristics, "ideals," to aim for the desired *ideal* for individuals. But there is

> no organisation without intellectuals, that is without organisers and leaders, in other words, without the theoretical aspect of the theory-practice nexus being distinguished concretely by the existence of a group of people "specialised" in conceptual and philosophical elaboration of ideas. But the process of creating intellectuals is long, difficult, full of contradictions, advances and retreats, dispersals and regroupings, in which the loyalty of the masses is often sorely tried. (Gramsci 1971, 643)

Even though attaining critical self-consciousness implies, politically and historically, the creation of an *élite* of intellectuals (Gramsci 1971, 643), the self-conscious space is not independent of what was emancipated from since a "new" culture means the diffusion in a critical form of truths already discovered (Gramsci 1971, 629), e.g., for each individual is

> the synthesis not only of existing relations, but of the history of these relations. He is a précis of all the past. It will be said that what each individual can change is very little, considering his strength. This is true up to a point. But when the individual can associate himself with all the other individuals who want the same changes, and if the changes wanted are rational, the individual can be multiplied an impressive number of times and can obtain a change which is far more radical than at first sight ever seemed possible. (Gramsci 1971, 670–671)

Consequently, the individual must become individuals with a semblance of similar ideals to create the "grand ideal," if the self-ideal is to hold credence. Thus, one must potentiate and develop when transforming societal structure, but doing it individually is an illusion and an error, as what is necessary is modifying external relations with nature and other men (Gramsci 1971). Additionally, with capital's journey to a post-industrial global economy, a strongly defined self within a cultural-historical-political context which pays attention to difference and power is required, inciting consciousness of self as the basis of critical consciousness (Ledwith 2009). Basically, individuals are points of intersection, disadvantaged along some axes, simultaneously advantaged along others, in their quest for recognition (Buckel and Fischer-Lescano 2009).

 Gramsci argued that man (sic) "cannot be conceived of except as historically determined man, i.e., man who has developed, and who lives, in certain conditions, in a particular social complex or totality of social relations," but "the will and initiative of men (sic) themselves cannot be left out of account" (1971, 244). Thus, a human combination of "Stone Age received wisdom and intimations of a better future society" (Gramsci 1971, 324), and a performance that battles hearts and minds so individuals may achieve a fresh conception of themselves and society (Leggett 2013, 309). For

> what is man? what we mean is: what can man become? That is, can man dominate his own destiny, can he "make himself," can he create his own life? We maintain therefore that man is a process, and, more exactly, the process of his actions. (Gramsci 1971, 668)

Speech

Man (sic) as process, or to "process" man, requires articulation through the medium of sounds spoken and received by others, and simultaneously received for the spoken self for self-monitoring of what one is saying, via the power of words. That is why before the creation of something or thing, be it movement, action, inaction, a structure or structural formation, such as society, words are needed to guide the process from conception to ongoingness. In other "words," words and speech are the running commentary of how to practice, perform, to be, in society, and the word prevents society from becoming a "dociety." For instance, conception of an utterance to create is the beginning of creation, and language is the medium of beginning as it carries the authority of "how to" and "not to" via the speaker as an individual, and speaker as an individual representing an organized group aiming for similar ends. Hence, speech beginnings function to produce difference (of one project compared to another) and continuity of deciding what comes after, so beginnings are acts of power (McCarthy 2013). Correspondingly, to speak and speech are also acts of power.

Who does the speaking and who does the listening are significant in how effective these acts of power are, since the degrees of separation between them in terms of societal position and interrelated psychological position enhance the power differential. Also, regardless of religious or secular beginnings, separation of the power centers from the everyday of ordinary people is marked by diversity in speech and language, diversity that increases as the language of the ruling groups grow to be more ossified, florid, i.e., purely rhetorical, a style that is merely literary and affected and solipsistically concerned with its own formal rules of speech and syntax (Gramsci 1975). Simultaneously, this crafted language of power is more and more removed from social life, so, difficult to possess by the people (Lo Piparo 1979; Salamini 1981), and the rise and decline of the vernacular reflect the rise and decline of relative power of lower classes in a given society (Gramsci 1975).

Gramsci recognized that "truth" of communication only reaches historical and political consequence through absorption and propagation through a social group or society. In this fashion, the consequence is generated and achieved by speech, language, and rhetoric to persuade people and gain their consent (Fontana 2000); a movement from feeling to knowledge or the movement from a particular (pre-political) to a hegemonic (political) consciousness (Gramsci 1971, 1975).

Therefore, the underpinning of politics and the state is reason and speech, i.e., the formula signifying the union of ratio and oratio from Cicero (Ryan 1983), in which Cicero observes:

> not only that rhetoric is not merely a technique and method by which power may be acquired but also that, precisely as a means to power, rhetoric presupposes the simultaneous existence of a determinate political, moral, and social order within which it acquires meaning and value. (Kennedy 1972, chaps. 1 and 3)

In this manner, utility and effectiveness of rhetoric is itself a function of a particular moral-intellectual culture, what Gramsci calls a conception of the world and a way of life (Fontana 2000). For example, in the democratic polis (the ancient Greek city-state) rhetoric equated to power and liberty, and its modern representation of rhetorical performance is the construction of ideological and cultural power structures (Fontana 2000). Accordingly, the voice and content of cultural narrative is powerful by

> virtue of its elevated or superior position to authorize, to dominate, to legitimate, demote, interdict, and validate: in short, the power of culture to be an agent of, and perhaps the main agency for, powerful differentiation within its domain and beyond it too. (Said 1983, 9)

Thus, "owning" rhetoric is central or key to an individual's position in the power dispersals and concentrations of society, and in the everyday living and law limitations that "guide" the process of domination and subordination.

Law

Jurisprudence is the theory of law incorporating law and legal systems principles and their underlying philosophical basis (Butterworths 2010). Hence, law is the subject matter of jurisprudence and, due to its complexity, enjoys diversity of definition depending on the specific jurisprudential method utilized:

> Schools of legal sociology emphasise the social significance of the law and its relevance to politics; positivism focusses on the framework of rules and regulations governing society. Natural law examines metaphysical issues of the precise

essence of law and relationship between law and morality, and positive law and natural law. (Butterworths 2010, 252)

So, law as a complex spoken word of how society is through politics, rules, regulation, morality, and "naturalness," is engaged with by Gramsci within the "lawful" philosophical basis of how law processes are rhetorical materialism put into practice to enforce designed behavioral patterns. This is a power play of hegemonic proportions, of creative speech and sound put into practice as the "real" of society.

Accordingly, the law is "in reality struggle for the creation of a new usage" (Gramsci 1991, Q6§98, 791). This is reflected in the state's endeavors to create and sustain a certain type of coexistence and individual associations, to ensure particular "ways of being" (Seddon 1972) and ways of behavior dematerialize and propagate alternatives (Buckel and Fischer-Lescano 2009, 447). In this way, the law and schools are the mediums to accomplish this (Gramsci 1991, Q13§11, 1548):

> If political leadership has to create a social conformism, then it is actually the "legal problem" to "educate" the "masses" (Q6§84, 777) or "a question for the 'law'," through which "the educative pressure on the individuals is exercised, so as to attain their consensus and collaboration" (Q13§7, 1544). This does not mean a traditional political "control concept," but the "educative, creative, formative character of the law" (Q6§98, 792). (Gramsci 1991)

From this, behavioral dematerialization and materialization of legal relation-ships re-creates itself as a sole operator, a closed system (Luhmann 2004), and an automatic response of social relations results (Buckel and Fischer-Lescano 2009). Consequently, the "individuals" of society in the everyday interaction with the closed system of the law performance generally accept the law as the Law of Society, and the closed exclusivity shuts the general demographic outside of law creation, construction, and implementation. Hence, their participation is by responding to it reactively rather than proactively, and their will and action demonstrate automatic responses toward it (Buckel and Fischer-Lescano 2009). Essentially, the law itself determines what law is (Fischer-Lescano 2006).

The coercive and consensual "double face of law" produces a bourgeois di-alectic of law (Buckel and Fischer-Lescano 2009, 447) that Gramsci saw as an ethical conception (Cutler 2005, 529):

"ethical conception" here means the stimulation of self-technologies, the elaboration of a form of the relation to oneself that enables the individual to constitute itself as subject of a particular way of living. (Buckel and Fischer-Lescano 2009, 448)

Constituting oneself within the legislation of societal constitution, or subjecting and subjugating oneself to it, leads to a specific way of living, namely the living "style" dictated by the historical bloc one lives or has lived within. An historical bloc is the whole set of material forces (content) and ideologies (form), in which "the ideologies would be individual whims without the material forces" (Gramsci 1991, Q7§21, 877). However, state power does not wish for individual whims along its hegemonic law journey, so it overrides these collective individual whims within its uniform collective whim. For instance, Gramsci indicated a set of social forces' dealings, where the assorted legal, economic, political, and ideological relations are networked, incorporating feeling and thinking, of a mutual life way covering the assorted forces (Demirovic 2001). Essentially, since legislation is crucial to an understanding of law, and it is impossible to engage with law without learning about legislation (Hall and Macken 2009), in Gramscian speak, however, this legislation has already been preordained; e.g., one is disempowered by its empowerment.

Time of the Now and History

Coercive and consensual power structures of the now, similar to law, retain a timed dual face, a face of the present and a face of the past(s) or faces of the past. It is these prior faces of power, built within their own epochs or historical blocs, that leave durable traces of ideological and material essence and substance. Characteristics of these traces will not only enjoy a sustained sameness but also difference, depending on the particular sociocultural environment a bloc functions by:

> Every real historical phase leaves traces of itself in succeeding phases, which then become in a sense the best document of its existence. The process of historical development is a unity in time through which the present contains the whole of the past and in the present is realized that part of the past which is "essential"—with no residue of any "unknowable" representing the true "essence." (Gramsci 1971, 409)

It is the "essential" that power players are interested in to indulge in the power game during their particular lifetimes. For example, what have been the powerful practices and performances within blocs that have seen effective results and continue to see them—i.e., those that gave the society of the time their structure, and thus from this knowledge why change a formula that works, just simply add to it to suit the present structural environment and discard the residue that does not measure up. For instance, the unknowable can create risk, deviation, and distraction from the powered course of events and a negativity that should be avoided or discarded, i.e., an error. To illustrate, mechanical historical materialism denies error but assumes that political acts are controlled, instantly, by the structure, thus as a real and permanent (achieved) alteration of the structure (Gramsci 2000). From this, the structured historically based time of acts or structured acts through time limit the political, echoing the limiting performance tensions between structure and agents. So, the political in society can be thought of as a superstructural agent existing due to the existence of its attendant structure, and, within the roots of time, superstructures and structures produce a "historical bloc," i.e., a connectivity of superstructure as being a complex, contradictory, and discordant ensemble, reflecting the ensemble of the social relations of production (Gramsci 2000, 192).

The performance of societal sense of being is a praxis of absolute "historicism," the absolute secularization of thought, an absolute humanism of history (Gramsci 1971, 465). Therefore, the legacies of the human now are saturated by what went on before, which also signifies acknowledging that the very mental processes that created ideas, inventions, adaptations, and innovations are not absent in the present. For instance, it is their very presence that changes historical direction, but of which perhaps some aspects are above and beyond the history complex. For example, the "'social' element of a work of philosophy may be rooted in the past, yet there may remain a 'residue' that cannot be explained by the historical context" (Femia 1981, 124), i.e., it is the unity of the human spirit, that is, the unity of history and nature, that allows men (sic) to create new history…in other words without this unity:

> philosophies would not become "ideologies," they could not, in practice, acquire the fanatical granite solidity of "popular beliefs," which have the equivalence of "material forces." (Gramsci 1996, 194–195)

Within the philosophy of praxis, the structure does not break from the superstructure, both being intimately connected, interrelated, and reciprocal, according to

Gramsci (2000, 193), who continues by saying that the structure is not a "hidden god," even metaphorically, since it is ultrarealistic. Thus, from this perspective, structure is the ongoing material powerbase that powers history and, in turn, is powered by history. However, powered history is not of a simplified form, as Gramsci (1995, 374) states:

> the past is a complex thing, a complex of the living and the dead, in which a choice cannot be made arbitrarily, a priori, by an individual or by a political current...What will be conserved of the past in the dialectical process cannot be determined a priori, but will be a result of the process itself and will be characterized by historical necessity, and not by arbitrary choice on the part of so-called scientists and philosophers.

So, the processional choice is an ideological choice; therefore, for the governed ideological illusions and for governing a knowing and willed deception and within the philosophy of praxis,

> ideologies are anything but arbitrary; they are real historical facts which must be combatted and their nature as instruments of domination revealed, not for reasons of morality etc., but for reasons of political struggle: in order to make the governed intellectually independent of the governing, in order to destroy one hegemony and create another, as a necessary moment in the revolutionizing of praxis. (Gramsci 2000, 196)

Every historical undertaking is something of an adventure, since it is never guaranteed by any absolutely rational structure of things (Merleau-Ponty, quoted in Said 2000, 10). This "loose" undertaking of what went on before and what to draw on from the past to profit the present and future immediacies is a purposely selected filtered process, and historical materialism is the tool of filtered choice. Gramsci's (1996) view of historical materialism incorporates the value of the physical properties of matter, both mechanical and chemical, as an economic factor of production. Hence, an object of production and property and a crystallization of a social relation coinciding within a particular historical period. So, historical materialism is a commodifying and commodified legacy that floods into the present and future, retaining the power of materialistic usage choice, consequently retaining power in society. Fundamentally, it allows one's time of the now to be powerful, assuming the praxis is governed, since the "philosophy of praxis is precisely the concrete historicization of philosophy and its identification with history" (Gramsci 1971, 436).

Faithful Religion Church

To be powerful as a subject or individual, or agent to an object that represents a distinct aspect of society (military, church, religion, education, economics, employment, political party, the political system itself, or all these taken together as the whole of societal structure), the subject must possess faith. For instance, faith in oneself and faith in the prominent institutions of society, i.e., the distinct objects listed. This is because faith reflects confidence, trust, reliance, conviction, belief, and assurance and faith is sustained and empowered by devotion, loyalty, fidelity, allegiance, and belief; e.g., faith can move mountains, metaphorically speaking, and keeping those mountains intact and in place, depending on the individual motivation to act, mime, and "in-act. "

Mime in this sense is appearing to do something, but it is actually doing nothing, and only maintaining the status quo, which is worse than in-act(ion) as it gives other individual devotees hope but does not deliver. Hence, it is the promise of delivery but not delivering, since it is in the in-between space and place that does not progress any further. This "in-betweenness" is the power of the unknown and unknowable deliverance at the other end, e.g., end of life, which offers a promise of betterment that keeps the masses in line and keeps the "messengers" of faith, hope, and "clarity," perhaps not charity, in employment, e.g., employment that retains power and retains the power of the object the messengers work within:

> Faith in a secure future, in the immortality of the soul destined to beatitude, in the certainty of arriving at eternal joy, was the force behind the labour for intense interior perfection and spiritual elevation. True Christian individualism found here the impulse that led it to victory. All the strength of the Christian was gathered around this noble end. Free from the flux of speculation which weakens the soul with doubt, and illuminated by immortal principles, man felt his hopes reborn; sure that a superior force was supporting him in the struggle against Evil, he did violence to himself and conquered the world. (Gramsci 1971, 648)

(Note: The Beatitudes are the eight blessings recounted by Jesus in the Sermon on the Mount in the Gospel of Matthew. Each is a proverb-like proclamation, without narrative. Four of the blessings also appear in the Sermon on the Plain in the Gospel of Luke, followed by four woes that mirror the blessings.)

Faith gives the subject power of conviction, a sense of what is right and what is not. The sense is "guided" by religious doctrine to believe in a certain way, to conquer the world in a certain way, e.g., religious faith and faiths on a global scale of tensioned powered production. To illustrate, the tensioned can be thought of one faith clashing with another or clashing with its particular state or states, as the space of faith is not restricted to the one place of state. For example, there takes place in society what Croce labels the "perpetual conflict between Church and State," with the Church representing totality of civil society, but actually it is only an element of diminishing importance within it (Gramsci 1971, 506). To combat the diminishing, a State-Church dualism emerges:

> when the Church has become an integral part of the State, of political society monopolised by a specific privileged group, which absorbs the Church in order the better to preserve its monopoly with the support of that zone of "civil society" which the Church represents. (Gramsci 1971, 507)

In essence, keeping the faith of a power base, and in this case the power base of the object of faith, of religion, and of the church,

> religion, or a particular church, maintains its community of faithful (within the limits imposed by the necessities of general historical development) in so far as it nourishes its faith permanently and in an organised fashion, indefatigably repeating its apologetics, struggling at all times and always with the same kind of arguments, and maintaining a hierarchy of intellectuals who give to the faith, in appearance at least, the dignity of thought. (Gramsci 1971, 651)

Hence, miming the appearance of thought as if it were for the good of the subjects that follow a particular church or religion , who by remaining faithful and think they are constructively thinking, may inadvertently create a 'good' process. However, to remain within this 'good' space, a subject should just do not think too much, which will allow oneself to contently stay inside the hegemony produced.

State and Civil Society

Defining the "State" or "civil society" as definitive or as definitive structures is a slippery and elusive undertaking. For instance, state and civil and society are fluid and within their apparent stability there is ongoing movement to maintain stableness. This is a paradox of state and civil society, since movement keeps the stillness and the stillness allows for movement, and it is these fixed and fluid "state" of affairs that keep the state and societal system a going and ongoing concern. Therefore, a lack of progress, advancement, and development can stifle the system somewhat. Gramsci (1971, 447) did not succeed in finding a single, wholly satisfactory, conception of "civil society" or the state, but perhaps that is the point. For example, it may not be possible to do so, and, if "accomplished," only reductive, narrow, and limited understanding may result. Additionally, as the state and civil society are invisible and visible manifestations of power at work and play, singular conception to address both is not adequate enough, since a multiplicity of process is required to attain some semblance of the meaning(s) of the state and the civil society and, hence, their attendant power performances.

Gramsci (1971, 504) postulates that

> the State is the entire complex of practical and theoretical activities with which the ruling class not only justifies and maintains its dominance, but manages to win the active consent of those over whom it rules.

Consequently, to become the state is to become the force, creating space of control in a centralized, concentrated form, that once established as a powerbase can gather in the rest of societal space to its way of thinking, being, and doing. The concentrated form may begin with just the individual, which due to particular vulnerabilities in the societal character and strength during unguarded moments, manipulated or not, can allow access to that power for that individual. However, preparation and motivation to want societal power is key, and the individual requires others of like-minded attitudes to achieve their own power version over another individual or group that is not of their own. Accordingly, one's group, if successful, becomes the state or at least runs the state within their specific agenda. Success or the

> supremacy of a social group is manifested in two ways: as "domination" and as "intellectual and moral leadership." A social group is dominant over those antagonistic groups it wants to "liquidate" or to subdue even with armed force, and it is leading with respect to those groups that are associated and allied with it. (Gramsci 1975, III, 2010)

So, the power and existence of the state appear to endure through the dualism of dominion and ideological manipulation, and utilizing both the human embodied forms of physical and mental susceptibilities. This is a two-pronged attack to influence one's will and bodily action to certain ways of behavior and acceptance.

Gramsci calls this sociopolitical order an "integral State"; a hegemonic equilibrium of "combination of force and consent which are balanced in varying proportions, without force prevailing too greatly over consent" (Gramsci 1975, III, 1638–1639). Thus, force must be present to get people's attention, but pure force usage can be an eventual self-defeating strategy, as resistance builds. So, to attempt negation of or at least reduce resistance, consent is a weapon of choice since if people generally agree (i.e., difficult to achieve total consent) with what is being presented to them as state and civil society, power of resistance can be managed. In this manner, the attempt at negation is present, if not absolute in its results. Therefore, consent and force and leadership and domination compose the political, so the state in Gramsci is constructed by two distinctive, but entwined, realms (Fontana 2000, 308): "dictatorship + hegemony," and "political society + civil society," where the synthesis of the two spheres denotes the meaning of "state" (Gramsci 1975, II, 763–764).

Hence, the synthesis indicates that the civil society is a subset of the state, but in actual reality the civil society and the state are one and the same (Gramsci 2000). For instance, considering state and government as an economic-corporate form and representing blurred boundaries between civil and political society, the imprecise notion of state retains impressions of notion of civil society, i.e., State = political society + civil society, in other words hegemony protected by the armor of coercion (Gramsci 1971). Civil society for Gramsci is used in various ways and means such as occasionally meaning economic life (Gramsci 1971, Q17§51, 266–267), occasionally counted as under the state (Gramsci 1971, Q8§190, 261), and as the handmaiden of state and economics, relating to hegemony (Glasius 2012, 671).

Therefore, civil society is a source of strength of state power, where the state's political and ideological leadership is primed by civil societal networks (Patnaik 2012). These networks offer a range of nexuses, since for Gramsci, civil society provides "backward linkages" (inputs) for the state while it receives "forward linkages" (outputs) from classes (Patnaik 2012, 579). Thus, civil society occupies a space in between class and the state (Femia 2002). Also, the state is a negative phenomenon, and the civil society is a positive phenomenon (Bobbio 1988), but Gramsci suggests that both positive (like moral/intellectual) and negative functions (like ideological/political) coexist within the domain of civil society (Patnaik 2012, 579), which provides "rationalization (intellectual or morale elaboration) of class-state (negative element), on the one hand, and ethical-state (positive element), on the other hand" (Gramsci 1971, 262–263). So, concerning the ethical state (the cultural state) is such that every state:

is ethical in as much as one of its most important functions is to raise the great
mass of the population to a particular cultural and moral level, a level (or type)
which corresponds to the needs of the productive forces for development, and
hence to the interests of the ruling classes. The school as a positive educative
function, and the courts as a repressive and negative educative function, are the
most important State activities in this sense: but, in reality, a multitude of other
so-called private initiatives and activities tend to the same end—initiatives and
activities which form the apparatus of the political and cultural hegemony of the
ruling classes. (Gramsci 1971, 526)

Hence, civil society as a network of apparatus serves the societal state apparatus
as if both were one entity, i.e., one "common" purposeful space of power making,
and indeed this "oneness" may be the actuality of the social process.

War

Gramsci's narratives on state and civil society incorporate a significant connectivity to military language (Glasius 2012, 671):

when the State trembled a sturdy structure of civil society was at once revealed.
The State was only an outer ditch, behind which…stood a powerful system of
fortresses and earthworks. (Gramsci 1971, Q7§16, 238)

These bastions of fortressed power in combination with their networked power
lines of earthworks demonstrate an overlapping and enfolding defense system.
A "state(us)" system of in-depth proportions layered to be able, or enabled, to
withstand a military assault from without by another state or states, and within,
by those who wish to reimage the state to their self-reflective version. The former
"without" is overt violence in nature and form, a direct assault, and one that can
be seen and joined in battle in a candid manner. The latter "within" is covert in
its formless nature, an indirect offensive that is circuitous, and difficult to get
a hold of as it is meandering, convoluted, and devious. Gramsci calls to mind
Gandhi, generally regarded as the founder of civil resistance (Glasius 2012,
671), to highlight the warfare metaphor for political struggle: "war of movement,
war of position, and underground warfare." For example, the underground can
be thought of as the covert, but that is not to say the overt approach does not
contain "underground" aspects to undermine the opposition, since for both the

direct and indirect aspects, the movement, position, and underground would be part of their offensive and defensive strategy and armory.

Along these lines, a prominent part of Gramsci's social theory is his dialogue of political strategy of "war of manoeuvre" through military insurrection, and "war of position," characterized by evolved capitalism by a cultural fight of significantly greater complexity and duration (Egan 2014, 521). Thus, in the art of politics as in the art of military:

> war of movement increasingly becomes war of position, and it can be said that a State will win a war in so far as it prepares for it minutely and technically in peacetime. The massive structures of the modern democracies, both as State organisations, and as complexes of associations in civil society, constitute for the art of politics as it were the "trenches" and the permanent fortifications of the front in the war of position: they render merely "partial" the element of movement which before used to be "the whole" of war, etc. (Gramsci 1971, 503)

So, the entrenched and "trenched" positional war of politics reinforces (more military jargon) the fortresses and earthworks metaphor and also reflects a spatial war of position that represents the majority of the space of the sovereign society, both physically and hegemonically, with only the peripheries having a greater ability to maneuver. This is an apt descriptor, since challenging the political societal space and civil space would generally feel movement and fluidity at their respective peripheries, and keeping a sense of positional permanence for the remainder:

> In war it would sometimes happen that a fierce artillery attack seemed to have destroyed the enemy's entire defensive system, whereas in fact it had only de-stroyed the outer perimeter; and at the moment of their advance and attack the assailants would find themselves confronted by a line of defence which was still effective. The same thing happens in politics. (Gramsci 1971, 489)

As the concept of war correctly adheres to the social as permanently contested, Gramsci infers a single political space essentially separated into two camps (e.g., the fundamental classes) (Laclau and Mouffe [1985] 2001). However, this "single" space or finite space of position and movement is more than the binary of class since it can be of multiple, diverse forms (Leggett 2013, 302), which simultaneously can be a strength and weakness of military and political capabilities, potentials, and actualities.

Once the strategic goal in military war is accomplished, of destroying the enemy's military capability and taking over their living space, peace results, i.e., a clear-cut resolution. However, political war is far more complex, since the "defeated army is disarmed and dispersed but the struggle continues on the terrain of politics and of military 'preparation'" (Gramsci 1971, 481), and the "single" political space becomes a space of blockade, a cordon. For example, the new group in charge which has "defeated" the old group and occupied the "vacant" space, or the old group which has emerged victorious and still occupies the nonvacant space, both use their respective version of hegemony to "block" the other or others. Additionally, the extent and intensity of blockade reflect the war of movement and position and their proportions thereof in the same physical and political space of contention:

> in politics the "war of position," once won, is decisive definitively. In politics, in other words, the war of manoeuvre subsists so long as it is a question of winning positions which are not decisive, so that all the resources of the State's hegemony cannot be mobilised. But when, for one reason or another, these positions have lost their value and only the decisive positions are at stake, then one passes over to siege warfare; this is concentrated, difficult, and requires exceptional qualities of patience and inventiveness. In politics, the siege is a reciprocal one, despite all appearances, and the mere fact that the ruler has to muster all his resources demonstrates how seriously he takes his adversary. (Gramsci 1971, 495–496)

Accordingly, politics and retaining power within this space are an ongoing siege; as if not being subjected to another's attacks via movement, position, and underground, one is subjecting the other to the same strategies. But

> to fix one's mind on the military model is the mark of a fool: politics, here too, must have priority over its military aspect, and only politics creates the possibility for manoeuvre and movement. (Gramsci 1971, 486)

Hegemony

Hegemony is a network of values and ideas created by a group influenced by organic intellectuals (McCarthy 2013). An organic intellectual is an intellectual member of a social class, as opposed to a member of the traditional intelligentsia that regards itself as a class apart from the rest of society (wikitionary.org). However, it is the class-apart space that is telling in hegemonic construction, as hegemonic realization and actuality rely on separation and distancing between societal individuals and groups, and it is this separateness and remote performance which allow for the space(s) of hegemony to perform. To illustrate, the hegemonic performance needs spaces of action since Gramsci saw that it requires forging across differential political geographies that will be at once coherent but loose enough to allow for the different temporalities, the uneven patterns of development, and the complexities of modernity across those spaces, be they spaces of politics or spaces of culture (Said 1993). Forging is an apt descriptor for those who forge and those who are forged by hegemonic processes, i.e., building, shaping, fashioning, forming and associated falsifying and counterfeiting. However, having a class or group apart is not conducive to long-term control and retaining power, as the class apart must not be an obvious spatial differentiation to the rest of society, so, better to hide the exclusivity behind hegemony. In this fashion, *hegemony* refers to the ability of a ruling bloc to exercise leadership and control over subordinate social groups (Ekers, Loftus, and Mann 2009, xx) through

> bringing about not only a union of economic and political aims, but also intellectual moral unity, posing all the questions around which struggles rage not on a corporate, but a universal plane. (Gramsci 1971, 182)

Thus, a union, unity, and universal collective imagery designed to bring all together, to make all feel they belong in and to the one group, e.g., the group of society. This accord is all the more effective if people, all the people, believe in it.

A necessity to influence all the people to a particular way of seeing and being is Weltanschauung (worldview), on which the preferences, taste, morality, ethics, and philosophical principles of the majority are based (Buckel and Fischer-Lescano 2009). The aim behind this "world effort" is a question of obedience, as Gramsci saw that in modern bourgeois societies rule by authority and command means is not fruitful. For instance, obedience of itself does not work that well, but can from a necessarily ideological proof of its "necessity" or "rationality" (Gramsci 1991, Q15§4, 714). The decisive thing is for the

> hegemonic group to represent a theoretical self-perception, a "philosophy," which must not be just the exclusive possession of a restricted stratum of intellectuals, but has to become a Weltanschauung, manifested implicitly in art, the economy, politics, and, specifically, in law too, in all "molecular" and collective expressions of life. (Gramsci 1991, Q17§51, 1890)

Power requires differentiation to work since if everyone is the same, of a clone-like society of one status, one economic capacity, one mental ability, and equality of all the other markers of and how agents are in society, and, most importantly, of equal power, not much obedience would occur or be basic to societal functionality. Consequently, power differentiation is present because "there really are the governed and the governing, leaders and led" (Gramsci 1991, Q16§4, 1713). Essentially, politics is the art of how one can most effectively lead and, on the other side, recognize the line of least resistance, in order to secure the obedience of the led or governed (Gramsci 1991, Q16§4, 1713).

For a person to become political, or a political commodity in the game of hegemony, is realized and recognized if caring to look or having the potential to look through a hegemonic filtered perception. In other words, hegemonic consciousness, as opposed to hegemony, reveals the power production, of the application of fraud and deception recognized by Gramsci (Fontana 2000). As a result, the public-private divide becomes apparent through the hegemonic intrusion to individuals in civil society (family, community, schools, formal religions) (Ledwith 2009). From this, individuals or social actors are constructed as complex nonunitary subjects who are interpellated by various and contradictory discursive practices (Gottfried 1994; Sotirin 1997).

Thus, making the hegemonic project move beyond "simple" domination as consent, to embodying possibilities (Mumby 1997, 369) of degrees of domination and consent. For example, modern societal power relationships are polycentric, centered on particular subsystem conditions of exploitative rule interlaced with plurality of multiple technologies of power and composed together with them (Buckel and Fischer-Lescano 2009). Therefore, a "sensus communis" (Jay 1984, 160) (a sense held to unite the sensations of all senses in a general sensation or perception [Merriam-Webster, n.d.]) that, conjoined with Gramsci's historicist understanding of language, helps produce an idea of hegemony as an intersubjectively constructed meaning, and being more important (because more effective) than truth as an a priori postulate (McCarthy 2013).

Gramsci pointed out that not all social forces have equal chances of becoming hegemonic, as the heritage of past struggles is a structurally inscribed strategic selectivity that favors some struggles over others (Jessop 1990). The "concrete" heritage points to the necessity of hegemony needing tangible material to perform social relations of production (Morton 2003, 139), i.e., a concrete "earthliness of thought" (Gramsci 1971, 465), in which the tangible material in an "earthy" form or natural resource capacity is translated into economic measurement. Therefore, although hegemony is ethicopolitical, it must also be economic and must necessarily be based on the decisive function exercised by the leading group in the decisive nucleus of economic activity (Gramsci 2000).

Therefore, concerning the leading group(s) in society, the political and legal leadership personnel perform repressively and hegemonically (Buckel and Fischer-Lescano 2009, 444) within their three societal tiers of power; e.g.,

> naturally, all three powers are also organs of political hegemony, but to differing extents: parliament is the most closely tied to civil society, judicial power represents the continuity of the written law (even against the government), while government in the technical sense is the most repressive form of state power. (Gramsci 1991, §81, 773)

However, a diverse political hegemony of economics can also diversify beyond society to the global sphere of economic activity in the guise of neoliberal globalization, and this process is not just economic domination of world societies, but an encumbrance of monolithic thought strengthening vertical difference, and limiting agents from imagining diversity in egalitarian, horizontal terms (Ledwith 2009). To clarify, capitalism, imperialism, monoculturalism, patriarchy, white supremacism, and the domination of biodiversity have coalesced under the current form of globalization (Fisher and Ponniah 2003), and, in international politics, "the great power is a hegemonic power, the head and guide of a system of alliances and ententes" (Gramsci 1975, III, 1598).

To sum up, Gramsci's hegemony emphasizes four different but related concepts: (1) the economic preeminence of civil society over the state; (2) the supremacy of the private sphere over the public sphere; (3) the increasing importance of consent and persuasion as instruments of political legitimation and social integration; and (4) the consequent perception of the decline in the role and utility of force/violence as the necessary instruments of state action (Fontana 2002, 158). Consequently, hegemony is a powerful force if only one just notices, assuming hegemonic processes have not become so powerful that it is indeed not possible to notice through one's individuality among the masses, living pathways of speech, law, time and associated history, faith, state and civil society, and war.

CHAPTER 9

Husserl

Power Is Not Located Anywhere

To perceive power is to feel it, as the perceptive process can recognize that a phenomenon is occurring that impels an agent or agents to perform in a certain manner or range of certain manners of a similar type, but not exactly the same as each agent retains partial uniqueness. The perceptive process cannot see the presence of power; it can only see the resultant actions caused by it. Again, the resultant actions will be perceived and experienced slightly diversely (or more than) by the involved agents. To reiterate, these differences in perception of the "same" thing (experience or object) happen because of the elusively powered presence as well as agents being not quite the same, but commonly same, as all are part of the universal human complex. Also, not being quite the same within the actual self of the one, since the one is an agent of multiple recognizing capacities.

Attempting to center oneself to perceive power is fraught with difficulties in perception, as not only power is decentering in trying to grasp its sense and essence, i.e., a constantly moving presence, the person's center is also momentary. For example, momentary as a "fixed" presence of positional perception evaporates, almost as soon it is established, to a new perceptual moment quickly replaced by another, and so on. The difficulty is compounded by trying to imagine how other agents view power from their decentered moments of perception, and how they view one's power attitude(s). Hence, the problematic of locating power is acknowledged as, according to postmodern semiotics, not to be located anywhere (Mickunas 2010). So, how to perceive this nonlocation is a challenge, as a consciousness of what establishes power in consciousness is required and why the lack of its locat(ability).

Husserl ([1907] 1999) looks at the beginning of the perception journey through the natural attitude. " Beginning" is a deliberate inclusion as agents in society would see the natural attitude as the beginning and end in and of itself, of what is being looked at and experienced:

> We begin our considerations as human beings who are living naturally, objecti-
> vating, judging, feeling, willing "in the natural attitude."…I am conscious of a
> world endlessly spread out in space, endlessly becoming and having endlessly
> become in time. I am conscious of it: that signifies above all, that intuitively I
> find it immediately, that I experience it. (Husserl 1999, 60)

The natural attitude implies that the world can be experienced and observed through a "natural" attitude, but the natural attitude is different for different types of community members and is in fact one thing for the leaders of the community and another for the "citizens" (Husserl 1935, 9). "Natural" is perceived, and all that loaded term implies in its fluidity of moments, from the base line of human original existence, is an historical connectivity going back to its "beginnings" and of a behavioral type of formal universality

> within which the actual normative style of culture-creating existence at any time,
> no matter what its rise or fall or stagnation, remains formally the same. In this
> regard we are speaking of the natural, the native attitude, of originally natural
> life, of the first primitively natural form of cultures. (Husserl 1935, 8)

So, seeing the natural as a beginning and end in and of itself, when perceiving what is around, would appear "natural," and that is how things are and are comprehended. However, just relying on the natural order of understanding has an unnatural quality about it, since the process of perceiving is mediated by the person, individual, or agent. Hence, Husserl contends that there is more to it that can even push the natural aside, or to the background, in the quest of seeing and appreciating what is really seen and how to see it.

In this way, what is really seen and how to achieve that heightened state of sensing, is aimed for when the agent steps "outside" of their natural attitude to a gazed fluid positionality retaining a sense of independence and, thus, not relying greatly on one's embodied or corporeal existence, which can limit perception. To be outside, Husserl visualizes the philosopher as not cogitating themselves and their thoughts as essentials or origins within the natural world; thus, thoughts are not restricted to objective time and space, standing in causal relations with other physical objects (Baldwin and Bell 1988, 28–29). Accordingly, this situating of oneself outside in the space and place of pure consciousness is Husserl's phenomenology.

Phenomenology considerations are not part of the world, not investigating the empirical subject; instead, the non-worldly, transcendental subject, and as preceding to the world, cannot be perceived in worldly stipulations (Mensch 2010). So, to differentiate between the natural and phenomenological approaches to interpretation, natural sense-perception works with the material space as the known reality, and understanding is evidenced on perception accuracy and objective knowability of the word as "real" (Keen 2009, 68), whereas phenomenological understanding is evidenced by "presuppositionless" of the "phenomenological reduction" (Husserl 1962, 96–103, 155–167). This is a pure consciousness of absolute Being (Husserl 1962, 194), consciousness of any given thing that appeals for its meaning as an "intentional object" (Husserl 1962, 242–243), and an intentional object is something that has already been chosen and grasped, grasping being an etymological connotation, of *percipere*, the root of "perceive" (Husserl 1962, 105–109).

Giving to the Pregiven

The given thing becomes a pregiven thing since the person cannot be self-constituting as they are natural beings depending on tradition, and both nature and tradition belong to what Husserl labeled as the *pregiven world* (Crowell 2010, 47). Thus, to say that the world is pregiven is to say that

> it is experienced as having already been there, in these and those ways, before I take up what is—givenl to me to do. That is, the world is not just—the given, or—what is, but rather what is presupposed as being in these and those distinct ways in every sort of experience that I, as engaged in this world, have. (Crowell 2010, 48)

However, there may be an inconsistency here in the transcendental phenomenology project, namely, that "there is for us no other world than the one that gains its Seinssinn (the full and true sense of being [Ingarden 1972, 28]) in us and from out of our own consciousness" (Husserl 2008, 444). So, the challenge is how must we understand the subject of the pregiven world? (Crowell 2010).

Through understanding of the pregiven world, it is what the agent gives to the process that formulates what the world presents through re(present)ations. For instance, the world of power or power flowing in the world does not stand out or stand alone from this all-encompassing, all-involving interpretive process of what the world is. This is because power is made, perceived, experienced, resisted to, and applied through what the agent gives to the endeavor. It is a giving perspective, and to give is to receive a resultant reaction, a reaction of and to power. Consequently, a person's "giveness" allows integration with the world, experiencing the world from one's innateness, one's perspective:

> Whatever in the perceived thing comes forward in the actual intuition does so in such a way that every genuinely intuitive moment has its mode of givenness; for instance, what is visually given will be in a certain perspective. And with this, the perspective again immediately points towards possible new perspectives of the same thing, and we are again drawn, only looking now in another direction, into the system of possible perceptions. (Husserl 1997, 227)

A certain or particular perspective is received in a unique form precisely because one's givenness is unique. To illustrate, one's given position is unique to oneself and creates an alteration, expansion, and development of one's given potential when repeating the perception process of directing attention to the other possible perceptions. Also, if looking at these other perceptions, one by one, without prior memory of doing so, would create perceptual difference if looking at these "same" perceptions with memory retention. This is because every fresh perceptual experience would add to the givenness bank of experiences within memory retention and that knowledge would create different giving results that constantly build on itself. Accordingly, the givenness itself will become more and more complex, as one's givenness exponentially grows through one's time and space of being. Thus, the givenness at one's beginning in life is being constantly overlaid with updated gives until one's ending in life.

To receive from one's givenness is meaningfully possible if what is given back to the person by the world is recognized as a given product or thing. For instance, Husserl asks what is constitutively and structured as a necessity for a world to be experienceable by someone at all (Poellner 2007): for, "there would be *for us*...no real and no ideal world. (but) Both of these exist *for us* thanks to evidence or the presumption of being able to make evident and to repeat acquired evidence" (Husserl 1977, §27, 96/60). Therefore, "Objects exist *for us* and are *for us* what they are only as objects of actual or possible consciousness" (Husserl 1977, §30, 99/65), and evidence for this equates to one's level of givenness potential at whenever one is in one's lifetime. To clarify, "Evidence" (Evidenz) is a Husserl technical label showing the direct presentation or "self-givenness" of the intentional object in experience (Husserl 1973, §4).

Powered Horizon

To have intention or to be intentional, is to attach meaning, purpose, and aim, and Husserl ([1913] 1982) regards sensory information as animated by intentions, which interpret them. Furthermore, to sense the intention is to apply and supply belief toward the object and encompass it within one's comprehensive tendencies, as if the self is surrounding it with one's mental grasp within a three-dimensional manner trying to ascertain all possibilities, all angles of perceptual probing that is sensorially humanly possible within that individual. Thus, "the authentic appearance of an object of perception is the intentional act in as much and to the extent that this act is interwoven with corresponding sensational data" (Bernet, Kern, and Marbach 1993, 118).

However, the interwovenness of perception and sensing through a three-dimensional filtered performance cannot be appreciated within the one moment in one's time-space existence, since a number of one's moments are required to gradually build up that objective three-dimensional image and reproduction of the real object. It is a similar performance when appreciating the true nature of power, or at least as close to the truth of what power is and does as one possibly can (since, one's givenness can be limiting as well as empowering). For instance, to get a "true" picture of the power one is experiencing can and does take time, as each part of the power jigsaw is gradually placed together as one perceives it from every updated fresh givenness, since every new givenness feeds off every previous one as the amalgamation of the previous ones allows tuning and fine tuning of the current one. As power experiences can be a plurality in one's life, since individuals can experience diverse power domains throughout daily living, perceptions of these will vary in intensity and understanding. In this fashion, the greater the engagement with the time spent considering a particular powered domain, the more of its three dimensions will be revealed. Hence, the power is beginning to be laid bare.

However, revealing the naked power and objects is a work in progress, since only a profile, an "adumbration" as Husserl labels it, can only be seen at the one moment. Therefore, to extend the one-sided depiction in physical form, or felt form if power is applied to the oneself from outside, to more than the one perceived side, a phenomenologically generated perception would maintain that "a physical

thing" is necessarily given in mere "modes of appearance" in which necessarily
a core of "what is actually presented" is apprehended as being surrounded by
a horizon of "co-givenness" (Husserl [1913] 1982, sec. 44). "Horizon," in this
context, distinguishes between the internal and external horizons of a perceived
object (Husserl 1973, sec. 8).

Internal are parts of an object (behind and within) that are co-given, and external
incorporates objects other than the presented, which are co-given and belonging
to the surrounding environment. The givenness of the person and the given-to by
the object and support objects, to the person, generated from the internal/external
presence, shows how power works from its dichotomous covert and overt nature.
For example, the former needs its covertness to plan the power movement and
to acquire the power for it to move without too much resistance, and the latter
is the physical and mental results of the movement. Yet, not necessarily just
affecting the targeted object, which may be a natural or synthetically produced
resource, and human resource, but affecting what is in proximity to these. For
instance, the proximity may extend to the world horizon, of which the world is
pregiven and individual things are given, but of a diversity that exists between
them of how agents are world-conscious and conscious of things or objects; a
diversity of indivisible unanimity:

> Things, objects (always understood purely in the sense of the life-world), are
> "given" as being valid for us in each case (in some mode or other of ontic cer-
> tainty) but in principle only in such a way that we are conscious of them as things
> or objects within the world-horizon. Each one is something, "something of" the
> world of which we are constantly conscious as a horizon. (Husserl 1970a, 143)

The ontic process relates to entities and the facts about them, relating to real as
opposed to phenomenal existence. When relating to the real, the performance to
do so can be thought of as relatively straightforward, as what one sees is what
one gets, presumably! But when relating to the phenomenal, a fantastic approach
or fantasy approach is required.

Phantas(y)ie

"Phantasie, another intentional act, does not present the world as a perceptual
real and actual, but rather making present that which is non-present...a solitary
nexus to irreality...through imagining consciousness" (Aldea 2010, 158).

To elucidate, imaginative contents cannot bestow particulars, but "eidetic singularities" (Poellner 2007, 26), and eidetic relates to or denotes mental images that retain unusual vividness and detail, as if actually visible. So, to avoid confusion, a real spatial particular retains an objective spatiotemporal position (Husserl 1973, §40, 203/173, §91, 430/355), whereas an imagined material object does not, within objective time (Husserl 1973, §39, 197/169). As a result, the imagined or phantasie way of seeing a reality of irreality can be a powerful mental process and can eclipse the really real of seeing and experiencing.

The real object in perception can be altered in an abstract fashion, which may be a potential forerunner to actual change for, and in the object, as it is this imagining through the filters of phantasie that can actualize the potential of power. For instance, phantasie enjoys unlimited creativity, only limited by the imaginative potential of the individual wielding their inventiveness and is, in a sense, both aspatial and atemporal, so not restrained by spatiotemporal objectivity. From this, phantasy is an inventive rather than a positing act, and the characteristic of actual existence, which first marks something as concrete and individual, is not something that I can invent (Husserl 2005). So, even though actual existence cannot be phantasied, it can act as a catalyst for the phantasied experience, as there will be something in the concrete that sets off the abstract mental capabilities of the person. The setting off does not have to be within the now of the moment of object perception, since a memory can start a phantasie performance that overrides the present concrete space one is embodied within, and for the moment and next set of moments the mental person is disembodied from themselves, i.e., off to a timeless and spaceless floating plane of self-made reality:

> When I shift from perception, memory, or expectation into phantasy, I am aware that I have entered a null world in which what I imagine is not taken as presently existing, as having existed in the past, or as coming into existence in the future. (Husserl 2005, 360)

Accordingly, there would be a sense of time and space of one's own making, lasting as long as the phantasie lasts. Also, there would be repetition of the same phantasies, as an internal or external stimulation catalyzes their reappearance, or perhaps not quite the same, as the phantasies would evolve along their own story line. It is these imaginative phantastic movements that create ideas, many of which can and are translated to power and its attendant performance.

Husserl suggested imagination is strongly analogous to "thetic" or "positing," i.e., belief-involving, "presentifications" (*Vergegenwärtigungen*), of which episodic memory is a paradigm case (Poellner 2007, 25). However, "just as the thetic component in sense perception is neutralized in the awareness of something *as* a perceptual illusion, so imagining is a form of 'presentifying' something absent where the belief component of episodic memory is lacking" (Husserl [1913] 1982, §111). Thus, phantasie fills gaps or adds more to what objective reality can potentially produce as and of by itself, and human engagement is required to alter the state of affairs of the object and objective place and space, with the human potential creating the actual or adapting the actual to a new and newer actuals. With the constitutive of imagination, the "images" involved should be *experienced as clashing* with perceptual representations and, thus, as "occluding...something in reality" (Husserl 1980, appendix 51, 485). The occluding can be paradoxical in the sense that on the one hand the perceptual object is partially blocked as of itself by the perception, but on the other, there is a freeing up of perception that goes beyond the perception.

Husserl uses three phrases to incorporate phantasy's unique personality: "as it were" (gleichsam), "as if" (als ob), and "quasi-." For instance, "I am conscious of what is phantasied, as if it were being actually experienced" (Husserl 2005, 659). Also, everything that can occur in perception—and much that cannot occur there—can make an appearance in phantasy, always with the index of the as-if (Husserl 2005, xxxv):

> Memory is also the consciousness of something as-if, but remains in touch with an actual past and therefore with actual being. Phantasy's as-if, is directed against actual existence (673). There are no phantasy objects—understood as existing objects (671). The consciousness of being that characterises actual existence, has been emasculated in phantasy (606). (Husserl 2005, xxxv ii, Translator's Introduction)

(NB: the three numbers indicated in the quote are the corresponding location page numbers in Husserl 2005.)

Essentially, the actual has been weakened and the phantasy has been empowered, and this empowerment may create newer strengthened actualities.

Bracket

To bracket or to place barriers around something implies that the thing or object contained within these semicircular symbols have a protective essence of their own. For instance, protected from "outside" influences that may and can distort and limit what these objects and things can do and, consequently, free up their potential to do so. The shape of the semicircular brackets enclosing their thing or object as a metaphoric symbol, both as separate to each "end," i.e., ( ) and joined together (), invokes a sense of power exclusion and inclusion simultaneously. To illustrate, the curve is more resistant than the straight when pressure is applied, and the joining together to make an oval or stretched circle does not have any weak sides as there is uniformity of strength all around the curved edge with each point of the curve reinforcing the next and prior. The point is that by bracketing, power can be retained and used within the bracketed confines, and other power plays from the outside can remain outside. Thus, the power retained within the bracket can be of an uncontaminated type, in the sense of there is no prejudgment of what it may look like since it is just power as of itself, in its truest form or formlessness.

Husserl expounds the concept of bracketing or what he terms *phenomenological epoché*. Consequently, offering that one is thought to be able to suspend judgment regarding the general or naïve philosophical belief in the existence of the external world and, therefore, look at phenomena as they are originally given to consciousness (Husserl [1913] 1982). Since consciousness is the "awake" form one is, when absorbing the world around, awareness of what consciousness itself is would be crucial to how the surrounding world is absorbed and of the manner it dictates how the world is seen and experienced. The implication here is the world is seen, but not heard, i.e., a purposely filtered process, and the challenge is the communication breakdown between what is perceived and what actually is.

Therefore, to assist with the challenge and subsequently to limit or negate the involvement of the consciousness filter, it is bracketed. Thus, some parts remain within the bracket and some parts without, and those that are "sent out" are all assumptions concerning the existence of an external world, with the parts that stay in allowing the expulsion of all assumptions concerning the existence of an external world. However, in practice, controlling the spaces of consciousness to such an extent may be somewhat of an ordeal, for how can one know of their own extent of consciousness, which, like power, is elusive and only certain aspects of its potentiality and actuality capacity are "consciously" apparent along life's moments. Fundamentally, to put up brackets one has to know what is being bracketed and, thus, what to exclude and what to include, essentially shutting out or shutting in.

However, if it is feasible to bracket in a totalizing manner, one can attain epoché. *Epoché* (ἐποχή epokhē, "suspension") is an ancient Greek term typically translated as "suspension of judgment" but also as "withholding of assent," and to suspend or withhold implies a reduced capacity. Accordingly, when looking at the world as is, to gain an epoché epistemological reduction, there is a requirement to furnish this positing of a transcendent world with "an index of indifference" (Husserl 1999, 30). Hence, with the phenomenological epoché, "we put out of action the general positing which belongs to the essence of the natural attitude; we parenthesize everything which that positing encompasses with respect to being" (Husserl [1913] 1982, sec. 32), e.g., parenthesize to powerize.

How of the World

> The exclusive and persisting direction of our interest lies in how...the world gets constituted for us. (Husserl 1970a, §38, 147/144)

The phenomenological problem of the relation of consciousness to an objectivity has its noematic side, in which the noematic senses are the diverse particulars of which objects are presented or given to the individual. Noema in phenomenology stands for the object or content of a thought, judgment, or perception, and noema in itself has a connection to an object through the noema's own "sense." However,

> if we ask how the "sense" belonging to consciousness comes to the "object," i.e., its own object, and how that object can be "the same" in manifold acts with very diverse noematic content, and if we ask how we see this in the sense, we find that new structures present themselves, structures whose extraordinary meaning is patent. (Husserl 2014, 255)

This unobstructed process allows for an expansive tendency, and of one that can be developed and enlarged in space and place and as rewritten space and place, i.e., new or at least overlaid spaces and places. Just as old power(s) can be overrun or overlaid by new power(s), creating newer places and spaces as the noema performance evolves, the power can become more powerful if multiple, interconnected noema or noeses are added together to focus on the same object. Thus, their totality of a prior exposure from a number of epochés will encourage greater comprehension of the truth of the said object, and the corresponding epochés if reflected, alternatively, on their parallel noeses will target

> the question of what consciousness' "pretension" of actually "referring" to something objective, of being "on target"...in reality says...and how objective

> relations of "validity" and "invalidity" may be clarified phenomenologically in
> terms of noesis and noema. (Husserl 2014, 255)

To clarify, noesis gives meaning to intentional act and noema is a meaning that is given to intentional act. For instance, all acts of intention involves an "I-pole" or noesis (origin of the noesis) and "object-pole" or noema, and noema seems to be whatever is intended by acts of perception or judgment in general, whether it be "a material object, a picture, a word, a mathematical entity, another person" precisely *as* being perceived, judged, or otherwise thought about (Sokolowski 2000, 59). Also, both noesis and noema, within an act, are not considered as that act object.

Within this transcendental reflection, the focus process is not inevitably introspective, since the reflection involves not only a thematizing of the subjective, noetic moment of a current experience but, *necessarily prior* to this, of its noematic component, i.e., the intentional *object* just as it is experienced (Husserl 1970a, §§50, 51). Husserl extends this by emphasizing that the utmost thematic focus is on the *relations* between the structures of the object as it is given and the structures of conscious subjectivity that are necessary conditions for the object thus to manifest itself (Husserl 1970a, §§41, 51, 53, 155/152, 177/174, 182/179). Like so, relations create the bridge between the person and the object and between the person and their essence.

Essence

> At first "essence" designated what is to be found in the very own being of an
> individuum as the What of an individuum. Any such What can, however, be "put
> into an idea." Experiencing, or intuition of something individual can become
> transmuted into eidetic seeing (ideation)—a possibility which is itself to be
> understood not as empirical, but as eidetic. What is seen when that occurs is
> the corresponding pure essence, or Eidos, whether it be the highest category or
> a particularisation thereof—down to full concretion. (Husserl [1913] 1982, 8)

Pure essence can be attributed to pure energy or pure power, and deviation from these true pathways is not possible, once tapped into their essence. In other words, an Eidos of pure essence (pure essence of pure essence), being at one with the purity of pure power. The What of an individuum, of the individual, is the actuality of that person, i.e., the true essence lying within, that seldom emerges to the surface of consciousness but when it does, or circumstances make possible its emergence, the one of the person syncs with the true power of oneself, in whatever form(s) that takes. Even though it may be only a momentary experience or one of several or numerous moments, it is nonetheless a fertile ground for ideas to form and come to fruition.

The momentary unitary or several of these replicated moments add essence to the initial or unitary one. This initial unitary is the single or first power. For example, just as a unitary state is a state governed as a single power in which the central government is ultimately supreme, and through this supremacy the central government may create administrative divisions, but only as units applying powers that the central government chooses to delegate, the unitary power does the same. Thus, the essence of power requires a beginning, a spark or act of recognized cognition, e.g., recognized in the sense that an opportunity for power is possible, and simultaneously recognizing that there is such a thing as power, for the former to be "possible. "

To recognize is to see, acknowledge, accept, and be on familiar terms with. It is this acceptance that is the self's gatekeeper that has opened, as what enters the person is admitted as the Real in individual form. The Real holds spatiotemporal existence, an actuality existing in the moment(s) of an individual's time-spot. So, retaining this

> particular duration of its own and a real content which in its essence could just as well have been present in any other time-spot: posits it as something which is present at this place in this particular physical shape where yet the same real being might just as well, so far as its own essence is concerned, be present at any other place, and in any other form, and might likewise change whilst remaining in fact unchanged, or change otherwise than the way in which it actually does. (Husserl [1931] 2002, 10)

It is this Husserlian essence that can be extended to the essence of power, and power is Real as long as it remains within the limits of the spatiotemporal, but the spatiotemporal does not belong to the power itself. For power, in its human form, only exists for as long as the human wields it, wishes it, and imagines it, and if this ceases, human-generated power ceases to be; i.e., it has outlived its human spatiotemporal form or essence. Natural power would be the same, since if life beyond human form and capacity, which is the vast majority of the life process anyway regardless of the presence or absence of human presence, ceased, power within that context would also cease. In other words, power requires the materiality of things, as mediums, to retain a sense of being, and particularly preferable is the materiality of the spatiotemporal, i.e., having matter to latch onto which has duration.

Power's shape-shifting in size and duration when "latching on" has potential of being in one and many places simultaneously as a saturated space of being. This is by "being" recognized and experienced through the adumbration (one-sided) process. For instance, the process to feel power is not restricted to the individual moving through the moments of their lives in an adumbrated way and absorbing more and more of what power means as its sides and layers are increasingly revealed, for it may be many individuals sharing an aggregate moment of adumbration (many sides produced from one's one-side), which tells the fuller power experience. This would occur all in the same moment of their moments. Therefore, the moment of the power, and its moment would be their moments in which the difference in the experience would be theirs, not the power itself; e.g., it is their sense and essence of spatiotemporal uniqueness that produce adumbration of the power, and adumbration in this case is all the sides contributing to the "one-side" that is the power. Fundamentally, its essence.

Seeing an essence is also precisely intuition (Husserl [1913] 1982, 9), e.g.,

> of whatever sort intuition of something individual may be, whether it be adequate or inadequate, it can take the turn into seeing an essence; and this seeing, whether it be corresponding adequate or corresponding inadequate, has the characteristic of a presentive act…implicit in this…is that…the essence (Eidos) is a new sort of object. Just as the datum of individual or experiencing intuition is an individual object, so the datum of eidetic intuition is a pure essence. (Husserl [1913] 1982, 9)

So, the individual object of pure essence began this essence segment, it also ends it. It is an instinctual and being instinctual unitary state of affairs, an instinctual sixth sense or clean sense of non-preconception, and an unpolluted spiritualness.

Spirit

One's spirit is one's essence. One's soul, life, life force, and inner self, so one's spirit is one's center and one's centerpiece. Everything that one can recognize is made possible by the spirit, and to live and appreciate that one is living is assisted by the spirituality of the individual. Husserl (1935) observes that one lives within a social framework in community, a communal space that sets the

horizons of the perceptual possibilities of family, nation or international community. However, to live within this reductive to expansive space (which does not
necessarily imply that the order of spatial growth reflects an expansive positioning
and movement of one's spirit, perhaps the opposite) is such that to "*live* is not
to be taken in a physiological sense, but rather as signifying purposeful living,
manifesting spiritual creativity—in the broadest sense, creating culture within
historical continuity" (Husserl 1935, 2), e.g.:

> Every spiritual image has its place essentially in a universal historical space or
> in a particular unity of historical time in terms of coexistence or succession—it
> has its history. (Husserl, Vienna Lectures, 1935)

So, for spirituality to have history, both from the past and the making of history
in the present, it needs to coexist with something physical, something that can
show evidence of spiritual existence in a seeing or touched form. For example,
"human spirituality is based on the human physis, each individual human soul-
life is founded on corporeality, and thus to each community on the bodies of the
individual human beings who are its members" (Husserl 1935, 2). Since corporeal
describes something that has a physical form, it is the apparent opposite of the
spiritual, apparent in that maybe it is not. This is because for the physical form,
movement and performance maybe the outward appearance of spiritual intent
since one's spirit powers one's corpo(reality). Accordingly, it is this embodied
process of body-spirit that creates the human-powered unit, of a dual unitary
individual as something real, at least as long as the body functions. However,
who is to say that the spirit does not endure beyond the demise of the bodily
"taxi" and is the conduit of power performance. Hence, along these lines the
spirit powers the body and "mindful" decisions and, hence, allows power to be,
e.g., the spirit as gatekeeper of power.

As a consequence, spirit as a powered source and as a conduit of power has
to be powerful in itself to perform these functions, and its lack of objectivity
assists with powered retention:

> There never has nor ever will be an objective science of spirit, an objective theory
> of the soul, objective in the sense that it permits the attribution of an existence
> under the forms of spatio-temporality to souls or to communities of persons. The
> spirit and in fact only the spirit is a being in itself and for itself; it is autonomous
> and is capable of being handled in a genuinely rational, genuinely and thoroughly
> scientific way only in this autonomy. (Husserl 1935, 19)

Thus, spiritual autonomy is its power. This is particularly so, for the spirit alone is immortal (Husserl 1935). The implication is that from the point of view of soul (spirit), humanity has never been a finished product, nor will it be, nor can it ever repeat itself (Husserl 1935).

There are parallels with one's spirit as the powered center of oneself and one's ego:

> To every living body [Leib], including that of the animal, belongs an ego-centering and a universal structural form that circumscribes everything psychical, thanks to which the one and identical ego of this living body lives in a multifarious ego-life, a life that has—the character of…ego-centered intentionality (consciousness of)—Living subjectivity in this sense—is in a primitive [erster] sense personal ego. (Husserl 2008, 274)

And there is the supernatural, extrasensory, subliminal. and subconscious performance of the ego that produces intimate intuition for the individual, i.e., intimacy of one's "I":

> I exist for myself and am constantly given to myself, by experiential evidence, as "I myself." This is true of the transcendental ego and, correspondingly, of the psychologically pure ego; it is true, moreover, with respect to any sense of the word ego. (Husserl [1931] 1960, sec. 33)

"I" and ego and spirit can be of the same essence, an essence of spatiotemporality and an essence that possibly can go beyond the limits of spatiotemporality. Thus, time is of the essence.

Time

Time is the most powerful force. It has permanency and will outlive or outlast anything else, except the background space that manifests as the physical form that time actually exists, and, within this duality, time and space can be thought of as one. Additionally, space, without time, would be inconceivable, for how would it exist or retain a spatial being without a length of perceptual duration to make that so. For instance, the length only has to be present for the instantaneous moment to provide "life" to that space, be that fleeting. In other words, if that moment is not there, there is no space either. Similarly, when considering time without space, if space is not there time cannot be seen or felt. Similarly, but not the same, is deliberate since time will still operate in non-space, i.e., a "space" perhaps of nonexistence of anything or any life form, or simply, the space of time or the time of space in which the only life existing is time itself. As can be surmised, within this circular argument of time-space, the time of itself with its "non"-space, is still a space, but perhaps the essential difference of time-space and time/non-space is that the latter has a lifeless quality. Nonetheless, the point is that time can outlast any living thing except itself.

Husserl sees a world that is conscious of time and space in the dealings of individuals and their temporal objects of curiosity, and to assist with illustrating this, transcendent and immanent temporal objects are engaged with. Transcendent is seen or intended by the individual, and intended acts are immanent to consciousness, so, "on both sides, that is, both in the immanent and in the transcendent spheres of reality, time is the irreducible form of individual realities in their described modes" (Husserl 1991, 284). This is because all temporal objects possess duration, which, being the object's time, and thus duration, as of time, is the form of individual objects (Husserl 1991). In this fashion, duration is particular to the object, whether the object is of concreteness or of an individual, and the temporal object enjoys a particular temporal location (Husserl 1991). Thus, the temporal of power possesses duration and location. Also, power requires space and time to perform, to be, and if space and time ceased to be, so would power.

Individuals perform along various time measurements, of different time frames internal and external to the individual. The internal maybe of 5-second duration, or 8 seconds, or whatever duration up to the duration when life for that individual ends. However, the measurement of "second" might be inappropriate, for the intensity of the internal durational experience cannot be reduced to mere seconds of reflection, since the power/force/passion of the "timed" experience can override the timing aspect, making it variable in duration. The external is of objective time independent of the individual, i.e., existing prior, during, and after the individual. This time is measureless, as it is endless to the past, present, and future. Indeed, it is only the positionality of the individual within their temporal time-space that provides a reference or comparison point in time to objective time. Hence, when speaking of time-consciousness, what is accepted is

> not the existence of a world time, the existence of a concrete duration, and the like, but time and duration appearing as such…also assume an existing time… not the time of the world of experience, but the immanent time of the flow of consciousness. (Husserl 1964, 23)

Therefore, multiple times operating within the "same" timeframe, and speculating how they operate within that by trying to establish

> how time which is posited in a time-consciousness as Objective is related to real Objective time, whether the evaluations of temporal intervals conform to Objective, real temporal intervals or how they deviate from them. (Husserl 1964, 23)

From that, the exercise and extent of human power is measured and calculated by time-consciousness as objective, working within the real of objective time, in which there are short-term powered gains and losses within the "expanse" of one's objective time duration, be that of a temporal nature.

So, the time of "now" is central to the powered time process, and among the modes of temporal appearance the now has a certain privileged status (Husserl 1991, 37), for it is the point of reference of the temporal experience. Following on from this, bodies are defined in their ultimate individuality by their absolute location in absolute space and time, of the position of observation and measure (Lobo 2010). Thus, within the now of one's internal time scales,

> Subjective time becomes constituted in the absolute timeless consciousness, which is not an object (Husserl 1991, 117).

Further

> the flow of modes of consciousness is not a process; the consciousness of the now is not itself now…therefore sensation…and likewise retention, recollection, perception, etc. are nontemporal; that is to say, nothing in immanent time. (Husserl 1991, 345–346)

And the power of the nontemporal is seen through phenomenological endings and beginnings.

Phenomenology as the Journey from One's Beginning to One's End

Phenomenology (from Greek *phainómenon* "that which appears" and *lógos* "study") is the philosophical study of the structures of experience and consciousness, and the Husserlian engagement throughout the chapter has as its central theme the study of what appears, i.e., appearance without frills and embellishments and appearance of the naked real and irreal. These are pure phenomenological experiences that imply

> abstention from all prejudgments stemming from scientific or other privileged spheres of experience which could render one blind to that which phenomenological reflection actually lays before us, actually makes available to us a progressive cognisance-taking that from the beginning proceeds by pure intuition, that is, one that from the beginning is an explication of examples in all their dimensions, of the purely mental moments implicit in them. (Husserl 1997, 219)

So, the pure intuition and the purely mental moments discovered or unearthed within this direct perceptional performance, of which "the contents are, in principle, not fully linguistically encodable" (Poellner 2007, 1). It is this action of nonaction of prejudgment that encourages a nonabsolute encodability, and not to prejudge removes the limitations of language on how, and to what extent, one perceives. This is because one is not being coded by oneself, which, by definition, allows oneself sense and essence freedom, a freedom of pure intuition.

Negation of prejudging also negates the object being scrutinized as an externality and as clues to what it is. Instead, what emerges is an assemblage of perception and functionality, inferring one another under the notion of a precise object or "type," and precision is key to reach for the heart of what power does, is, and adapts to, in evolving circumstances. The evolvement may involve consequences of power application in how it deliberately changes objects, things and the associated spatial environment, and unforeseen changes that power itself must cope with and accordingly self-adapt to maintain its domination. Like so, knowing the precision of power

> lays bare the "sources" from which the basic concepts and ideal laws of pure logic "flow," and back to which they must once more be traced, so as to give them all the "clearness and distinction" needed for an understanding, and for an epistemological critique, or pure logic. (Husserl 1970b, 6–7)

It may well be that when discovering and having discovered the pure logic of power, its supposed rationality, sensibilities, and soundness may appear flawed. For instance, possessing clearness and distinction capabilities would reveal that power, of itself and left to itself, may well be in possession of these three, but within the human context of power, the three are abused and distorted. This is because human intentionality is of a biased impurity, and powered processes and performance are often irrational, foolish, and unsound. Fundamentally, the difference between the flawed and pure of power, as with looking at any object through the phenomenological regressive inquiry (Husserl 2002) and bringing a new world to light, lies within the correlation between objectivity and subjectivity (Husserl 2002, xxix). Therefore, the "new world" may have been present all along but never or seldom purely perceived, due to the filtered, judging way people look.

The phenomenological regression or reduction enables the phenomenologist to go "back to the things themselves" (Husserl [1900/1901] 2001, 168), the actuality of experience. It is here that Husserl offers his Principle of All Principles, of which

> every originary presentive intuition is a legitimising source of cognition, that everything originally (so to speak, in its "personal" actuality) offered to us in "intuition" is to be accepted simply as what it is presented as being, but also only within the limits in which it is presented there. (Husserl [1913] 1982, sec. 24)

And intuition has flowed through this Husserlian chapter, emerging time and time again as a legitimate cognitive tool and allowing for "personal actuality." In clarification, one can emerge from one's potentiality as one's phenomenological potential beginnings can be transformed into endings of actualities. Added to this is the productive originary, which implies causing existence, and is primitive, primary, and original, i.e., the Beginning, the Beginning of and to the End. In other words, a static to constitutive movement of reverting or returning to one's origin to allow access to one's progression, e.g.,

> Is not static phenomenology precisely the phenomenology of leading clues, the phenomenology of the constitution of leading types of objects in their being. (Husserl 2001, 644)…

and…

> within a static register now, one moves regressively to constitutive phenomenology. (Husserl 2001, xxxv)

Since "constitutive" means having the power to establish or give organized existence to something, phenomenological immersion allows one's initiative empowerment to legitimately be at one with power, being immersed in its essence journey within one's beginning to end.

CHAPTER 10

Nietzsche

Morality

To have morals implies one possesses ethical prowess; i.e., one is good, right, honest, decent, and principled. These are honorable words, set or located within value systems that deem them as such, and how power can be applied or exercised is set against a backdrop of moral difference, or indifference. Accordingly, the variances of the moral range moving from differences to indifferences will determine how the application of power is perceived as mild, moderate, or extreme. Like so, the context of these three felt conditions operates within both good and evil intentions and results, which simultaneously may occur at the same moment(s) depending on how the initiator and recipient regard the performance. Also, simultaneously, what is regarded as good by one may be regarded as evil by the other. This nonspecific labeling of which one of the two is being referred to is deliberate, since the fixity of intended position can be reversed, and this reversal can be among different powered action contexts, or within the same one along its powered duration. An implication is that good and evil are of a similar disposition as one feeds into the other and ultimately creating the same performance and, thus, resulting in their distinguishability becoming problematic.

Actually, the agents in this powered game of good and evil, of the fixations and reversals, would not even know about the concepts of good and evil, if it was not for the learned "valued" system agents lived within. For example, another value system may not have definitions of good and evil, with the act of power simply regarded as an act to live, and die, by; i.e., no judgment is expected, or not expected to be expected, as the act of power just is, and accepted and predicted. Thus, power is normalized without the scrutiny of its why and not placing emotional value on its existence and effects. Moreover, the lack of judgment of agent performance implies a lack of morality or moral existence. However, the human project does not have to concern itself with a nonmoral state of being, since it is full of morality, a moral endeavor saturated with fixity and reversibility of what good and evil morality represents. It is this saturation that supplies the fuel to power up power and the ongoingness of the consequences of this, i.e., an animalistic drive that has always been present in the human makeup from its origin.

This is a rawness of attitude that Nietzsche regards as the perverse nature of the human animal, of being labeled the sick animal (Nietzsche [1887] 1996, GM III, 14). For example, there is so much in man that is horrifying! The world has been a madhouse for too long (Nietzsche [1887] 1996, GM II, 22). When considering the sick, the horrifying, and the mad, it can be appreciated these are not the most stable of characteristics to determine what power is and how it should be practiced. Alternatively, (perhaps paradoxically) to possess sickness, horrific capability and be madness-exemplified can also be coping mechanisms to deal with what power can do along its cruel intentions and, thus, retain the ability to apply power in this manner; e.g., the human mental capacity needs these three to do power:

> What we take to be "spirit" or "mind," as that which distinguishes the human animal from the rest of nature, is the product of a long constraint, involving much violence, arbitrariness and nonsense (Nietzsche [1886] 1998, BGE, 188); modern European morality is herd animal morality which considers itself to be the definition of morality and the only morality possible or desirable. (Nietzsche [1886] 1998, BGE, 202)

Mentioning the herd animal morality correlates to the beginnings of human thinking and being, coming full circle from the ongoing now to the initial commencement of human life tens of thousands of years ago. Of course, this is only applicable if assuming that the descriptor can be thought of as a circle (the line of the curve following a human pathway through the generations of life and after life), as it may be that in the human heart of hearts, the animal has never been left to permit a return to. Perhaps a better shape imaginary is of a circle of reduction, as the circumference reduces and the living space within becomes increasing dense in form, practice, and sense of being, until the resultant sphere is a sphere of density. From this, the suggested outcome is one in which the human center, being the animal has not traveled anywhere, since it is only the animal exterior, in the guise of the morality performance and what others in the human herd see of that performance at the surface-skin level, that has traveled through a series of technological evolvements. In other words, the human periphery adapts and changes, and the human core remains the same. Nietzsche regards the prehistory of the human animal important, of a prior time labeled "the morality of custom," predating world history, where and when this "decisive historical period" determined the character of man (Nietzsche [1887] 1996, GM III).

An implication is that the power of man and woman, and the power in man and woman, were present at human conception and were designed as a part of the human physiology, psychology, and spirit. Nevertheless, whatever way the animal in human was created or evolved into the form that has lasted to the present, power was part of the arrangement, and how this "given" power is used and perceived in the judgment of its usage, its moral application, depends on the cultural generation wielding it. This is because gauging moral application is a risky undertaking, since a reductiveness can cloud the judging process of one culture and time period over another, indeed, within the same cultural time and within cultures, let alone culture to culture. For instance, a culture is not necessarily coherent in all of its belief systems, and when speaking of "an erudite form of true belief in the prevailing morality," the conclusions reached are only "a part of the state of affairs within a particular morality" (Nietzsche [1886] 1998, BGE, 186).

"A part" is twofold. To illustrate, (1) "a part" implies only a partial grasp of what the morality really is or means, partial in only certain members of the societal group grasp it along similar lines, for others will have their interpretations; or partial in that the individual only grasps certain significances of the moral performance. (2) The "a part" creates an imagery of being separate from the moral process, literally apart. This detachment may not be perceived on the surface, which may favor a cultural togetherness, a learned mutual moral position, and an appearance that perhaps is not the actual that creates the "real" attitude toward the moral action, since the real one could reside within the animal core of the human —for instance, one that has a different attitude of morality to its surface counterpart, or not be moral at all. Thus, producing a power struggle occurring within the one of the person—one animalistic and, the other, intellectual. Either way, judging the "same" power process fashions multiple conclusions as to its moralistic measurement, be that good, bad, or evil, or nothing of consequence.

Reflecting the inner and surface of human moral appreciation, Nietzsche sees three phases of morality within the human life course. Firstly, from the initial animal stage to becoming man/woman, actions are no longer directed to the procurement of momentary well-being but to enduring well-being, attuned to utility and purpose (in which) the free domination of reason first breaks forth. Secondly, a higher stage is reached of acting to the principles of honor, in which an arrangement occurs in regard to others, so submitting to common sensibilities, i.e., a utility of what is thought of others and what they think of that person in return. At the third or highest stage, the action or acting is based on one's own standard with regard to men and things, of a self-determination for themselves and others of what is honorable and useful and a becoming of the lawgiver of opinion as a collective individual (Nietzsche [1878–1880] 1986, article 94, 50). Consequently, there is an evolvement of returning, but also of amalgamation, occurring along these three phases, in which the individual begins of the powered moment of self-short-lived advantage, then of shared powered advantage, then back to the self-powered advantage, but taking the societal remainder of people along within their powered version; e.g., it becomes their version to react to and react with.

Therefore, those who hold the moral "high ground" or should that be *a* moral high ground which has emerged as the current, *the* morality, instigate and sustain expected behavioral patterns of limited dispositions. Consequently, individuals are frowned upon who move beyond the set moral parameters that society goes by. Thus, morality is a controlling force of a mental and emotional method of production, a mass production of conformity and obedience, and a hierarchal producing environment, e.g.,

> morality is the doctrine of the order of men's rank, and consequently also of the significance of their actions and works for this order of rank: thus, the doctrine of human valuations in respect of everything human…The unconditional importance, the blind self-centredness, with which every morality treats itself wants there not to be many moralities, it wants no comparison and no criticism, but rather unconditional belief in itself. (Nietzsche 2003, 35(5), 17)

So, those who wish to hold the ultimate power in society, that of controlling the other humans in society, as much as one feasibly can, pursue a doctrine of moral unconditionality, and multiple moralities are not encouraged to operate within the same time and space. The existence of multi-moralities is supported by Nietzsche, who challenges the assumption that there is a single morality valid for all (Nietzsche [1886] 1998, BGE, 228). Nonetheless, moral competition is not required for the moral soloist, with emphasis on the "solo" when it comes to power implementation and distribution.

Relating to the animal heart of the matter of human action and tension with the surface-skin analogy, when doing the morality performance, Nietzsche's attitude of morality practice also flows along an absolute engagement to not so absolute nonengagement with it. He proposed that no one is ever morally motivated by utilizing the equivalence between "moral" and "unegoistic" (Nietzsche [1878–1880] 1986, HA, 133), but from later thinking admitted that human beings are sometimes morally motivated, insisting that when they are, errors move them to their actions (Nietzsche [1881] 1982, D, 103). These errors are clouded by custom:

> Morality is nothing other (therefore no more!) than obedience to customs, of whatever kind they may be; customs, however, are the traditional way of behaving and evaluating. In things in which no tradition commands there is no morality. (Nietzsche [1881] 1982, D, 9)

Customs are a cornerstone of societal norms and values, maintaining the powered structure that is in-placed and in place. In-placed denotes a deliberate act of placing "preferred" ways to be and resultant ways of being as ingrained in society, and so the placing becomes valued. It is the values of morality, when experiencing errors, that Nietzsche regards as the real problem (Nietzsche [1887] 1996, GM1, 1). For instance, morality as "merely sign language, merely symptomatology" (Nietzsche [1889] 1998, TI, VII, 1), the symptomatologic error of the combined signs, markers, or indications of a disease or disorder. A disease in how society is disordered within how values of morality are promoted, i.e., a suffered discrimination, in which those who cause discrimination, or value difference, have power to do such an act. From this, the "discrimination of values has arisen either amongst the powerful, the rulers, or amongst the ruled" (Nietzsche [1886] 1998, BGE, 260) and is the typical character traits by which a ruling class defines and affirms itself that Nietzsche focuses on (Nietzsche 2017b, I, 16); e.g.,

> the possession of a consciousness of difference results in feelings of delight and pride. The nobles have a consciousness of wealth that seeks to give and bestow. By contrast, the slave type of morality, which characterises the oppressed and those who suffer from life and seek a metaphysical solution to the problem of suffering, results in a pessimistic suspicion about the whole human condition. The eye of the "slave" and the weak person turns unfavourably towards the virtues of the powerful; they value those qualities that will serve the needs of their existence, such as pity, patience, industry and humility. (Nietzsche [1886] 1998, BGE, 260)

Accordingly, the "slave" or powerless in society becomes dependent on the moral values of the powerful, all in the name of quality of survival. This quality applies to both the ruling and the ruled of society, as each wishes to sustain, maintain, and improve on what quality of survival they already possess. This is a valued quality of difference, but also one of connectivity between the two. Thus, a symbiotic powered relationship "powered" by different moral perspectives.

However, if one stands beyond the moral compass, does that imply empowerment of an individual character, since the free human being is immoral because in all things they are determined to depend on themselves and not on a tradition? (Nietzsche [1881] 1982, D, 9). In this way, depending on oneself or being independent and creating values for oneself can be a powerful experience and create motivation to attain more of the same, as feeling of delight and pride emerge, i.e., echoes of the ruling attitude. Therefore, a dependence on delight and pride may be addictive, fueling the powered process, and maintaining this position to receive ongoing powered pleasing fixes. As a result, this self-valuation of man's (sic) pleasure justifies "self-glories, actions, intentions and states towards himself and, especially, towards his surroundings" (Nietzsche 2003, 35(17), 18). Subsequently, ordering desire orders morality, so

> the accepted order of rank of desirable things, according to whether a low, higher or highest egoism desires the one or the other, (although; my emphasis) not erected or altered in accordance with moral consideration, now determines whether one is moral or immoral. (Nietzsche [1878–1880] 1986, article 42, 36)

This, after the fact, morally based decision on whether one is "morally desirable" can be a personal estimation of success or failure, a self-appraisal. This is an often-flawed process, for the "motives and intentions behind it are seldom sufficiently clear and simple, and sometimes even the memory seems to be muddled by the success of an act, so that one foists false motives on one's act oneself, or treats inessential motives as essential" (Nietzsche [1878–1880] 1986, article 68, 44). Thus, when an act is realized through desire, one's power capacity to do so may not be fully appreciated by the oneself when acting. To illustrate, since one's powered possession is not clear and simple within the understanding of what it can do in terms of its potential and actuality, and the resultant change in one's surroundings, as others and material are altered, could be beyond human capacity. Thus, a partial comprehension of what results can be expected is possible, but not the full consequence of powered action.

Powered partiality of expectation, as one's limited mental capacity, points to an incomplete appreciation of what morality is or aspires to be. So, as "success often bestows upon an act the whole honest lustre of the good conscience, (and) a failure casts the shadow of pangs of conscience over the most estimable deed" (Nietzsche [1878–1880] 1986, article 68, 44), selective considerations of power consequences add to the limits of mental capacity, when considering it after the action is completed. This is, as well as before and during the powered experience, and what is recalled or "remembered" can assist with continuing or discontinuing the currently experienced and practiced power action, depending on if the desire is being fulfilled or not; if the desire is valid, i.e., "success is supposed to be a substitute for greater validity" (Nietzsche [1878–1880] 1986, article 68, 44). This mental process of limitation also applies to the spectator of the powered action, when gauging the extent of its performed moral presence. For instance, to learn to limit the limitation, "we have to learn to think differently—in order at last, perhaps very late on, to attain even more: to feel differently" (Nietzsche [1881] 1982, D, 103). Nevertheless, possessing limited mental capacity can be advantageous since it

> prevented man from despising himself as man, from turning against life, and
> from being driven to despair by knowledge: it was a self-preservative measure. In
> short: Morality was the great antidote against practical and theoretical Nihilism.
> (Nietzsche 2017a, 1, Nihilism, article 4, 4.)

Nihilism

Nihilism can be thought of "As an Outcome of the Valuations and Interpretations of Existence Which Have Prevailed Heretofore" (Nietzsche 2017a, 1; Nihilism, article 1). So, up to the present time, or taken literally, there is involvement of the total time and space of human existence, to create an outcome perceived as nihilism. However, it is not *the* outcome of the human product of being from conception up to the present, since human belief systems are a complex and competitive performance and process. For instance, long-term ingrained doctrines are problematic to displace as many in society perceive them as natural and so retain little or no capacity to critically think beyond their spatial influence. This is because it does not occur to them to do so, unless an experience or event happens that causes perception alteration, i.e., a perceptive moment that raises questions and doubts about the current ways of being and doing, although this does not imply that all the ingredients of the established doctrine are necessarily of negative natures to how one has been socioculturally sculptured. Also, some elements can remain, and others not practiced further in time, or at the least, altered to suit one's updated and updating perceptual capacity. Accordingly, a process of nihilism implying "that the highest values are losing their value. There is no bourne. There is no answer to the question, 'to what purpose?'" (Nietzsche 2017a, 1; Nihilism, article 2).

The bourne implication of no limit or boundary, or no goal or destination, is one suggestive of ongoing expansiveness in human perceptive capabilities. In other words, boundless empowerment in how one can think which is not tied to the shackles of prominent dominant personalities in society, or ones encountered though daily life processes, i.e., not tied to societal expectations of conformity, as there are alternate ways to be that can constantly be revised, or at the least, reviewed. However, this is not to say that in practice the potentially limitless ideas of nihilism will not be tempered by others, since "others," implying those who would aim for limitless thought potential and those who wish for the status quo, would also be stakeholders within this inexhaustible space of belief(s). Thus, an inbuilt limitation system, as each contends with the rest to have their "unlimited" beliefs as *the* belief of the rest, as those who wish for the "status quo" are well practiced and versed in possessing the "right" to retain the "top spot" of the belief system that the rest adhere to. In addition, they would be aware of the existence of nihilism and the danger it retains of undermining their positions of power in society, particularly if nihilism is practiced in a systematic manner, e.g., in-depth, exhaustive, comprehensive, and utter. For instance,

> thorough Nihilism is the conviction that life is absurd, in the light of the highest values already discovered; it also includes the view that we have not the smallest right to assume the existence of transcendental objects or things in themselves, which would be divine or morality incarnate. This view is a result of fully developed "truthfulness": therefore, a consequence of the belief in morality. (Nietzsche 2017a, 1; Nihilism article 3)

Nihilism relates to a sense of freedom, freedom from the mindfulness of others to create mindlessness in oneself, and it allows the one to reach for the "truthfulness" of themselves. "Truth" from Nietzsche's perspective is not a benevolent God, but nature, second nature (Nietzsche [1908] 2005, xviii), and the well-being of the human sense of being can be attained through truth, and as long as "we are strong enough...then everything has to turn out best for us" (Nietzsche [1908] 2005, EH, "Wise," 2), "for which the credit should be given, not to anything supernatural, but to our own practical and theoretical skills in interpreting and arranging events" (Nietzsche [1882–1887] 1974, GS, 277). Mentioning one's strength, particularly the inner strength of one's mental and spiritual capacity, is key to the nihilistic process. This is because one's strength of purpose in discovering what is best for oneself needs to overcome others strength of purpose in ensuring one does not do it their way(s). Everyone would have this potential to become powerful in how life can be perceived without looking through the filtered, selective process of others, but not too many actualize that potentiality.

When searching for the "truths" of nihilism how the external world is perceived is central to the process and, indeed, how much nihilism is taken on board. For instance, the effect of the external world is telegraphed into our brain, arranged, given shape, and traced back to its cause: then the cause is projected, and only then does the fact enter our consciousness (Nietzsche 2003, 34(54), 4), so the world of appearances, Nietzsche continues, appears to us as a cause only once it has exerted its effect and the effect has been processed; we are constantly reversing the order of what happens (Nietzsche 2003, 34(54), 4). Therefore, effects of the world become the causes that are reacted to, as if we are reacting to the "after the fact" external world and always playing catch-up and perhaps not ever fully catching up, which may point to why established doctrine can be, and is, powerful in its permanency, and the subsequent nihilistic difficulty to move beyond the active now(s) of the external world particularly if even ever reaching the now(s), let alone going beyond.

Adding to the mix of nihilistic cause and effect reversals is the selected admittance of what is desirable, which assists with retention of an overall view. So, "in our conscious mind there must be above all a drive to exclude, to chase away, a selecting drive—which allows only certain facts to be presented to it" (Nietzsche 2003, 34(31), 9). This selection process is an inclusivity and exclusivity process, simultaneously engaging with external stimuli, essentially the heart of the matter of nihilist process when looking at the outcome of valuations. Thus, selected valuations that are conceptualized which can lead to power. So, conceptual human valuations in terms of

> logic, sense of time, sense of space, are prodigious capacities to abbreviate, for the purpose of commanding. A concept is an invention which nothing corresponds to wholly, but many things slightly. (Nietzsche 2003, 34(131), 9)

This evaluation is carried through by the seizing of signs, and this apparatus of signs is

> man's superiority, precisely because it is at the furthest possible distance from the individual facts. The reduction of experience to signs, and the ever greater quantity of things which thus can be grasped, is man's highest strength. This intellectual world, this sign-word, is pure illusion and deception. (Nietzsche 2003, 34(131), 10)

So even though nihilism attempts to break though the barriers of illusion and deception of powered valuations of society, it paradoxically runs the risk of producing its own illusions and deceptions.

Awareness of illusions and deceptions assists one's perspective when considering a benevolent God, which is perhaps the most potent sign-word floating in the background and foreground of human as being and as beings. To illustrate, human tendency is to search for meaning in life and meaning of life; doing so allows one to believe that it is worthwhile to do power as meaning gives purpose to power. Also, if there was no meaning to life, in that anything one did does not make any difference as it is destroyed by the march of time, and doing power then becomes powerless, at least within the human context. However, beyond human power may be a different story, as lack of time to be in existence might not be a consideration, i.e., a timelessness capacity to be powerful. God is said to be timeless, and the benevolence shown or hoped for from God is one that promises external life beyond death. Death can be perceived as a condition recognized by current human medical practice, showing the corporal representation of human anatomy as decaying, but unknown concerning human mind and spirit beyond death. Along these lines, humans see the possibility to continue their mind and spirit through the benevolence of God, i.e., to continue onward, to retain the ability to continue life after death, be it of an assumed altered form and format. This is life as power and power as life, and if in doubt about God's existence, the tools of illusion and deception assist in negating that doubt and going for the powered life goal. However ,

> if the world had a goal, it could not fail to have been reached by now. If it had an unintended final state, this too could not fail to have been reached…But the old habits of thinking about all events in terms of goals, and about the world in terms of a guiding, creating God, is so powerful that the thinker is hard-pressed not to think of the goallessness of the world as an intention. (Nietzsche 2003, 36(15), 23)

This is where nihilism takes issue with goals, for that implies an ending, a limit to what may be possible, and thus leaving God behind and impressing upon the world the

> faculty for eternal novelty, that is, impose upon a finite, determinate force of unchanging magnitude like "the world" the miraculous capacity to refashion its shapes and states infinitely…to possess not only the intention, but also the means of guarding itself from all repetition. (Nietzsche 2003, 36(17), 24)

Hence allowing for human power to possess infinite possibilities during the now of life before death, since afterward the opportunities to do so may not be present. For example, as Nietzsche says of the Christian doctrine of personal immortality (Nietzsche [1888] 1968, AC 41, xxv), "the emphasis of life is put on the 'beyond' rather than on life itself—when it is put on nothingness…the emphasis has been completely removed from life as such" (Nietzsche [1888] 1968, AC, 43, xxv).

So, Nihilism, as a tool to power, advocates "that there is no truth, no absolute state of affairs". It finds that the "value of things are not real, but only a symptom of strength on the part of the valuer, a simplification serving the purposes of existence" (Nietzsche 2017a, Nihilism, article 13). Therefore, the power of Nihilism is that

> values and their modifications are related to the growth of power of the valuer. The measure of disbelief and of the "freedom of spirit" which is tolerated, viewed as an expression of the growth of power, (and) Nihilism viewed as the ideal of the highest spiritual power, of the over-rich life, partly destructive, partly ironical. (Nietzsche 2017a, Nihilism, article 14)

To attain an over-rich life, or living life to the full, in respect to Nihilism, in that "it is the negation of a real world and of Being, and might be a divine view of the world" (Nietzsche 2017a, Nihilism, article 15) is ironic, as it adds to or replaces the role of God, depending on the degree of individual acceptance of Nihilism.

Perceiving Instincts

The theory of milieu is that everything exerts an influence, and the result is man himself (Nietzsche 2003, 34(12), 1). To clarify, milieu or the environment, background, location, is the life-giving influence producing what the human is and possibilities offered of what can be accomplished. Accomplished in the sense of creative manipulation of the milieu to extract its materiality, and from this action, further materiality can be wrought. Since humans alter milieu, the latter can be viewed differently as from previous milieu and as allowing the creative imagination of human exploitative drive to produce altered material resource. This process repeats in an endless cyclical upgrade of technological evolvement. For example, from fire creation and self-crafted stone hand tools, to the hand tools of buttons that are pressed on mass-produced computer keyboards. Or from food gathered or killed by hand to feed oneself and one's family or local tribe, to owning vast tracts of land to grow food and keep livestock in which the livestock consumes much of the food, for humans to then eat the livestock and its dairy by-products. Thus, commodifying milieu, which in turn commodifies humans. As a result, as many humans as possible are commodified by a few commodifiers, who retain the economic clout to do so. Fundamentally, an instinct to dominate milieu and other humans, over the existence of humankind.

Therefore, an ego-generated instinct in which "egoistic actions have hitherto been by far the most frequent actions and will continue to be so for all future time" (Nietzsche [1881] 1982, D, 148). In this fashion, when considering the opposing instinct of the unegoistic, Nietzsche perceived that as the "great danger to mankind, its most sublime temptation and seduction—temptation to what? To nothingness?—precisely here I saw the beginning of the end" (Nietzsche 2017b, 5). Hence, a concern that the "unego" performance undermines human potential to be powerful and instead heading toward an underlining tendency of nonexistence, nonbeing, and emptiness. Consequently, power itself is at risk, heading toward its finish along the unegoistic course. Essentially, ego is necessary as a source and driver of power and its value is required, since

> the value of ideal selfishness is a matter of its role in human flourishing: "continually to watch over and care for and to keep our soul still, so that our fruitfulness shall come to a happy fulfillment." (Nietzsche [1881] 1982, D, 132)

Happy fulfillment is integral to human instinct, whether partially or wholly associated with the fulfillment of power gratification; e.g.,

> at the bottom of all belief there lies the sensation of the pleasurable or painful in respect to the subject experiencing the sensation…in our primary condition, all

that interests us organic beings in any thing is its relationship to us in respect of pleasure and pain. (Nietzsche [1878–1880] 1986, HA, article 18, 21)

Experiencing a state of happiness is achieved at diverse levels of feeling and intensity within the one person and between people. Also, it does not follow that what makes a person content will not necessarily do so again, as higher levels of that stimuli may be required next time to achieve similar "happy" outcomes, if they are reached at all. These "higher levels" could be a reason why many people seek further and further power acquisition to attain that happy fix and why people experience the "same" stimulus for happiness in dissimilar ways as their level of power acquisition would be at different stages of development.

Additionally, happiness as a state of mind is central for its appearance and perceived appearance. However, "sense-perception happens without our awareness: whatever we become conscious of is a perception that has already been processed" (Nietzsche 2003, 34(30), 1). So, it is one's instinct that has done the work of processing, that primary animal component within the core of humans that has already assessed the stimuli as pleasure or pain in which the conscious perceived the perception after it had been perceived and processed by the unconscious; i.e., the decision has been taken already. Nevertheless, this may be a protective measure, so the self can handle the stimuli, can live with it and its consequences, both for oneself and for others. Accordingly, protecting one's intensity of powered pleasure or pain from the debilitating effects and affects its stimuli can cause to others and the self, when ordering a perceived (by some) despicable act; e.g.,

> much that is horrific and inhuman in history in which one can hardly bear to believe is likewise ameliorated when we consider that he who ordered it and he who carries it out are different people: the former does not see it and his imagination therefore receives no strong impression of it, the latter obeys one set above him and does not feel responsible. (Nietzsche [1878–1880] 1986, HA, article 101, 54)

In this way, distance in space and time is created by the one causing the powered action, to those experiencing its effects. In other words, the "powerer" is removed from direct contact with those the order affects, and there is a time delay in the communication from one to the other, so the other cannot respond immediately, if at all. If there is a delayed response, it may be of a relatively powerless nature of gestures and symbolism and in which the messengers of power, the go-betweens, retain distance of accountability. So, from this process, the recipients have to absorb the order the best way they can. Essentially, all three in the performance enjoy the protection of variability within this a prior powered perception process, a dissimulation process; e.g.,

> the intellect, as a means for the preservation of the individual, develops its chief power in dissimulation. In man this art of dissimulation reaches its acme of perfection: in him deception, flattery, falsehood and fraud, slander, display, pretentiousness, disguise, cloaking conventions, and playacting in front of others and in front of himself…all these things are so much the rule, and the law. (Nietzsche 1997, 88)

These acts of concealment, suppression, and camouflage assist with one's perceptual instinctual unity. For example, to be in harmony and accord with oneself in the powered milieu of life, allows life to be bearable within its inauthenticities, and one's instinct carries the day. This is the authentic part of the self that allows unity among everyone's conscious disunity:

> If I have anything of a unity within me, it certainly doesn't lie in the conscious "I" and in feeling, willing, thinking, but somewhere else: in the sustaining, appropriating, expelling, watchful prudence of my whole organism, of which my conscious self is only a tool. (Nietzsche 2003, 34(46), 2)

Consequently, a wholesome instinct, of which "egoism is not evil, because the idea of one's 'neighbour' is very weak in us" (Nietzsche [1878–1880] 1986, HA, article 101, 54).

Good and Evil

Hence, considering if egoism is not evil, when acting out power, both for the instigator and receiver, values can be applied to the act of power in terms of good and evil, but can a meaningful differentiation between the two terms be reached? For instance, a good evil or an evil good, a good evil act or person or thing, an evil good act or person or thing, or "good, a preliminary stage of evil; a mild dose of evil" (Nietzsche 2003, 34(174), 12). Nietzsche speculates on this interlocking duality:

> Can all values not be turned round? And is good perhaps evil? and God only an invention and finesse of the Devil? Is everything perhaps in the last resort

false? And if we are deceived, are we not for that very reason also deceivers? (Nietzsche [1878–1880] 1986, HA, 7)

To know what the difference is between good and evil, if indeed there is difference, can be attributed to one's "place" in society and what one has absorbed as the cultural makeup of that society. This learned cultural makeup is labeled one's Second nature, as First nature, in this context, is one's primary animalism or original, one's original being, casting oneself back to prehistory, of good and evil resided firstly in the soul of the ruling tribes and castes and possessing the ability to requite. This revengefulness allowed for ability to see good with good, evil with evil, and those who requited were good, and those who could not, were bad (Nietzsche [1878–1880] 1986, HA, article 45, 36–37). Accordingly, the good are a caste with power, the bad as power-less people with no sense of belonging together…good and bad was perceived as noble and base, master and slave (Nietzsche [1878–1880] 1986, HA, article 45, 37).

From this, modern judgments of good and evil or bad are based on the original, tainted by second-nature considerations. However, this is not to say that the origins of humanity would not have possessed their Second nature running alongside the First, just as humans do today. For instance, the culture(s) of that conceptive time and space would have championed requite-ness based on the harshness of life encountered, and thus encouraging the First-nature and Second-nature practice that would have built on and alongside each other, almost as an indistinguishable oneness of being. However, as technology has developed over the ages, the "gap" between first and second nature appears to have drifted apart, since evolving technology can protect against the harshness of life. Nonetheless, appearance can deceive and be the deceiver, as First nature is simply hidden behind the veil of Second nature, but that does not dismiss second nature as integral to the process of engaging with good and evil, since in order to

> become who we are, we must be honest with ourselves not merely as pieces of nature, as animals in an undersigned world, but as pieces of "second nature," as animals whose character and circumstances are significantly constituted by culture. (Nietzsche 2005, xii)

So, natures of humans are dictated by their living environment, be that of human and natural construction, and both are transformed by the rigors of time. Yet, since humans are fallible, their natures possess strengths and weaknesses, and to deal with these long and shortcomings Nietzsche sees humans as giving style to themselves, practiced by those who survey

208

Not Losing Face

all the strengths and weaknesses of their nature and then fit them into an artistic
plan...Here a large mass of second nature has been added; there a piece of original
nature has been removed. Here the ugly that could not be removed is concealed;
there it has been reinterpreted and made sublime. (Nietzsche [1882–1887] 1974,
GS, 290)

Therefore, this artistic plan allows one to do acts that otherwise may be discounted
since one feels uncomfortable in what one is doing or being, and it makes the
performance of power easier to deal with as the uncomfortable aspects are
hidden from others and from oneself. This secreted action is applicable to both
the powered and those that receive it as each have their artistic way of dealing
with power from acceptance through to resistance and diverse degrees of these
simultaneously within both.

The receivers when submitting "abjectly to capricious laws" have only done
so because of the "tyranny of such capricious laws," with the "probability being
that this is 'nature' and 'natural' and not that laisser aller" (Nietzsche [1886]
1998, BGE, 188). So, not apathy or sloppiness, but a purposeful reaction to
capriciousness when aiming for the similarly worded laissez aller, hence implying
lack of constraint and freedom, i.e., a second-nature reaction of active forces. For
instance, active forces are regarded as a cut above, since they create difference;
reactive forces create nothing except ressentiment and bad conscience (Deleuze
2006, x). In the tensions between master and slave, Deleuze utilizes Nietzsche's
division of affirmation and negation, regarding the active master forces as "I am
good, therefore you are evil," and the slave reactive forces as "you are evil, therefore I am good" (Deleuze 2006, x). To illustrate, one likes to think of themselves
as being in the "right," righteousness, and goodness, and it is one's other that
experiences difficulties with achieving that standard, that superior perspective,
from the one looking outward or downward on them. The result is that good and
evil arrive at the same time and place of action and reaction, but from diverse
directions, and define the "same" re(action) together. Power can also be said to
experience the same re(action).

Egoism is not evil, but it is also not good, it just is, and a First nature tempered
by a Second nature of culturalness. So, since culture is saturated with what is
acceptable and unacceptable, individuals operate within this group dynamic by
an egotistical anxiousness of not being caught out or not being caught. From
this, a cultural peer group powered pressure ensures a conformity of sorts with
each individual conforming, within their hidden states of reactiveness, to the
active culture:

No one has ever done anything that was solely for the sake of another and without a personal motive. How indeed could he do anything that was not related to himself, thus without an inner necessity (which simply must have its basis in a personal need)? How could the ego act without ego? (Nietzsche [1878–1880] 1986, HA 133)

Consequently, a personal need to protect what power one has, be it great or small. For instance, one is "Going Beyond Good and Evil" (Nietzsche, BGE, [1886] 1998) and ceasing falsehoods about oneself and to accept falsehoods about the world, for example, that it is governed by providential reason and goodness (Nietzsche [1882–1887] 1974, GS, 277). Thus, ceasing falsehoods about what power is and perhaps being governed by providential, or indeed prudential, reason and goodness or evilness, e.g., power just is!

Zarathustra Will to Truth

The power of the aesthetic ideal "the harmful ideal par excellence," i.e., the human will, has been the solitary ideal until challenged by the counter-ideal of Zarathustra; e.g., man wills "nothingness," rather than not will, but the appearance of the Nietzschean Zarathustra figure transforms this (Nietzsche [1908] 2005, EH,). For instance, Zarathustra appeals to the man of the future, who will redeem humanity from the curse of its reigning ideal and from all those things that arise from it, notably nihilism and the will to nothingness (Nietzsche [1908] 2005, II, 24). Accordingly, the "will to truth" transformative process involves will becoming conscious of itself as a problem in us; consequently, Christian morality will destruct involving a drama that will be "the most terrible and questionable" but also "the one most rich in hope" (Nietzsche [1908] 2005, III, 27). Additionally, a new will for man is to be uncovered and posited to sublimate the principal ideal that has hitherto reigned on earth (Nietzsche [1908] 2005, III, 28). This transfer or redirection is a timed work in progress, a "premature-born" and as yet "undemonstrated future" (Nietzsche [1882–1887] 1974, GS, 382, [1908] 2005, EH, "Thus Spoke Zarathustra"). Hence, a power struggle is in movement, within time and space, between established beliefs in religious doctrine, reinforced by 2,000 years of presence and consolidation, and the recent emergence, of a couple of hundred years or so, of nonreligious willing.

So, a freeing of one's expression of self beyond religious limitations of expected behavior and cognitive development, an empowermental process and performance assuming one is not content to be within the religious umbrella, basically an anti-degeneration project; i.e., Zarathustra asks, "tell me, my brothers what do we consider bad or worst of all? Is it not degeneration?" (Nietzsche 1976, 187). To counter degeneration, it is necessary to reassert that all that is natural and healthy are dependent on the ruthless extirpation of those antinatural ressentiment sources of degeneration that have thoroughly weakened and falsified the natural and aristocratic bases of life (Aschheim 1997). Ressentiment is a sense of hostility directed toward an object that one identifies as the cause of one's frustration, i.e., an assignment of blame for one's frustration (TenHouten 2018). Since extirpation means to remove or destroy totally, do away with, an implication to treat degeneration of the human will and becoming is to remove one's sense of hostility on a permanent basis. Hence, strengthening and truth-defining one's natural and noble way of being, cleansing oneself of power dogma, allowing one's natural power to surface, and returning oneself to one's natural state that may be different for every individual. To illustrate, a collection of Zarathustra speaks:

> I teach you the overman. Man is something that shall be overcome. What have you done to overcome him? The overman is the meaning of the earth…remain faithful to the earth, and do not believe those who speak to you of otherworldly hopes! Poison-mixers are they, whether they know it or not. (Nietzsche 1976, article 3)

> Man is a rope, tied between beast and overman—a rope over an abyss. A dangerous across, a dangerous on-the-way, a dangerous looking back, a dangerous shuddering and stopping. What is great in man is that he is a bridge and not an end: what can be loved in man is that he is an overture and a going under. (Nietzsche 1976, article 4)

> One still works, for work is a form of entertainment. But one is careful lest the entertainment be too harrowing. One no longer becomes poor or rich: both require too much exertion. Who still wants to rule? Who obey? Both require too much exertion. No shepherd and one herd! Everybody wants the same, everybody is the same: whoever feels different goes voluntarily into a madhouse. (Nietzsche 1976, article 5)

> Behind your thoughts and feelings, my brother, there stands a mighty ruler, an unknown sage—whose name is self. In your body he dwells; he is your body.

There is more reason in your body than in your best wisdom. And who knows
why your body needs precisely your best wisdom. (Nietzsche 1976, On The
Afterworldly)

This collection is a journey of human power, e.g., overcoming the power of
others, overcoming the tension of the animal within and the intellectual without,
overcoming the need to demonstrate power over others, overcoming the oneself
by the true self, and, ultimately, overcoming power.

Will to Power

To overcome whatever one regards that is needed to be overcome requires a
focused strength of purpose, a purposeful will to drive process, and sustain and
develop it, once obtained. It is the will that alters things, people, and the self,
and the act of willing brings together an assortment of feelings, e.g., the "feeling
of the state to be left, the feeling of the state to be reached, the feeling of this
leaving and reaching itself, the feeling of the duration of the process, feeling of
the muscles" (Nietzsche 2003, 38(8), 36). However, feeling the ways of one's
will is not an easy task to accomplish along the willed journey, since the origin to
destination is fraught with sensations, emotions, and reactions, i.e., attitudes that
produce a fluid, volatile mixture that roller-coasts one's will, as one constantly
thinks the process. For example, "in every act of will, a thought commands";
however, "the will is not only a complex of feeling and thinking, but above all
also an affect: that affect of command" (Nietzsche 2003, 38(8), 36).

   In this way, it is will translated into command that actualizes the potential
of will. For example, this form of willpower has its seeds in one's thinking
of an initial idea that can direct others toward desired ends, and "feeling"
one's way through the performance. However, the willed performance does
not necessarily have to involve others, as it may be a solitary experience. On
the other hand, if others are involved, this does not necessarily indicate that
they have been considered in one's willed act, e.g., considered in terms of
moral harm. The reason for this is that the act may be so single-minded that
the fortitude of the consideration crushes any objection or resistance—i.e.,
the thinking and feeling aspects—when willing is limited to one's egotistical
aspiration. What is being suggested is that thinking and feeling, when willing, are not constants within the one person since one's thinking and feeling
journey "will" depend on the type of will required within particular situations

and decisions. To clarify, will is contextual, will is pliable, and so the wills of all individuals will be pliable and, hence, not consistent in intensity with other people's wills.

One may ask, why is will present in an individual's character? Without will one would be stationary in life, even drifting backward from one's beginning. For instance, "each step on earth, even the smallest, was in the past a struggle that was won with spiritual and physical torment" (Nietzsche [1887] 1996, III, 9). So, with no will, one would have trouble existing, but also have no trouble in exiting life since having no defense against life's torments. In other words, the will is required to power one's life, and in a sense the will to power is simply being alive; i.e., "there is nothing on earth which can have any value, if it have not a modicum of power...granted, of course, that life itself is the Will to Power" (Nietzsche 2016, 51). Therefore, the act of being alive is the starting point of the will to power, and being alive provides the power to will. Hence, from the commencement of life, the will to power is in constant alertness to initially survive the person it is within, which in turn allows it to survive, and then once established, thrive the person to whatever level that person can judge to, beyond consciousness; e.g.,

> you shall become who you are (Nietzsche [1882–1887] 1974, GS, 270)...your judgement has a pre-history in your instincts, likes, dislikes, experiences and lack of experiences, indeed, that you take this or that judgement for the voice of conscience...may be due to the fact that you have never thought much about yourself and have simply accepted blindly that what you had been told ever since your childhood was right. (Nietzsche [1882–1887] 1974, GS, 335)

Along these lines, the "right" will of others must be taken into account when the will of the self is active, as the self's thinking and feeling capacities can suffer limitations due to what is thought and felt may be because of the will activities of the said others and their accompanying thinking and feeling.

Forcing the active will to power is not a question of force, since force does not power one's will; rather, one's will powers force. To illustrate, Nietzsche offers the following:

> The victorious concept "force," by means of which our physicists have created God and the world, still needs to be completed: an inner will must be ascribed to it, which I designate as "will to power" (VP II 309/WP619). The will to power alone is the one that wills, it does not let itself be delegated or alienated to another subject, even to force (VP I 204, II 54). (Deleuze 2006, 49)

In this fashion, will to power involves "an insatiable craving to manifest power, or to employ, exercise power, as a creative drive" (Nietzsche 2003, 36(31), 26), and this willful craving, for it to be successful, must "out crave" other competing wills to power. For example, "the weaker pushes its way to the stronger... conversely, the stronger repulses the weaker, it doesn't want to perish this way... the will to power in every combination of forces—resisting what's stronger, attacking what's weaker" (Nietzsche 2003, 36(21), 25). From this, the weaker force obeys within a relation (Deleuze 2006, 51). Essentially, "force is what can, will to power is what wills" (Deleuze 2006, 50).

It is possible to have more than one will to power within the same person, a numbered set of wills, each championing their cause from the diversity of thinking and feeling one retains, being a human. These will be dependent on the lived evolving time-space context, circumstance, environment, moral inclination, nihilist tendency, instinct, one's good and evil, one's Zarathustra—one of one's will, and will overpowering of another by one's will (at least temporally). The temporality may be just of the moment or extending onward to moments of whatever time duration is required to realize the will of that moment(s) and perhaps often revisited to sustain and enhance it. Fundamentally, one's central will to power capacity drives its subset wills, within their own "mini" will, to power one's drive for life. For instance,

> for us to become aware that we are suffering from the vehemence of a drive presupposes the existence of another equally vehement or even more vehement drive, and that a struggle is in prospect in which our intellect is going to have to take sides. (Nietzsche [1881] 1982, 11, 109)

Thus, our intellect or thinking and feeling processes taking sides with one mini will to power over another, at least maybe only for the short term, then another takes a turn, but all always driven by one's centered will. In this manner, Nietzsche considers that "life itself to be an instinct for growth, for endurance, for the accumulation of force, for power: when there is no will to power, there is decline" (Nietzsche [1888] 1968, AC, 6).

CHAPTER 11

The Art of War or the Art of Power

The expression of power within whatever scale of operational space one practices it can be thought of as a performance of war, in which war can be thought of as two antagonists opposing each other on a field of battle. The consequences of this encounter create conflict, combative tendencies, confrontation, competition, a campaigning attitude, and the resulting crusade involving victory or defeat or an unsubstantiated outcome. Considering that war, in its "traditional" sense, views the two antagonists as one nation-state(s) against another nation-state(s), or one principality against another, or civil war which splits a nation-state, or colonialism versus the targeted precolonials—i.e., all examples being essentially one group, e.g., militaristic in character, fighting another group—this traditional view does not go far enough in expressing the spatiality of war and attendant spatiality of power. What is implied by this is that in one's everyday "ordinary" existence, one can be thought to be at war with the living environment one exists within, which creates a sense of inevitable survival and engagement with life and to struggle for a piece of power by expressing one's power. Even though the capacity of such an expression of power may be small or insignificant to the scale achieved by country-sized conflicts, similar tactics can be applied to achieve a degree of individual victory in the power game. So, if one wishes to practice the art of power and be successful at doing so in terms of accumulating power, studying the art of war may be advisable.

The context for the art of war content is drawn from Sun Tzu's "The Art of War." The origins of this text came from China roughly 2,600 years ago, in which thirteen directives on how to "do" war were offered as guidance to be success-ful at it, hence keeping one's power intact and consolidating it. Therefore, the chapter will look at these thirteen guiding principles in turn of how to be power-efficient, and since this is the last chapter of the book, before the Conclusion, it is appropriate to complete the powered themed chapters with a consideration of how to do power. "Doing" so demonstrates that power is indeed an art form, which takes practice to perform well, but a practice that is well grounded in preparation within an ongoing preparatory nature. Also, that the act of power is the act of life and everyone does it, be that of unequal dispositions since power is a competition. Thus, the power performance is of who we as humans are, or wish to be, both as instigators of power and its recipients.

However, the aims of the power performance are different for everyone. For example, one individual may wish to rule over all others, while some are content with protecting what they have as best they can and perhaps acquiring a bit more to be comfortable in life, and others may be obliged to fight for some power, simply to survive. Nonetheless, whatever one's "station" in life, one "arts" to power. However, the purposeful intentional irony for those who prepare efficiently for war utilizing "The Art of War" is to maintain the peace, and this irony can be extended to the art of power. For example, peace can be thought of as others not threatening one's power capacity, as they know it to be resolute and prepared for conflict, so not to be unwisely trifled with. Within the thirteen directives or principles, when appropriate, Shakespearian war context quotes will be added to the narrative. These additions will add depth of insight to how the war/power process and performance are a calculated complexity of interactions with others and the interaction with the conscious of oneself. Thus, showing that power play and life itself are mentally demanding and disturbing.

(Note: Shakespeare quotes are sourced from Shakespeare (1990) *The Complete Works*, so to avoid repetition of this citation, quotes will acknowledge their respective play).

Laying Plans

"The art of war is of vital importance to the state. It is a matter of life and death, a road either to safety or to ruin. Hence under no circumstances can it be neglected" (Tzu 1983, 9). Like so, the risk of neglecting one's power potential is also of vital importance, as doing so can significantly affect one's life chances and may lead to decline in the ability and opportunity to accomplish things. The art of war is ruled by five perpetual components, which are the Moral Law; Heaven; Earth; the Commander; and Method and Discipline. First,

> Moral Law causes the people to be in complete accord with their ruler, so that they will follow him regardless of their lives, undismayed by any danger;

Heaven signifies night and day, cold and heat, times and seasons; Earth comprises distances, great and small, danger and security, open ground and narrow passes, the chances of life and death; The Commander stands for the virtues of wisdom, sincerity, benevolence, courage, and strictness; Method and Discipline is the marshalling of the army in its proper subdivisions, the gradation of rank among the officers, the maintenance of roads by which supplies may reach the army, and the control of military expenditure. (Tzu 1983, 9–10)

These five elements are metaphors of how one can live a life of quality, quality in terms of possessing strength of character, resolve, and not straying from the "rightful" path to succeed. Staying rightful is following one's moral compass and being in complete accord with one's choices, assisted by an acute awareness of one's "Heavenly" environment, i.e., one's physical living background and what it is doing at any time. Also, adopting a cautious approach through one's life pathway, as it is fraught with danger and risk when one aims for great and small targets of accomplishment through inclusive (open ground) and exclusive (narrow passes) places and spaces. Therefore, retaining control and dominion of oneself when traveling through life by utilizing and staying true to the five virtues of the Commander, so one can indeed live a virtuous existence. This existence is aided by choosing one's selected method and maintaining discipline to sustain that method—i.e., marshaling one's character traits for these to reach their potential in one's own diverse life spaces (home, work, and play), helped by knowing one's place in society (various gradations of rank) and keeping open one's "supply lines" (maintenance of roads) of uninhibited energy to achieve potential but also being aware of one's limitations (control of expenditure).

Practicing these five elements can draw out one's power, a power of one's well-being and of feeling comfortable and at peace with oneself but also possessing an awareness of availing oneself of "any circumstances over and beyond the ordinary rules (five elements) and modifying plans accordingly (since) all warfare is based on deception" (Tzu 1983, 11). This deception of one's competition also involves being honest with oneself. In other words, not deceiving oneself as being what one is not, which would be a fatal flaw in one's aimed-for power acquisition as one must know oneself to be an effective deceiver; i.e., "False face must hide what the false heart doth know" (Act I, Scene VII, Macbeth).

On Waging War

> Never forget: When your weapons are dulled, your ardour dampened, your strength exhausted, and your treasure spent, other chieftains will spring up to take advantage of your extremity. Then no man, however wise, will be able to avert the consequences that must ensue. (Tzu 1983, 13)

One's power can be of a temporary nature depending on how it is exercised, so care must be taken to ensure it is sustainable and can last over the course of one's lifetime. For instance, power enjoys a finite capacity to be effective, regardless of its size, so must not be overused and abused. Even though one may argue that if someone or an organization or an army has immense resources to practice power, and their "finite" power capacity can retain resistance to being dulled, dampened, exhausted, and spent, they may be as vulnerable to being taken advantage of as the individual player who possesses much less power. This is because their particular powered space may retain a significant number of weaknesses as well as strengths due to its immense size; i.e., "All that glisters is not gold" (Act II, Scene VII, The Merchant of Venice), which implies that what is perceived on the surface of a powered entity (individuals included) and the ensuing performance may be just an act or surface facade, but actually concealing a power vacuum beneath. Thus, relating to the art of deception.

Given that one's powered capacity is finite, time is literally of the essence because

> only one who knows the disastrous effects of a long war can realise the supreme importance of rapidity in bringing it to a close, (also) the value of time—that is, being a little ahead of your opponent—has counted for more than either numerical superiority or the nicest calculations with regard to commissariat. (Tzu 1983, 13)

(Commissariat, within Tzu's milieu, is a department for the supply of food and equipment.) Thus, one's "store" of substances and materiality, ready to supply one's power capacity, may not be as advantageous as it sounds in practice, as compared to creating opportunities out in the "field of life" in terms of antici-patory advancement of a situation ahead of the competition. For instance, the delay in getting one's powered supplies "battle ready" can be offset by acquiring extra power capacity that would have gone to someone else, if not for a speedy act. In addition, the extra power can be utilized to gather in fresh substances and materiality; therefore, "a wise general makes a point of foraging on the enemy"

(Tzu 1983, 14). Hence, a wise power player sorties into the powered fields of their competitors to see what can be assimilated, and doing so makes the former stronger and the latter weaker, and not doing so leads to nothing ventured, nothing gained, as "Nothing can come of nothing" (Act I, Scene I, King Lear). Thus, acquiring power needs an active pursuit.

The Sheathed Sword

Alternatively, there are other methodologies that can be implemented to achieve power that appear to minimize the active component. For example,

> the skilful leader subdues the enemy's troops without any fighting; he captures their cities without lying siege to them; he overthrows their kingdom without lengthy operations in the field. With his forces intact he disputes the mastery of the empire, and thus, without losing a man, his triumph is complete. This is the method of attacking by stratagem of using the sheathed sword. (Tzu 1983, 16)

The strategy utilized here is one of fighting without risking one's fighting materiality, so retaining one's implied potency of purpose. This purposeful potency makes it clear to the opposition that the threat of one's power potency is such that it should be taken seriously, and if actually challenged, there is a great risk of being defeated by it. Accordingly, it is the retracted and shrouded "sword," that potential of unleashed power, which can win over or subdue the opposition as its quality is made known to them, enhanced by deception, e.g., "let not light see my deep and dark desires" (Act I Scene IV, Macbeth), which may be enough to achieve one's aims without harming oneself or the opposition. Thus, one can acquire the "undamaged goods' of another's power while not compromising one's own power "goods." Hence, "breaking the enemy's resistance without fighting" (Tzu 1983, 15), since the enemy experiences a continuous anxiety of being physically punished; e.g., "From toe to crown he'll fill our skins with pinches, Make us strange stuff" (Act IV, Scene I, The Tempest), and "I shall be pinched to death" (Act V, Scene I, The Tempest).

There are five main ingredients for victory and, consequently, that person will win

- Who knows when to fight and when not to fight
- Who knows how to handle both superior and inferior forces
- Whose army is animated by the same spirit throughout all its ranks

- Who, prepared himself, waits to take the enemy unprepared
- Who has military capacity and is not interfered with by the sovereign.

(Tzu 1983, 17–18)

Therefore, the self should be calculating when deciding whether to encounter or not to encounter the competition, possess a fair measure of appraisal of where one stands within the social hierarchy and the subsequent resultant varieties of how to treat others, retain fighting spirit in all situations, practice to create the necessary mental toughness to play the power game, and have the potential to acquire and possess power assisted by the noninvolvement of another who could take charge. This last one is important since many individuals, if not the majority in society, are not able to express or pursue power in a meaningful manner as another is in charge of them. The "another" can be an individual, an organization, a field (see Bourdieu), or the society itself. This circumstance, of course, is the crux of the matter of how power works in terms of its unequal distribution in society, since the result limits the power capacity of many as the eyes of authority are watching, perhaps unseen, while doing so, i.e., during Prospero's ocularcentric regime, where the sovereign's unrevealed scrutiny expects that the spirit should be "subject to no sight but thine and mine, invisible to every eyeball else" (Act I, Scene II, The Tempest); e.g., the spirit may equate to the specter of concealed surveillance.

Tactics

To be a successful powerbroker, one must have strategies in place designed for that to be so. These constructed maneuvers should be mentally rehearsed for all possible scenarios that may befall the tactics carried out in practice; hence, be flexible in nature, as neglecting this planned preparation of tactical application will leave one vulnerable to defend one's position in society and, simultaneously, leave one with an inability to challenge anyone else. Alternatively,

> the general who is skilled in defence hides in the most secret recesses of the earth; he who is skilled in attack flashed forth from the topmost heights of heaven. Thus, on the one hand, we have ability to protect ourselves; on the other, to gain a victory that is complete. (Tzu 1983, 19)

Occasionally, it is also advantageous to "hide" oneself when attacking, since if the competition is unable to perceive an attack and the identity of the instigator of the said attack, it becomes problematic to defend against such an action. There-fore, "To be or not to be, that is the question" (Act III, Scene I, Hamlet), or to be seen or not to be seen doing power, that is the question depending on the conflict context. Also, after the act has been completed, the instigator is protected due to their anonymous status and, hence, revenge and retaliation may not eventuate or indeed be possible, and additionally no one else will be aware of one's increase in power, which when kept hidden is also protected since no one else will yearn for it.

Keeping one's powered hand close to one's chest is advisable, since its helps with negating the possibility of making mistakes; i.e., "making no mistakes is what establishes the certainty of victory, for it means conquering an enemy that is already defeated" (Tzu 1983, 20). Also, this "a prior" defeat would have been constructed and contrived by the tactics implemented. However, it still befalls to the enemy to create unintended openings, perhaps due to one's tactics and perhaps not, that allows for a possibility of victory. Essentially, one can be sure of oneself given time and practice, but never 100 percent sure of the enemy. For instance,

> to secure ourselves against defeat lies in our own hands, but the opportunity of defeating the enemy is provided by the enemy himself. Hence the saying: One may know how to conquer without being able to do it. (Tzu 1983, 19)

Energy

Energy is the material and immaterial substance that supplies the fuel for power. Material, within this context, can be thought of as food and drink and the pos-sessions one has gathered over the course of life, i.e., property (residential and commercial), land, money, and other people. The immaterial is the energy that derives from ideas, drive, ambition, acquired experiences, and (hopefully) an increasing capacity for wise courses of subsequent decision-making and action. The immaterial energy can produce material outcomes, which in turn may create fresh scenarios for the immaterial self to work on to produce further materiality and immateriality. Furthermore, energy is potential and kinetic or an actuality, when it is demonstrated in practice. This is because it becomes a fact, a reality, and a certainty that can be perceived and reacted to. Hence, energy becomes power, and power equates to energy; i.e., one is of the other.

Knowing when to use energy, e.g., when to use power, is a vital decision-making process of timing and quantity of energy utilized when implementing power. Indeed, perhaps the quality of energy utilized is more important than its quantity, as for instance "the quality of decision is like the well-timed swoop of a falcon that enables it to strike and destroy its victim. 'Therefore the good fighter will be terrible in his onset, and prompt in his decision'" (Tzu 1983, 22), but both quality and quantity of energy still need to be involved as an amalgamated product for the decision to have substance, since "energy may be likened to the bending of a crossbow; decision, to the releasing of the trigger" (Tzu 1983, 22). In other words, the energy of power "loaded up" by the drawing of the metaphoric crossbow, quivering and vibrating in its insistence to be released as an intense bolt of power, awaiting the decisive trigger moment.

This energetic decisive "trigger moment" can result in a purposely direct or indirect encounter with one's competition, when defending one's powered position or attacking one's competition power capacity. To illustrate,

> to ensure that your whole host may withstand the brunt of the enemy's attack and remain unshaken, use maneuvers direct and indirect. In all fighting, the direct method may be used for joining battle, but indirect methods will be needed in order to secure victory. (Tzu 1983, 21)

"Your whole host" can be thought of as the holistic self in the context of the individual; i.e., the whole of the self is utilized to practice power effectively (a combined effort of the self, by the self), and to achieve success in one's power, the circumnavigated pathway is the subtle power of choice. Hence, when actualizing this "combined circled" powered space, while utilizing energy,

> his fighting men (or the fighting components within oneself) become, as it were, like rolling logs or stones. For it is the nature of a log or stone to remain motionless on level ground, and to move when on a slope; if four-cornered, to come to a standstill, but if round-shaped, to go rolling down. Thus the energy developed by good fighting men is as the momentum of a round stone rolled down a mountain thousands of feet in height. (Tzu 1983, 24)

Weak Points and Strong Points

> That the impact of your army may be like a grindstone dashed against an egg, use the science of weak points and strong. (Tzu 1983, 25)

The weak and strong points' performance is intimately bound up with the direct and indirect fighting methods. In this manner, possessing knowledge of one's opposition's weak and strong points allows one to exploit that knowledge, and eventually if enough of the weak points have been assailed, the strong points will be undermined and subsequently become weak points themselves. This process of exploitation is augmented by retaining intimate knowledge of one's own weak and strong points, so one can calculate to optimum efficiency offensive and defensive courses of action, or indeed at times inaction. Speaking of "at times," an example of one's strong and weak points when compared to the powerful ravages of time is illustrated thus: "Golden lads and girls all must, As chimney-sweepers, come to dust" (Act IV, Scene II, Cymbeline); i.e., one can begin life full of vigor, energy, will power, and strength, but as the autumn years catch up and one's personal immaterial and embodied power slowly fades, what remains is weakness and eventual nothingness of energy and power. Therefore, "And nothing is But what is not" (Act I, Scene III, Macbeth), signifying what is not nothing is something, e.g., has potential for energy, but nothing in and of itself is "nothing. "

To perceive what is strong and what is weak when assessing one's opponent, one's perceptible capacities should become liquefied, i.e., flexible and retain the ability to adapt and mold oneself to the playing fields of power. Along these lines,

> military tactics are like unto water; for water in its natural course runs away from high places and hastens downward. So in war, the way is to avoid what is strong and to strike at what is weak. Water shapes its course according to the nature of the ground over which it flows; the soldier works out his victory in relation to the foe whom he is facing. Therefore, just as water retains no constant shape, so in warfare there are no constant conditions. (Tzu 1983, 29)

In this manner, the "grindstone" of the self can leave one's other with "egg on their face!"

Maneuvering

One's maneuvering or one's movement is the mental and embodied demonstration of one's intentions, and the movement may be of kinetic disposition or of potential stillness. Each of these has its purpose to "outmaneuver" one's advisory or adversaries by placing him, her, or them at a disadvantage in terms of spatial environment, times of low fighting spirit, deception of apparent weakness, i.e., a vision "which, looked on as it is, is" indeed "naught but shadows/Of what it is not" (Act II, Scene II, Richard II), and being the first to a strategic location or simply not being around to fight. How one maneuvers within the game of power, and indeed if one does actually move and hence avoids becoming a passive recipient of others' maneuvers, will influence to an extent, success. This is, of course, tempered by what challenges and obstacles are placed in one's way by those one is in the "dance of movement" with. The process of tempering works simultaneously in two ways—the first is of moderating or mitigating one's movement, and, second, of hardening or toughening one's movements. The former because the advisory's movement is strong and shrewd, and the latter precisely because of the strong and shrewd environment faced, thus having to become annealed. To illustrate, with "tactical manoeuvring, there is nothing more difficult. The difficulty consists in turning the devious into the direct, and misfortune into gain" (Tzu 1983, 30).

Key maneuvering points that must be adhered to when powering oneself are as follows:

- Manoeuvring with an army, i.e., the holistic self, is advantageous; but with an undisciplined multitude, i.e., being of a self-conflicting disposition, most dangerous. (Tzu 1983, 31)
- We cannot enter into alliances until we are acquainted with the designs of our neighbours
- Not fit to lead on the march unless we are familiar with the face of the country
- We shall be unable to turn natural advantages to account unless we make use of local guides
- In war, practice dissimulation and you will succeed
- Move only if there is a real advantage to be gained
- Let your rapidity be that of the wind
- Your compactness that of the forest
- When you move, fall like a thunderbolt
- Let your plans be dark and impenetrable as night
- Ponder and deliberate before you make a move
- He will conquer who has learned the artifice of deviation. (Tzu 1983, 32)

Thus, creating power from movement or maneuverability is a dark, dangerous, and uncertain business. For instance, there are many facets that must come together, and not least is the timing of these facets as becoming one product at the optimum moment of tactical advantage, to allow one's power to be actualized. Essentially, power is always a work in progress, but one of flexible progress when facing the peaks and troughs of momentum (or lack of momentum) that characterize power struggles with others; e.g., "It is a military axiom not to advance uphill against the enemy, nor to oppose him when he comes downhill" (Tzu 1983, 34).

Variation of Tactics

To be tactful can deflect head-on encounters and softly parry the offensive intention, which may be far more preferential and less damaging than meeting direct force with direct force. For instance, the deflective movement can neutralize the attack and simultaneously put oneself onto the offensive, as the antagonistic offensive momentum has been disrupted and is momentarily weakened. Furthermore, an appropriate variety of tactics can then exploit the revealed weakness, but one needs to be quick, i.e., the thunderbolt analogy. However, the exploitation can only happen if an in-depth appreciation of tactics is comprehended:

> The general who thoroughly understands the advantages that accompany variation of tactics knows how to handle his troops. The general who does not understand these may well be acquainted with the configuration of the country, yet he will not be able to turn his knowledge to practical account. (Tzu 1983, 38)

In other words, even though one may know how the powered space is organized and disorganized, this knowledge cannot be of advantage if the application of transforming the theory into practical acts is not so well known; i.e., "A horse! A horse! My kingdom for a horse!" (Act V, Scene IV, Richard III); e.g., the inability to access a horse is a metaphoric inability to access the available tactical variety, even though the powered environment is known, e.g., one's kingdom. Basically, "in the wise leader's plans, considerations of advantage and of disadvantage will be blended together" (Tzu 1983, 38).

Consequently, possessing an awareness of the art of war or the art of power is not enough, for one must absorb the teachings of the art. For instance, if one does so, then the art teaches us "to rely not on the likelihood of the enemy's not coming, but on our own readiness to receive him; not on the chance of his not attacking, but rather on the fact that we have made our position unassailable" (Tzu 1983, 39). Therefore, preparation to power is vital, and knowing what it is capable of can steady oneself from its onslaught, hence reducing the resultant affects. For example, one's own faults should be recognized as part of this preparation, such as recklessness (leading to destruction), cowardice (leading to capture), delicacy of honor (an insensitivity to shame), a hasty temper (vulnerability to insults), and over-solicitude (leading to prolonged suffering in defeat and extension of the war) (Tzu 1983). Accordingly, one must know of tactical variation to be tactful when dealing with power.

The Army on the March

When the decision to implement power is taken, care must also be taken to nurture it to a peak level of effectiveness as possible. This is because power is on the march and engaging with other powers on their marches, with the result being an uncertain situation. Like so, preparation for this uncertainty and ways and means to produce certainty from it demonstrate that the individual wielding the power retains an effective possession of competency. To illustrate, that individual can read the space of battle, both its physical environment and the maneuverability of the opposition, with the aim of maximizing the best strategic positions and actions to exploit weaknesses and avoid strong points. For instance, "He who exercises no forethought but makes light of his opponents is sure to be captured by them" (Tzu 1983, 41), and

> all armies prefer high ground to low, and sunny places to dark, low ground is not only damp and unhealthy, but also disadvantageous for fighting. If you are careful of your men, and camp on hard ground, your army will be free from disease of every kind, and this will spell victory. (Tzu 1983, 43)

Therefore, when traveling along with one's power plays, carefully watch your adversary(s) to ascertain their power movements and counter movements, and counter these, but also select the best conditions to implement power. Doing so will free oneself of "diseased" movements that could significantly compromise success and perhaps cause failure and the loss of what power one initially retained. Consequently, "Now is the winter of our discontent, Made glorious summer by this sun of York" (Act I, Scene I, Richard III), suggesting that Richard was mentally vexed within his cold and damp state of mind, e.g., ill, but became better in the "sunny" dispositions of his actions.

So, one's state of mind receiving warmth from one's "sunny" actions will attract more warmth, i.e., positive movements toward and of success which breeds success. Although to reemphasize, one must always have awareness of the adversary to protect the gained success, since the warmth has potential to quickly become cold and unhealthy. Accordingly, having awareness is knowing that when the enemy is close at hand and remains quiet, he is relying on the natural strength of his position. When he keeps aloof and tries to provoke a battle, he is anxious for the other side to advance. If his place of encampment is easy of access, he is tendering a bait. (Tzu 1983, 44)

So, along these lines be cautious of when to engage with the enemy and when not to, i.e., beware of traps!, since "Humble words and increased preparations are signs that the enemy is about to advance" (Tzu 1983, 44), and, alternatively, "when envoys are sent with compliments in their mouths, it is a sign that the enemy wishes for a truce" (Tzu 1983, 48). Thus, when on the march, be flexible with one's power implementation.

Terrain

Knowing the topography that one's power operates within allows for the power to flow as uninhibitedly as possible, since this allowance will be tested by the terrain's characteristics of limitations and enhancements. For example, one should favor the enhancements offered and only encounter limitations when conditions are favorable for achieving the gains offered in such locations; otherwise, avoid them. There are six types of powered "grounded" terrain, which can also be disempowering if one is not cautious and does not retain enough experience to utilize the terrain as an ally. The six grounds are as follows:

- Accessible (ground freely traversed by both sides)
- Entangling (ground that can be abandoned but is hard to reoccupy)
- Temporizing (when the position is such that neither side will gain by making the first move, i.e., deadlock)
- Narrow passes (if you can occupy them first, let them be strongly garrisoned and await the advent of the enemy. Should the enemy forestall you in occupying a pass, do not go after him if the pass is fully garrisoned, but only if it is weakly garrisoned)
- Precipitous heights (if you precede your adversary, occupy the raised and sunny spots, and there wait for him to come up)
- Positions at a great distance from the enemy (if the strength of the two armies is equal, it is not easy to provoke a battle, and fighting will be to your disadvantage).

(Tzu 1983, 50–52)

These grounds are metaphoric positions that oneself can face when one's power is in states of potentiality and actuality, and depending on when a particular ground or grounds are favorable or not, the power moves back and forth between the two states. In this fashion, the self must decide which state to be in, but would still be influenced by the offered "groundwork"; e.g., "Men at some time are masters of their fates: The fault, dear Brutus, is not in our stars, But in ourselves, that we are underlings" (Act I, scene II, Julius Caesar).

Therefore, the terrain of oneself, i.e., how one conducts oneself during one's power movement and stillness, is just as important as the terrain one moves within, since "Uneasy lies the head that wears a crown" (Act III, Scene I, Henry IV, Part 2), and if this conduct is lacking, defeat will follow. Again, six terrains/ grounds are offered to illustrate one's terrain, e.g., neglect to estimate the enemy's strength, want of authority, defective training, unjustifiable anger, nonobservance of discipline, and failure to use picked men (Tzu 1983, 53), and these must be carefully considered and acted on. Essentially, these six qualities will test if the self has the capacity to be a strong and effective leader, which equates to being fair but resolute, of a sound and balanced nature, and maximizing one's power to meet situational demands, i.e., select the right "men/women" (one's that possess appropriate qualities of character) for the right task when empowering oneself.

The Nine Situations

A situation is a state of affairs, i.e., the circumstances and conditions one may find themselves in when doing the work of power, and one's awareness of these possible and foreseen situations will assist with avoiding or embracing them. However, if avoidance is not feasible, then possessing contingencies to extricate oneself from the undesired setting as quickly as possible without losing too much of oneself, i.e., limiting the damage to one's power capacity, is advantageous. The art of war acknowledges that nine situations, and as with the terrain considerations, are associated with the ground one finds oneself moving on and through:

- Dispersive (when a chieftain is fighting in his own territory, there is a risk of dispersion, since the soldiers, being near to their homes and anxious to see their wives and children, are likely to seize the opportunity afforded by a battle and scatter in every direction)

- Facile (when having penetrated into hostile territory, but to no great distance)
- Contentious (ground that is of great advantage to either side)
- Open (ground on which each side has liberty of movement)
- Intersecting Highways (ground that forms the key to three contiguous states, so that he who occupies it first has most of the empire at his command)
- Serious (when an army has penetrated into the heart of a hostile country, leaving a number of fortified cities in its rear)
- Difficult (all country that is hard to traverse)
- Hemmed in (ground that is reached through narrow gorges, and from which we can only retire by tortuous paths, so that a small number of the enemy would suffice to crush a large body of our men)
- Desperate (ground on which we can only be saved from destruction by fighting without delay).

(Tzu 1983, 56–58)

These nine are the spaces of encounter and conflict one must enter when doing power. Perhaps not all of them will be experienced when doing a particular "power trip," but as the course of one's power journey proceeds through life, all may eventually be dealt with to the best of one's ability (through experience and battle-hardening) and current (of that moment) level of power resources to draw on. Although, it may be that as familiarity increases of encountering one or more of the nine situations, and as one develops more power retention, they become easier to deal with. For instance, during some moments there will be setbacks that can be learned from, so one is stronger of mind and presence. However, some setbacks can deal a fateful blow that one struggles to recover from—such is the nature of the power game; i.e., "Come what come may, Time and the hour runs through the roughest day" (Act I, Scene III, Macbeth).

Attack by Fire

To ignite by fire and ensuring that the "wind" is blowing in the desired direction, i.e., toward one adversary, can be a blatant and brutal act and a direct assault devoid of the subtleties of deceptive warfare. Still, there are deceptive elements to it, as fire can cause panic, confusion, and fear, and through experiencing these, it becomes easier to deceive. For instance, the adversary is too busy reacting to the inferno enveloping them than thinking why, when, where, and how the fire was ignited in the first place. The metaphoric "wind" depicts favorable conditions that have come together at an opportune moment to release one's fiery attack. Even so, the wind's character must be carefully considered since fire can be indiscriminate and turn back on its "owner" with unfortunate results, as one's own fingers risk being burned; e.g., "Bloody instructions which, being taught, return To plague th'inventor" (Act 1, Scene 7, Macbeth).

There are five ways of attacking with fire; burn soldiers in their camp, burn stores, burn baggage trains, burn arsenals and magazines, and hurl dropping fire among the enemy (Tzu 1983). Essentially, weaken the adversary's materiality, level of resistance, and cause disruption and, hence, unbalance their countenance. Once the fire has begun, it will evolve into several potential developments one should be prepared for:

> When fire breaks out inside the enemy's camp, respond at once with an attack from without. If there is an outbreak of fire, but the enemy's soldiers remain quiet, bide your time and do not attack. When the force of the flames has reached its height, follow it up with an attack, if that is practicable; if not, stay where you are. If it is possible to make an assault with fire from without, do not wait for it to break out within, but deliver your attack at a favourable moment. (Tzu 1983, 85)

Fundamentally, fire is a fickle friend that may not guarantee hoped-for results because how the enemy reacts to its presence is key to whatever opportunities for exploitation present themselves, even at the zenith of its power. Thus, to use or not to use one's fire as part of one's power arsenal against an adversary(s) should be a cautious act, but once a fire is lit it can be difficult to extinguish, e.g.:

> Though well we may not pass upon his life
> Without the form of justice, yet our power
> Shall do a curtsy to our wrath, which men
> May blame but not control.
> (Act III, Scene VII, King Lear)

The Use of Spies

Having eyes and ears within the space of the enemy allows for access to their planning, state of mind, strength of purpose, and weaknesses and strengths, i.e., essentially the quality and quantity of their power. Knowing these intimate details will allow for opportune moments to enter this space to strike a decisive blow, assuming that opportune moments become feasible. However, an efficient spy network may be of such potency that it creates these valuable moments of enemy vulnerability. Thus, when this moment of decisiveness is reached, the covert movements become overt, with the revealed visibility of purpose and action detected too late for the enemy to respond to with effective countermoves. A successful spy network consists of five classes:

- Local spies (employing the services of the inhabitants of a district, i.e., enemy's space)
- Internal spies (making use of officials of the enemy)
- Converted spies (getting hold of the enemy's spies and using them for our own purposes)
- Doomed spies (doing certain things openly for purposes of deception, and allowing our own spies to know of them and, when betrayed, report them to the enemy)
- Surviving spies (those who bring back news from the enemy's camp. This is the ordinary class of spies, who should form a regular part of the army).

(Tzu 1983, 78–80)

It is within this shadowy world that power plays can be at their most powerful, and at their most cost-efficient, for it is inadvisable for the oneself to risk implementing and committing the bulk of their power to an action without ascertaining the lie of the land, i.e., the land of their enemy. Consequently, playing in the shadowy world only uses up a small proportion of one's power, when probing the enemy's power, but can reap immense dividends in terms of gaining power and limiting the damage inflicted on the self. It is in the shadows that deception can thrive and be "stage-managed":

All the world's a stage,
And all the men and women merely players:
They have their exits and their entrances;
And one man in his time plays many parts
(Act II, Scene VII, As You Like It)

Considering the many of these "many parts," it is the "spy" within all of humankind that greases the wheel of power plays that allows these many parts to perform. For instance, everyone, whether aware of doing so or not, actively engages with their surroundings to see what is out there and makes judgment calls accordingly. So, to activate oneself as a spy or getting others to spy for oneself is vital in the art of power, since "spies are the most important element in war, because upon them depends an army's ability to move" (Tzu 1983, 82), e.g., also the self's ability to move.

Power Is an Art Form

To do power and gain power one must be artful, and this cunning craftiness is achieved by following the thirteen principles. Additionally, it should be appreciated that even though the "Art of War" was written as a treatise of how a leader can marshal the resources available for his army to win, these same principles can be extended to the oneself, as wise counsel in how they can be a potential to actual and effective power player in society. Hence, one must access "wise" to be artful; i.e., "Lord, what fools these mortals be!" (Act III, Scene II, A Midsummer Night's Dream). As power is everywhere, and oneself is included in that "everywhere," so the one has no option but to be a part of that place and space. However, the paradox of being part of the art of power, and subsequently as part of the art of war, is the inevitability of the power eventually devouring oneself, i.e.

> Then everything includes itself in power,
> Power into will, will into appetite;
> And appetite, an universal wolf,
> So doubly seconded with will and power,
> Must make perforce an universal prey,
> And last eat up himself!
> (Act 1, Scene III, Troilus and Cressida)

Final Thoughts and Considerations

Whatever and however life is defined as in terms of its essence, its existence equates exactly to how power is and how power does. For instance, one is of the other since life is power and power is life, of which this statement incorporates the whole of existence, i.e., "whole" in the sense of the absolute limit of human perspective of how the space outside and inside of each person is appreciated and comprehended. However, the human perspective retains its own inbuilt limitations of how things really are, and the "whole" of creation would not be the true whole. This relates to the reality-making environment of ontological creation trying to emulate the epistemological that has been created or has simply been there all along within its timeless capacity, e.g., the myth making of the former overlying its representational abstract immateriality/materiality on top of the concrete immaterial/materiality of the latter.

There is a paradox at work here in this process of trying to get what life is really about, since the tools that are adopted by humans for that purpose are of a tangible disposition engaging with an insubstantial and unquantifiable presence. In other words, humans utilize their physical senses to probe what is around them and to situate themselves as a going concern of what is discovered based on their cultural heritage and attendant human characteristics, of which the latter would be common to all cultures. Essentially, the results of the probing need to be of a palpable, solid, and noticeable appreciation for it to have value, of which "value" varies for every individual, culture, and society. However, problems and challenges arise when attempting to access something that is insubstantial, for it cannot be quantified in an absolute sense, and what best can be hoped for is partial inroads toward its essence.

Hence, a mismatch is at work of something that is not of the other attempting to reach the other, but always falling short. Thus, always producing a gap in the knowledge of fully knowing the other. Since possessing gaps is an uncomfortable and unsatisfactory state to find oneself in, as humans, this is filled up or compensated by further abstractive processes adding to the abstractive picture already formed and adapted to. An irony here is that an insubstantial process is applied from a perceived substantial platform (from humans) to produce an apparent substantial conclusion of an unsubstantiated object or thing (namely, the life that surrounds humans). Insubstantial is purposefully offered as the epistemological presence of actuality (of life as it really is), because since it is of such a complex, timeless, limitless, and seen but also unseen formation, that its substantiality is perhaps only the surface covering of the veiled insubstantiality constantly in states of movement and stillness beneath. Additionally, these movements and stillness could be of an imperceptible difference as one blends into the other, fundamentally making them the same, i.e., a oneness of motion of nonmotion and vice versa.

The point of all this speculation of how life may be or is from human perspectives, and the actual that is life, is that this relationship between the human and their surroundings (from the immediate locality up to what is thought to be the universe, and beyond!) enjoys intimate relations with power and how some of that power can be siphoned off for human usage. Indeed, it may be that within the "mismatched" space of the ontological human endeavor reaching for the epistemological unreachable is where the creativity of abstract imagination is at its most fertile to do this thing called power. For instance, there is a survival and competitive instinct that fires up human thought processes to a heightened state of awareness that is only limited by the capacities brought from other humans who may counter or object to the thinking presented, the limitations from the environment, and limitations from life itself. However, the limit of limitations is not fixed, as is not the limits or limitations of power, for both can expand or contract depending on the performance, process, or contextual situation occurring.

The nature of power within the mismatch space that attempts to bridge the ontological to the epistemological is supplemented by the ontological space of humans and the epistemological space, e.g., everything else that is extra to humans. Actually, there is a paradox here because humans, whether they appreciate it or not, also belong in that epistemological space. The implication here is that they are part of the overall life process and, hence, also part of its attendant power process, as well as producing their own interpretive power plays, i.e., a double power play which, depending on the context, may complement or conflict with each other determined by what the epistemological space is favoring during particular moments. The "favoring" is highlighted, since it would be the epistemological of life that is of an enduring quality, and, subsequently, its power would be of an endless potential and actuality, and it would be the human-powered capacity that is vulnerable to its ageless plan, since the human input to power is ultimately of a momentarily existence; e.g., life as itself is forever, and those who frequent life are of an interim measure.

However, within this temporarily lived space, the human ontological performance to produce power plays is of diverse roles. From this, it may be that since humans are only alive or have only been alive for a very short time as compared to the Earth's existence, which of itself has not been around that long as compared to the time-space of the universe, and if human lifetime is broken down into generational time, humans may experience a sense of desperation to make their mark on life in the allotted time they can do so, for they only have moments to play with and utilize what diversity they can grasp. This diversity is rich in its array of perspectives, applications, attitudes, performances, and practices to engage with life and the power potential and actual that is on offer. Essentially, much of this diversity of how humans' power has been contemplated or mediated over through the chaptered faces of the book to offer a powered perspective that recognizes not only its complexity but also its singularity of purpose.

This complex singular consideration began with Aristotle and the attendant beliefs and values of his time and space that reflected the society then lived in. In a sense, this society can be thought of as a blueprint of how modern societies function, particularly in relation to the city-state that was the main focus of that time. For it is the city then and now that takes center stage as a powered concentrated place and is where many "seats of power" reside, especially if the city is the capital of a sovereign nation-state. It is significant that the philosophy of Aristotle's time drew inspiration from the Earth and Universe and their combined five elements that provide the essence of the material and immaterial of life and what makes life possible. It is recognized here that the creative forces that make life, and are life, allow humans a sense of being and allow them to be "human beings" and, thus, have an opportunity to play at power; i.e., human power is a power of proxy, and humans play an "understudy" role to the main actor, namely life itself.

"Significant" in that it was recognized that the real power or main power concentration was not from humans, but from the vast surroundings extending out to the "Heavens," of which humans tap into. Be that on a small scale of production in the immense scale and scheme of universal things. However, even if the production is "small" or "immense," and wherever a sentient being finds itself along the Ladder of Life and "chained" to its sense of being, this sense will produce potential and actual power possibilities. These considered and realized power plays will not only be influenced and driven by individualistic memory, ethics, happiness, and virtue but also tempered or enhanced by the group mentality the individual lives within. Essentially, the Law of Nature of which all beings are limited by. It is from this that the Rule of Law is constructed, but since human nature is saturated by ambiguity, law can be thought of as leaning toward the particular rather than universal consensus, even though it governs as if it is a universal space of power production and discouraged production; i.e., this "mis-production" is generated by human self-centeredness and specific versions of the "balance" of power and how this is maintained by the propaganda and propagation of deliberately designed educational text.

A classical and contemporary deliberately designed educational text is the Bible. It is perceived as a conduit of power, as it carries the Word of God in human form and language that humans may be able to understand. Since God (or an equivalent or similar living being) is believed by many humans over the last 2,000 years to be the Creator of Life and is Life, then it follows that this figurehead of life is where the essential power of existence resides; i.e., all power represented in an all-in-one (literally) transcendental entity. Since humans are self-centered (they cannot be otherwise, even if they are "serving" someone else or an organization, as they still get out of it what is possible for themselves), even *The Power* of God can be manipulated to the advantage of human power, by association. For instance, using religious doctrine to run society, for it takes a brave individual to question the "(right)eousness" of how and why power performances are as they are if sanctioned by the Word of God. Hence, power is secure by the advocacy of the theocentric world view and purposely causes the anthropocentric positionality and particular hierarchy anthropocentric positions to take center stage in the human societal power project.

However, since the Word of God and God retain the majority power, it follows that there is plenty of it to go around, if that is God's wish. Therefore, God's dunamis is available for any and everyone who wish to access it, and not just available for the "elite" powerbrokers to manipulate its symbolism. The dunamis is the potential and actual power that God possesses, which in turn God allows humans to tap into, in their quest to actualize their potential power source. As this powered energy originates from God who presumably has no need to favor one human being over another in terms of how much power an individual receives, it would be up to the individual to seek their own pathway to "goodness" by using the bit of power given to them, with "goodness" being of a personal preference of what is implied by it. Consequently, the formation of "goodness" would be an emotional, immaterial, and material expression of how one practices one's power. Essentially, the (G)ood of God or God's *Power* grants all other living beings a chance to do power within their "mini" scales of production and the freedom to imagine whatever form power may or can take, i.e., an openness and ongoing-ness of interpretation from one's Genesis to one's constant moments of now.

The backdrop of divine power and perhaps as some part of God's embodiment in a form that is perceived as "real" by sentient beings, humans included, is nature. A nature or the Nature as infinite color as it saturates the senses with its constant presence of emitted energy. For instance, the light energy that originates from the Sun in the Earth's local solar system supplies the Earth and all living beings on it, both flora and fauna, with the vast majority of energy required to survive, e.g., the main or dominant power source that allows things to be and not to be. Therefore, the nature of the Sun formulating and sustaining the nature on the Earth, or perhaps the nature near and on the surface of the Earth, that in turn allows humans and other surface and ocean dwellers to exist. It may well be that all known beings on Earth originally owe their existence to the properties of the Sun's light rays striking the Earth, i.e., the primary and constant source that powers up Earth's potential power into assorted actualized forms. For instance, at the macro level of the Earth itself, and the micro levels of its sentient beings.

The power of nature is constant within its varying inconsistency. What is implied here is that nature's processes appear to meander away from its "true" course through time and its space of production. Its space of production is emphasized, as nature can be regarded as power exemplified in physical form that all sentient beings must operate within. For instance, they can only perform to the limits of their potential and actual imagination of what it provides for them. From this, "unnatural" material, in terms of the human context of creativity, is constructed from the "natural" materiality of nature. Examples include various metals, tarmac, plastics, combustible engines, electricity, and singular and numerous combinations of chemicals from the human-invented Periodic Table of the Elements and what uses these may offer. The point is these "alien" materials "beyond" the naturalness of what nature is still draw on the storehouse of nature's resources and, therefore, still belong to nature's self. Thus, nature retains the store of material power, to power those who live within its space and dictates whether all these sentient beings will live or die. This is because if nature is suddenly not there, its life-giving properties are also not there, so no being can sustain themselves outside of its space.

Also, if the properties of nature change beyond what its present sentient beings have adapted to survive in, it will simply continue, and they will not. So, who really has the power? This is where nature's appearance of meandering away from its "true" course is significant. For instance, various human perspectives cause this "off course" meandering by instilling on nature human values and attendant behavioral patterns. Nature, or at least its surface places that humans can touch, becomes socialized. So, humans borrow power from nature or wrestle power from nature to build the social of nature resulting in a distancing and togetherness of the two, depending on human attitudes toward what they think nature is, i.e., from a political and economic struggle to an ecological political struggle. Regardless of where one is situated between these struggles, nature is a plurality of power perspective. However, since nature is the only constant and consequently is unlimited in its potential and actuality, e.g., the universe and beyond is also incorporated into the definition of Nature as well as the localized Earth's nature, it would possess a self-perpetuating course of being within its unlimited time and space, in which the meandering tendencies of human intervention would only be an almost unnoticed blip/inconsistency to its forever true course of performance.

Nature is of the grand scale, whereas humans are not, although many humans would not perceive themselves as just a "blip" along the never-ending course of existence. This is because humans possess limited spaces of knowing and are too preoccupied competing with each other to obtain bits of the finite resources of power that nature and the social of nature tease them with. This competition, in the context of Foucault, is of a personal level, i.e., person to person, nation to nation, the rulers to the ruled, and enjoys its own sense of grand scale since the thoughts and subsequent action processes take center stage in the person's life. As life is a competition of power, there will be those who win power and those who lose power, which includes all competitive spatial scales between humans, e.g., from the individual up to the global nations or one corporation against another. Thus, power polemics eventuate, which creates the parameters that humans perform with and from. This "poles apart" performance creates inclusion and exclusion, core and periphery, and those with a voice and those without. However, in the endless game of power, the poles apart also creates a genealogical attitude, implying an attitude of resistance that accompanies the power journey. The resistance injects errors into the dominant powered spaces and practices to undermine them and perhaps to eventually replace them as the new dominating power.

Errors are a matter of perspective, since those committing them would not see them as so, whereas errors for the dominant force(s) in society would be viewed as "outside" their purposefully set agenda of power. This agenda of power is archived as a statement or statements of "this is how life is" embedded into the societal materiality on show and used by the mass of population and also embedded into the nonmateriality of people, i.e., dictating what their conscious-ness and unconsciousness thought patterns are, or should be. One's episteme or thought frameworks are molded, so becoming an objective subject. The object is the norm and values set by the powers that be where one is subjected to it, and one's subjectivity to be is corrupted by that process. That said, all in society are corrupted by power at whatever level one may be at within the parameters of one's social system due to the nature of the power game, desired for or not, resulting in a disempowering of the self, including one's body, and of disempowered resistance. It would be through the capacity of one's knowledge of power that greatly influences how well one plays this competitive game and the resultant heightened awareness of the disempowering process. As Foucault says, power is a complex strategical situation.

The complexity of power can be manipulated by the speaking voice. A voice that "simplifies" or conceals the complex(ion) so that the language used essen-tially only allows restricted access to the inner workings of that spoken powered context. Thus, retaining the power through an articulation of language and, hence, demonstrating an articulation of restricted power to those who can speak that language, allow themselves to speak it, and disallow others. As Bourdieu's "voice" suggests, this vocal process is of an emblematic disposition. An interac-tive communication process representing the primacy of relations, and it is the relations between people, countries, and corporations that are the preeminent component of how power flows back and forth among them. Intimate to this symbolic disposition is violence or the veiled threat of violence, of which the latter can be more efficient and sustaining of wished-for and realized behavior patterns of submission, than the former. This is because those who are not "priv-ileged" to be a member of the knowledgeable speakers may not be aware of the submissiveness they are being subjected to and so will not react to it with any great force of resistance or will not show any force at all. Whereas direct physical violence does not leave much room for ambiguity, thus vulnerable to retaliation.

Power has its spatial centers of operation, with its tentacles reaching out beyond these concentrated power bases. These provinces of power or fields can be thought of as metaphoric medieval castles symbolizing the presence of their version of power and influencing the immediacy of the surrounding space. However, in the modern form, there would be many "castles" in the one settlement place, duplicated across the major to minor settlements belonging in the one nation-state (which is the powered Field all these other "minor" fields necessarily work with, or for), with the numbers and size of castles varying from numerous to a few, respectively. Examples of contemporary castles are political centers, economic/ commercial centers, health, law, and education. Each would possess biased field power to advantage their individual agendas. The "advantage" comes in the form of capitalization, i.e., a field's economic, cultural, symbolic, and social capacity. These will be enhanced, or not, depending on the amount of political capital they generate or can be generated for them and on the manipulated flexibility of professional access to capital. The levels of doxa (common belief and opinion) of those in the same society environment will greatly influence how much power these fields have, including both of individuals within and without the field centers of operation, and how this power is inhabited through one's habitus.

Fields are made up of those who use them (or are used by them), those who work in them (again, used by them, but perhaps also being used) or own them, and the field structure itself. The structure would have a legacy of evolvement and adaptation to sustain and maximize its power base generated from previous users, which produces its own life processes, and consequently the users or agents must adapt to that powered landscape production. As a result, as Giddens points out, there are tensions and compromises between structure and agents that need working through. Essentially, power plays between oneself and one's living environment of the macro national structure, and of the micro numerous structures encountered on a daily basis and over the course of one's life. Thus, an agent's life is saturated under the blanket of structuration, of social practices prearranged through time and space. Subsequently the agent is constantly dueling with life's encountered social structures and existing as one part of the duality of structure and agent, with evidently structure(s) being the other intimate partner in the powered process. Right from life's start, and probably before when being subjected to health checks while in the womb, the agent is born into social structure and has to deal with its powered limits of what the self can perform to, and to be, and hopefully from this be as uninhibitedly alive as possible.

However, when playing the powered game of structuration as limiting, with its accompanying space of a rigorously stationary appearance, both within material and immaterial contexts, the power potential inside of an agent can transcend these limitations. At least in the form of one's unlimited imagination and sense of spirit that can abstractly formulate endless capacities of power and accompanying possibilities of what may be. The potential inside oneself is important in the duality of structure and agent performance, for not only would have structure been invented and constructed by the imagination inside but also the imagination has power to transform structure. This is not to say that structure will be "imagined" away, since agents require structure to have something tangible to make sense of life. For instance, at the present time, agents cannot perform in a structureless environment, although perhaps the post-structural imagery is a half-way house to the structureless form of no form. In the consistent ongoing tensions and compromises between agency and structure, the agent (unless they have capitulated to the social structure) strives for ontological security sustainability. Namely, an establishment of one's self-identity and be comfortable with that to a point, and beyond, that one feels empowered, regardless of what the structure is doing.

Even though one can achieve a sense of comfortableness of who and what one believes one is, this is often outweighed or outmaneuvered by the actions of other agents and the stoic structural emplacement of, and in, society. One finds oneself subjected to the convenient labeling of others, so they feel comfortable with their generated-identity labeling of their others to conform to their ways of thinking and doing. The power of this labeling and its resultant hierarchical structural make up produces, via Marx's ways of thinking and doing, class. Class purports to make distinctive layers of "like-minded" agents who "conform" to similar behavioral patterns dictated by their analogous economic capacity (whether that be a lot, limited, or lack of). Whether a rigid class system is still in place in societies or agents regard themselves as autonomous (as much as one can be when living in a societal structure), it is generally one's economic capacity that dictates if one controls structure(s) or is controlled by it. In Marx's duality of class of fundamentally the ruling and the ruled, the ruling economic interests and the connected social relations (or nonsocial relations to their "outsiders") produced, and in turn produce, societal insulation. Essentially, a powered layer or boundary to the rest of the society agents "below," who assist with the "insulation. "

Consequently, these "below" agents are not insulated from the rigors and demands that "privileged" agents and their owned structures impose from "above," within this economic state of affairs, since this powered performance creates alienation. An alienation from the running of the structure and an alienation from oneself, as one becomes subsumed within the structural stampede, and to a point of awareness that perhaps one does not realize this has happened to them; i.e., the act of alienation becomes normalized, and one becomes commodified or as an actual commodity. This purposely powered performance to achieve alienation begins from primitive accumulation of capital that sets in motion ownership over power and the means to sustain and develop it; i.e., power is claimed and accumulated, and those who did not claim, miss out, and become subjects and subjected to it. As the primitive accumulation matures, that momentum and the generated internal power accumulated become self-sustaining, thus producing and reproducing the capitalistic relationship itself. This ensures that the timing and spacing of capital is constraining, i.e., constraining in the sense that both the rulers and the ruled cannot break out of this accumulation, even if they wished to.

Nevertheless, it is not entirely an absolute that individuals cannot break out or away from the accumulated primitiveness, but to do so would take immense strength of character and self-awareness of what society does to the individual. All would have this capacity, but only a few would have the wherewithal to seriously consider it and how to go about it. Gramsci spoke of ideological consciousness as a way to be aware of one's social living environment, which would give the oneself tools to excavate through the surface veneer of society and reveal the bare bones of power beneath. However, to do this successfully one must have a stable platform to work from to provide the strength and sense of purpose required to see the thing through. This stable platform can only originate from the self and knowing oneself at the level of one's bare bones of personal power, i.e., having a deep, or one's possible deepest, intimate encounter of the true self. From this intense experience, ideals emerge that may be perceived as idyllic, supreme, and the model to follow to reach the epitome, e.g., the quint(essence) and personification of the embodied self in practice. Thus, a self-actualization or at least a self-potentialization of the self as an optimal powered being.

Reaching one's self-potential, but perhaps not one's self-actual, is deliberately mentioned as there are other ideals at work. These ideals can temper one's ideals, unless some of these follow similar outlooks where there may be possibilities to work together to create a conglomeration of individual powers into a mass movement of joining and adjoining individual powers. Also, ideals face the challenge of being historically determined, since man and woman are historically determined, so another weapon to deal with when trying to break out of the social structure, change it, or become it. Humans are a work in progress, a process always in motion, in movement, and, consequently, will rarely find or achieve a sense of stability or peace (this may be peace of mind, i.e., peace of the oneself, and peace with others) because humans and their ideals are based around power, and since power is a progression process the only peace it finds is knowing that it is being used for its purpose of existence, i.e., to do power, regardless of how its power (or itself, being Power) is applied. In essence, Power is its own hegemony, of which human hegemony within its idealizing process taps into.

As power and humans doing power are processes and not fixed and nonmovable, it is problematic to situate with any great certainty the location of power. However, knowing how to quantify power—i.e., locating it, and actually if quantifying it makes doing power more powerful—would be relevant in improving its efficiency of performance, and if one could conclusively do so, one may be more powerful than power itself. However, perhaps all that one can hope for, in terms of the extents or limits of one's power location, is to get gradually closer to the essence of power by one's givenness that keeps giving to one's phenomenological capacity throughout life, adopting Husserl labeling. From this, when looking for the "trueness" of power, its situatedness, one can try the methodology of the powered horizon. This cannot look directly at the core or essential being of power itself, but what it can do is gather modes of appearance of this power in performance, to surround it by an horizon of co-givenness. The plurality of these modes can produce an informed appreciation of what power is, if not actually reaching or viewing into the heart of power.

The closest that one can get to the heart of power is perhaps through phantasie, i.e., trying to ascertain the reality of power through filters of irreality, since the perpetual filters of reality can only achieve so much in terms of comprehension. Doing phantasie can "open up" what is being focused on at a much deeper level of interpretation, and perhaps the deepest perspectival level that humans are capable of, which may equate to the epistemological Holy Grail of how reality really is, and revealing the unmediated power of power. Yet, to reach the epistemological pureness of power, bracketing out the cluttering of human sociocultural chatter is necessary to create a pure interaction. This is "seen" as a phenomenological epoché, of phenomena initially made available to consciousness. The initial act is important, as it arrives before other stimuli can cloud the experience. From this, one can use this clarity of experience and knowledge to make sense of the how of the world and of the how of power and, as a result, alter the fundamentals of how life and power is, or if that is not possible, the actual knowing of power fundamentals will subtly change the relationship of humans to power, which itself is a powerful step to take, i.e., one's essence or spirit being intimate with pure power, and given the time to do so.

Having time is essential to do things, experience things, and to do power. When doing power or wielding power, one may feel a sense of constraint of how much power to use and the way it is used. This constraint can be perceived as adapting structure and agency considerations to the question of morality, as these two will still have input into how one's morals should be. In the human collective, what is morally appropriate is questionable as Nietzsche indicates, since it is not a one-size-fits-all way of thinking, although those in charge often try to make it that way. Thus, from this, one's morals can demonstrate abuses of power, and the moral recognition from others that this powered act is of an abusive nature of which their own morals tell them so is itself an act of cultural education in how their particular society operates and moralizes. As morals in practice can be "good" or "evil," or both at the same time, as it all depends on

how one appreciates morals, they can drive the power process along unpredictable pathways —at least unpredictable to those receiving consequences who
may be of a different moral standing, but not unpredictable to those producing
the consequences, since the latter's performance is informed by their morals.

Attempts to place one's morals on another, as if this is the "correct" way to behave
and judge life's processes from, is a controlled and controlling performance. It is
effectively implemented if there is acceptance of this particular moral sense of being
and way(s) to be. However, this constructed moral framework can be undermined
if people question why these particular moral rules and guidelines to make society
functionable, not including the application of others, or having no morals at all.
As a result, one's "questioned" sense of feeling inhibited, marginalized, excluded,
or of not being counted as a member of society, can create a tendency to reject
morals and embrace nihilism. This is because nihilism champions limitlessness,
a freedom from attitude and the social boundaries that tie one inside a system of
someone else's construction, i.e., their ways and means of doing power. It is a way
of doing one's power and "doing over" the power of others and the social system
and willing oneself to truth. Nihilism is the instinctive truth of one's naturalness that
existed before sociocultural systems came into existence and before the primitive
accumulation of life's resources, including the human resource. Essentially, a will
to power the oneself within a nihilism form of moral attitude.

The numerous ways power is performed within the human context varies greatly
in terms of quantity and quality. In quantitative terms, the amount of power at
one's disposal, be that retained by the self or of an organization's resources, i.e.,
fields of power, may depend on one's inherited advantage. For example, what
standing or station in life one was born into, or if part of an organization, the
extent of its influence and standing in society that has already been established
through historical connectivity, i.e., one operated from positions of power already in-placed and in place. Retaining this already-established power quantity
is challenging, since the power game is also, but perhaps more so, for those who
wish to gain power quantity from positions of non-inheritance or disinheritance.
This is where the quality aspect comes into play. For instance, knowing how
to play the power game effectively, which implies an overall success rate that
creates and subsequently produces more advantages than disadvantages over the
course of one's life. Since being "successful" at power is individually subjective,
advantage and disadvantage would be of a personal perspective; i.e., one's quality
of performance and how that is measured can only be truly assessed by oneself.

That true measurement may be found within the center of the core of a person's
inner essence, or spirit, the place inside of everyone that is not contaminated

by sociocultural influences, but by one's natural instinctual influences, as if one had never been born into a human-constructed system of how to be. However, the paradox is that individuals are born into social systems and require the assistance of their most hidden essence, i.e., who they really are when stripped away of societal layers instilled on them, to function in the social space born into. It is this inner power in everyone that allows movement in their living space, to encounter the inner power of others born within that same time and space, and competing for that powered quantity and quality. To compete well, one must know of the Art of War or the Art of Power. It is from this awareness, both from its knowledge base and experience base and allowing oneself to constantly learn from these, that accumulates the art to be artful when it comes to power. This "art" may not be the methodology advocated through Sun Tzu's way of powered art, although much of that "artwork" may be present in similar forms, but as long as the oneself creates one's powered working art, "power on"!

Powering up and Powering Down

When considering Power, one requires power to do so. This latter power may not be of the same consistency as the former, but it retains membership to the former. This association can be applied to all the face types of power flirted with in the book, all others beyond the book's scope, and all power of unknown awareness, because the aggregate of all these equates to Power. Power is everything, everywhere, and everyone (all living beings, not just the humankind), and consequently it can be thought of as the Life Force. The Force of Life and the Force of Death that drive all processes, material and immaterial, along their impermanence, as they are born, live for a time, and then die or change form from one state of matter to another. As Power is the only permanency that is, it can be recognized as time and space since these also are of eternity, which is an apt description. Apt in the sense that Power operates within seen and unseen ways of being; i.e., the seen is the space, and the unseen is the time. In other words, it becomes quickly apparent of how one moves in space is negotiated through limitations, so power is seen and felt at work. However, time is not so visible when quietly going about its constructive and erosive tendencies, as one's life force powers up and powers down and eventually powers out; e.g., time's subtleness and time's space is its power, and is Power. One needs to face up to that and try and not lose face, or too much of it, while doing so, since Power itself outlasts everything else in their end, as its end is endless.

REFERENCES

Adams, D. 2010. "Karl Marx & the State." http://www.marxisthumanistinitiative
.org/alternatives-to-capital/karl-marx-the-state.html.

Adams, W. 1996. *Future Nature: A Vision for Conservation*. London: Earthscan
Publications.

Adams, W., and J. Hutton. 2007. "People, Parks and Poverty: Political Ecology
and Biodiversity Conservation." *Conservation and Society* 5:147–183.

Aichele, G. 2008. "Canon as Intertext: Restraint or Liberation?" In *Reading
the Bible Intertextually*, edited by R. B. Hays, S. Alkier, and L. A. Huizenga,
139–156. Waco, TX: Baylor University Press.

Aitken, S., and G. Valentine. 2009. *Approaches to Human Geography*. London:
Sage Publications.

Akard, P. 2001. *Social & Political Elites: Encyclopedia of Sociology*. Vol 4,
2nd ed. New York: Macmillan.

Aldea, S. 2010. "Phantasie and Husserl's Phenomenological Inquiry." Presented
at the 41st Annual Meeting of the Husserl Circle. Hosted by The New School
for Social Research, Theresa Lang Center, New York:56–173.

Alter, R. 1981. *The Art of Biblical Narrative*. New York: Basic Books.

Althusser, L. 1965. *For Marx*. New York: Pantheon.

Archer, M. S. 1982. "Morphogenesis versus Structuration: On Combining
Structure and Action." *British Journal of Sociology* 33:455–483.

Archer, M. S. 1995. *Culture and Agency*. Cambridge: Cambridge University Press.

Arendt, H. 1969. *On Violence*. New York: Harcourt, Brace & World.

Aristotle. 1934a. *Nicomachean Ethics*. Book 1, Chapter 7, 1097a15–1098b8.
Aristotle in 23 vols, Vol. 19, translated by H. Rackham. Cambridge, MA: Harvard
University Press; London: William Heinemann.

Aristotle. 1934b. *Nicomachean Ethics*. Book 2, Chapter 6, 1107a8–1107a17. Aristotle in 23 vols, Vol. 19, translated by H. Rackham. Cambridge, MA: Harvard University Press; London: William Heinemann.

Aristotle. 1983. *Physics*. Books III and IV. Clarendon Aristotle Series. Translated by E. Hussey, (and Introduction and Notes). Oxford: Oxford University Press.

Aristotle. 1998. *The Politics*. Translated by C. D. C. Reeve. Indianapolis, IN: Hackett Publishing.

Aristotle. 2004. *The Poetics*. Translated by I. Bywater. Last update April 2004. http://www.authorama.com/book/the-poetics.html.

Aristotle. 2009. *Politics*. Translated by E. Barker. Oxford: Oxford University Press.

Aristotle. n.d. *Metaphysics*. Translated by W. D. Ross. *Internet Classics Archive*. http://classics.mit.edu/Aristotle/metaphysics.html.

Arnold, D. 1996. *The Problem of Nature: Environment, Culture and European Expansion*. Oxford: Blackwell.

Aschheim, S. 1997. "Nietzsche, Anti-Semitism and the Holocaust." In *Nietzsche and Jewish Culture*, edited by J. Golomb, 3–20. New York: Routledge.

Atkinson, W. 2007. "Anthony Giddens as Adversary of Class Analysis." *Sociology* 41 (3): 533–549.

Atkinson, W. 2010. "Phenomenological Additions to the Bourdieusian Toolbox: Two Problems for Bourdieu, Two Solutions from Schutz." *Sociological Theory* 28 (1): 1–19.

Atkyns, R. 1688. [cited in Sherwood, Y. (2008)] "The God of Abraham and Exceptional States, or The Early Modern Rise of the Whig/Liberal Bible." *Journal of the American Academy of Religion* 76 (2): 312–343.

Austin, J. L. 1962. *How to Do Things with Words*. Oxford: Clarendon Press.

Baber, Z. 1991. "Beyond the Structure/Agency Dualism: An Evaluation of Giddens' Theory of Structuration." *Sociological Inquiry* 61 (2): 219–230.

Bach, A., ed. 1999. *Women in the Hebrew Bible: A Reader*. New York: Routledge.

Baert, P. 1998. *Social Theory in the Twentieth Century*. New York: New York University Press.

Baldwin, T., and D. Bell. 1988. *Phenomenology, Solipsism and Egocentric Thought. Proceedings of the Aristotelian Society, Supplementary Volumes.* Vol. 62, 27–43, 45–60. Oxford. Oxford University Press.

Bakker, K. 2010. "The Limits of 'Neoliberal Natures': Debating Green Neoliberalism." *Progress in Human Geography* 34 (6): 715–735.

Bakunin, M. 2005. *Statism and Anarchy.* Cambridge: Cambridge University Press.

Barker, P. 1998. *Michel Foucault: An Introduction.* Edinburgh, UK: Edinburgh University Press.

Barnes, J., ed. 1995. "Life and Work." In *The Cambridge Companion to Aristotle*, 16. Cambridge: Cambridge University Press.

Bauder, H. 2008. "Citizenship as Capital: The Distinction of Migrant Labor." *Alternatives* 33:315–333.

Bearman, P. 1997. "Generalized Exchange." *American Journal of Sociology* 102:1383–1415.

Behind the Name 2023. "Aristotle."

https://www.behindthename.com/name/aristotle.

Bell, C. 1992. *Ritual Theory, Ritual Practice.* New York: Oxford University Press.

Benton, T. 1989. "Marxism and Natural Limits." *New Left Review* 178:51–86.

Benveniste, E. 1971. *Problems in General Linguistics.* Miami, FL: University of Miami Press.

Bernet, R., I. Kern, and E. Marbach. 1993. *An Introduction to Husserlian Phenomenology.* Evanston, IL: Northwestern University Press.

Best, S. 2001. *Introduction to Politics and Society.* London: Sage.

Bible Study Tools. 2020. "Dunamis." http://www.biblestudytools.com/lexicons/greek/nas/dunamis.html.

Bielo, J. S. 2009. *Words upon the Word: An Ethnography of Evangelical Group Bible Study.* New York: New York University Press.

Biersack, A. 2006. "Reimagining Political Ecology: Culture, Power, History and Nature." In *Reimaging Political Ecology*, edited by A. Biersack and J. B. Greenberg, 3043. Durham, UK: Duke University Press.

Biesecker, A., and S. Hofmeister. 2010. "Focus: (Re)productivity, Sustainable Relations Both between Society and Nature and between the Genders." *Ecological Economics* 69:1703–1711.

Blau, P. M. 1974. "Presidential Address: Parameters of Social Structure." *American Sociological Review* 39:615–635.

Blau, P. 1977. *Inequality and Heterogeneity*. New York: Free Press.

Bloch, David. 2007. *Aristotle on Memory and Recollection: Text, Translation, Interpretation, and Reception in Western Scholasticism*. Philosophia Antiqua: A Series of Studies on Ancient Philosophy, vol. 110. Leiden, Netherlands: Brill.

Blommaert, J. 1999. "The Debate Is Open." In *Language Ideological Debates*, edited by J. Blommaert, 1–38. Berlin: Mouton de Gruyter.

Bobbio, N. 1988. "Gramsci and the Concept of Civil Society." In *Civil Society and the State*, edited by John Keane. London: Verso, 73-99.

Boer, R. 2013. "Between the Goat's Arse and the Face of God: Deleuze and Guattari and Marx and the Bible." *Journal for the Study of the Old Testament* 37 (3): 295–318.

Booth, A. 2015. "Marx's Capital: Chapter 26–33—The Origins of Capitalism." https://www.socialist.net/marx-s-capital-chapters-26-33-the-origins-of-capitalism.htm.

Bossman, D. 2014. "Ideology as Power in Biblical Religion." *Biblical Theology Bulletin* 44 (2): 66.

Bouchard, D. F., ed. 1977. *Language, Counter-Memory, Practice: Selected Essays and Interviews by Michel Foucault*. Oxford: Blackwell.

Bourdieu, P. 1977. *Outline of a Theory of Practice*. Cambridge: Cambridge University Press.

Bourdieu, P. 1979. *Distinction: A Social Critique of the Judgement of Taste*. Translated by R. Nice. Cambridge, MA: Harvard University Press.

Bourdieu, P. 1984. *Distinction: A Social Critique of the Judgement of Taste*. Translated by R. Nice. Cambridge, MA: Harvard University Press.

Bourdieu, P. 1985. "The Social Space and the Genesis of Groups." *Theory and Society* 14 (6): 723–744.

Bourdieu, P. 1986a. "Forms of Capital." In *Sociology of Education: A Critical Reader*, edited by A. R. Sadovnik and R. W. Coughlan, 83–95. New York: Routledge.

Bourdieu, P. 1986b. "The Forms of Capital." In *Handbook of Theory and Research for the Sociology of Education*, edited by J. G. Richardson, 241–258 (Chapter 1:15–29). Westport, CT: Greenwood Press.

Bourdieu, P. 1987. "Bourdieu What Makes a Social Class? On the Theoretical and Practical Existence of Groups." *Berkeley Journal of Sociology* 32:1–17.

Bourdieu, P. 1989. "Social Space and Symbolic Power." *Sociological Theory* 7 (1): 14–25.

Bourdieu, P. 1990. *The Logic of Practice*. Cambridge: Polity Press.

Bourdieu, P. 1991. *Language and Symbolic Power*. Edited and Introduced by J. B. Thompson. Translated by G. Raymond and M. Adamson. Cambridge: Polity Press.

Bourdieu, P. 1993. *Sociology in Question*. London: SAGE.

Bourdieu, P. 2000. *Pascalian Meditations*. Cambridge, UK: Polity.

Bourdieu, P. 2002. *Distinction: A Social Critique of the Judgment of Taste*. Translated by R. Nice. Cambridge, MA: Harvard University Press.

Bourdieu, P., and J. C. Passeron. 1990. *Reproduction in Education, Society and Culture*. London: Sage.

Bourdieu, P., and L. Wacquant. 1992. *An Invitation to Reflexive Sociology*. Cambridge: Polity.

Bratton, J., M. Callinan, C. Forshaw, and P. Sawchuk. 2007. *Work and Organizational Behaviour*. London: Palgrave Macmillan.

Brewer, A. 1990. *A Guide to Marx's Capital*. Cambridge: Press Syndicate.

Brockington, D., R. Duffy, and J. Igoe. 2008. *Nature Unbound: Conservation, Capitalism and the Future of Protected Areas*. London: Earthscan.

Brooks, S., M. Spierenburg, L. Van Brakel, A. Kolk, and K. Lukhoz. 2011. "Creating a Commodified Wilderness: Tourism, Private Game Farming, and 'Third Nature' Landscapes in Kwazulu-Natal." *Tijdschrift voor Economische en Sociale Geografie* 102 (3): 260–274.

Brown, J., N. Mitchell, and M. Beresford, eds. 2005. *The Protected Landscape Approach Linking Nature, Culture and Community*. Gland, Switzerland: IUCN.

Bryant, C. G. A. 1992. "Sociology without Philosophy? The Case of Giddens's Structuration Theory." *Sociological Theory* 10:137–149.

Bryant, R., and S. Bailey. 1997. *Third World Political Ecology: An Introduction*. London: Routledge.

Bryant, R., and M. Goodman. 2004. "Consuming Narratives: The Political Ecology of 'Alternative' Consumption." *Transactions of the Institute of British Geographers* 29 (3): 344–366.

Bryant, C., and D. Jary, eds. 2011. *Giddens' Theory of Structuration: A Critical Appreciation*. New York: Routledge.

Buckel, S. J., and A. Fischer-Lescano. 2009. "Gramsci Reconsidered: Hegemony in Global Law: Foundation of the Leiden." *Journal of International Law* 22:437–454.

Burawoy, M. 2012. "The Roots of Domination: Beyond Bourdieu and Gramsci." *Sociology* 46 (2): 187–206.

Butterworths. 2010. *Concise Australian Legal Dictionary*. Chatswood, Australia: LexisNexis.

Campbell, L. 2008. "Local Conservation Practice and Global Discourse: A Political Ecology of Sea Turtle Conservation." *Annals of the Association of American Geographers* 97:313–334.

Carrier, J., and D. Miller. 1988. *Virtualism: A New Political Economy*. New York: Berg Publishers.

Carrier, J., and P. West. 2009. *Virtualism, Governance and Practice: Vision and Execution in Environmental Conservation*. Portland, NY: Berghahn Publishers.

Carruthers, Mary. 2007. *The Book of Memory: A Study of Memory in Medieval Culture*. New York: Cambridge University Press.

Casey, K. L. 2005. *Defining Political Capital: A Reconsideration of Bourdieu's Interconvertibility Theory*. St. Louis: University of Missouri.

Christophers, B. 2016. "Risking Value Theory in the Political Economy of Finance and Nature." *Progress in Human Geography* 42:330–349.

Clarke, G. 2013. "The Bible and the State Constantine and Speaking Scripture to Power." *St Mark's Review* 225 (3): 1–7.

Clines, D. J. A. 1995. *Interested Parties: The Ideology of Writers and Readers of the Hebrew Bible*. Sheffield, UK: Sheffield Academic Press.

Coates, P. 1998. *Nature: Western Attitudes since Ancient Times*. Cambridge: Polity Press.

Colletti, L. 1975. *Introduction to Karl Marx: Early Writings*. Translated by Rodney Livingstone and Gregor Benton. New York: Vintage.

Colon, G. A. T., and C. A. Hobbs. 2015. "The Intertwining of Culture and Nature: Franz Boas, John Dewey, and Deweyan Strands of American Anthropology." *Journal of the History of Ideas* 76 (1): 139–162.

Cronon, W. 1991. *Nature's Metropolis: Chicago and the Great West*. New York: W. W. Norton.

Crowell, S. 2010. "Praxis and Passivity: A Hidden Naturalist Assumption in Husserl's Transcendental Phenomenology." Presented at the 41st Annual Meeting of the Husserl Circle, Hosted by The New School for Social Research, Theresa Lang Center, New York City:47–62.

Crump, D. 2013. *Encountering Jesus, Encountering Scripture: Reading the Bible Critically in Faith*. Grand Rapids, MI: Eerdmans.

Cutler, A. C. 2005. "Gramsci, Law, and the Culture of Global Capitalism." *Critical Review of International Social and Political Philosophy* 8 (4): 527–542.

Dahrendorf, R. 1959. *Class and Class Conflict in Industrial Society*. Stanford, CA: Stanford University Press.

De Angelis, M. 1999. *Marx's Theory of Primitive Accumulation: A Suggested Reinterpretation*. London: University of East London.

https://scholar.google.com/citations?view_op=view_citation&hl=es&user=KtHMtJ4AAAAJ&citation_for_view=KtHMtJ4AAAAJ:qjMakFHDy7sC updated

De Haas, F., and J. Mansfeld, eds. 2004. Aristotle: On Generation and Corruption. Book 1 Symposium Aristotelicum. Oxford: Clarendon Press.

Deleuze, G. 2006. *Nietzsche and Philosophy*. Translated by H. Tomlinson. New York: Columbia University Press.

Deleuze, G., and F. Guattari. 1988. *A Thousand Plateaus: Capitalism and Schizophrenia*. Translated by B. Massumi. London: Athlone Press.

Demeritt, D. 1996. "Social Theory and the Reconstruction of Science and Geography." *Transactions of the Institute of British Geographers* 21:484–503.

Demirovic, A. 2001. "Hegemoniale Projekte und die Rolle der Intellektuellen." *Das Argument* 239:59–65.

Derrida, J. 1991. "Des Tours de Babel: Poststructuralism as Exegesis." *Semeia* 54:3–34.

Derrida, J. (2003) 2005. *Voyous: Deux essais sur la raison* [Rogues: Two Essays on Reason]. In French. Translated by Brault Pascale-Anne and Michael Naas. Stanford, CA: Stanford University Press; Paris: Galilée.

Dickens, P. 1996. *Reconstructing Nature: Alienation, Emancipation and the Division of Labour*. London: Routledge.

Douglas, M. 1968. "The Social Control of Cognition: Some Factors in Joke Perception." *Man* 3 (3): 361–376.

Dressler, W. H. 2011. "First to Third Nature: The Rise of Capitalist Conservation on Palawan Island, the Philippines." *Journal of Peasant Studies* 38 (3): 533–557.

Dreyfus, H. L., and P. Rabinow. 1982. *Michel Foucault: Beyond Structuralism and Hermeneutics*. Brighton, UK: Harvester Press.

Eagleton, T. 1990. *Ideology*. London: Verso.

Ebenstein, Alan, and William Ebenstein. 2002. *Introduction to Political Thinkers*. Belmont, CA. Wadsworth Group.

Egan, D. 2014. "Rethinking War of Maneuver/War of Position: Gramsci and the Military Metaphor." *Critical Sociology* 40 (4): 521–538.

Ekers, M., A. Loftus, and G. Mann. 2009. "Gramsci Lives!" *Geoforum* 40:287–291.

Encyclopædia Britannica. n.d. "Byzantine Empire." https://www.britannica .com/place/byzantine-empire.

Engels, F. 1882. "Socialism: Utopian and Scientific Converted to eBook by Andrew Lannan." https://www.marxists.org/archive/marx/works/download /Engels_Socialism_Utopian_and_Scientific.pdf http://www.marxists.org/archive /marx/works/1880/soc-utop/index.html.

Engels, F. (1893) 1968. "Letter to Franz Mehring, July 14, 1893." In *Marx and Engels Correspondence*. Translated by Donna Torr. New York: International Publishers.

Escobar, A. 1998. "Whose Knowledge, Whose Nature? Biodiversity, Conservation, and the Political Ecology of Social Movements." *Journal of Political Ecology* 5:53–82.

Femia, J. 1981. "An Historicist Critique of 'Revisionist' Methods for Studying the History of Ideas." *History and Theory* 20 (2): 113–134, 142.

Femia, J. 2002. "Civil Society and the Marxist Tradition." In *Civil Society: History and Possibilities*, edited by S. Kaviraj and S. Khilnani, 131–146. Delhi: Cambridge University Press.

Figlio, K. 1996. "Knowing, Loving and Hating Nature: A Psychoanalytic View.' In *Future Natural: Nature, Science, Culture*, edited by G. Robertson, M. Mash, L. Tickner, J. Bird, B. Curtis, and T. Putnam , 72–82. London: Routledge.

Fiorenza, F. S., and G. D. Kaufman. 2008. "God." In *Critical Terms for Religious Studies*, edited by Mark C. Taylor, Chap. 6, 136–140. Chicago: University of Chicago.

Fischer-Lescano, A. 2006. "Global Constitutional Struggles: Human Rights between Colère Publique and Colère Politique." In *International Prosecution of Human Rights Crimes*, edited by W. Kaleck, M. Ratner, T. Singelnstein, and P. Weiss, 13–29. Berlin: Springer.

Fisher, W. F., and T. Ponniah. 2003. *Another World Is Possible: Popular Alternatives to Globalization at the World Social Forum*. London: Zed.

Fitzsimmons, M. 1989. "The Matter of Nature." *Antipode* 21 (2): 106–120.

Fontana, B. 2000. "Logos and Kratos: Gramsci and the Ancients on Hegemony." *Journal of the History of Ideas* 61 (2): 305–326.

Fontana, B. 2002. "Gramsci on Politics and State." *Journal of Classical Sociology* 2 (2): 157–178.

Forbes, C. 1997. "Coffee, Mrs. Cowman, and the Devotional Force of Women Reading in the Desert." In *Lived Religion in America*, edited by David D. Hall, 116–132. Princeton, NJ: Princeton University Press.

Foucault, M. 1973. *The Order of Things: An Archaeology of the Human Sciences*. New York: Vintage Books.

Foucault, M. 1975. *The Birth of the Clinic: An Archaeology of Medical Perception*. New York: Vintage Books.

Foucault, M. 1977a. *Discipline and Punish: The Birth of the Prison*. London: Allen Lane-Penguin Press.

Foucault, M. 1977b. "Nietzsche, Genealogy, History." In *Language, Counter-Memory, Practice: Selected Essays and Interviews*, edited by D. F. Bouchard, 139–164. Ithaca, NY: Cornell University Press.

Foucault, M. 1977c. *The Archaeology of Knowledge*. London: Tavistock.

Foucault, M. 1978a. "Politics and the Study of Discourse." *Ideology and Consciousness* 3: 7–26.

Foucault, M. 1978b. *I, Pierre Rivière, Having Slaughtered My Mother, My Sister, and My Brother*. London: Peregrine Books.

Foucault, M. 1979a. *Discipline and Punish: The Birth of the Prison*. DP. New York: Vintage Books.

Foucault, M. 1979b. *Discipline and Punish*. Translated by A. Sheridan. Harmondsworth, UK: Penguin Books.

Foucault, M. 1979c. "On Governmentality." *Ideology and Consciousness* 6:5–22.

Foucault, M. 1979d. *The History of Sexuality*, vol. 1. London: Allen Lane-Penguin Press.

Foucault, M. 1980. *Power/Knowledge: Selected Interviews and Other Writings, 1972–1977*, edited by C. Gordon. trans by C. Gordon (chap 6 'Truth and Power' 109-133 and chap 7 'Power and Strategies' 134-145 & K Soper chap 5 'Two Lectures' 78-108. . New York: Pantheon Books.

Foucault, M. 1981. "Questions of Method." *Ideology and Consciousness* 8:3–14.

Foucault, M. 1984. *Histoire de la sexualité*, vol. 2, L'Usage des plaisirs, Editions. Paris: Gallimard.

Foucault, M. 1988. *Philosophy, Politics, Culture: Interviews and Other Writings of Michel Foucault*, edited by L. D. Kritzman, PPC. New York: Routledge. Chap 2 'Critical Theory/Intellectual History' 17- 46.

Foucault, M. 1997. *The Essential Works of Michel Foucault, Vol. 1: Ethics: Subjectivity and Truth*, edited by P. Rabinow, EW1. New York: The New Press. 'Polemics, Politics, and Problematizations' 111-120.

Foucault, M. 1998. *Aesthetics, Method, and Epistemology, the Essential Works of Michel Foucault 1954–1984*, vol. 2, edited by J. D. Faubion, EW2. London: Penguin. 'Nietzsche, Genealogy, History' 369-392.

Foucault, M. 2000. *Power, the Essential Works of Michel Foucault 1954–1984*, vol. 3, edited by J. D. Faubion, EW3. New York: The New Press. 'So Is It Important to Think?' 454-458.

Foucault, M., and R. Sennett. 1982. "Sexuality and Solitude." In *Humanities in Review*, vol. 1, edited by D. Rieff. London: Cambridge University Press.

Fowler, J. 1981. *Stages of Faith: The Psychology of Human Development and the Quest for Meaning*. New York: Harper Collins.

Franklin, A. 2014. "On Why We Dig the Beach: Tracing the Subjects and Objects of the Bucket and Spade for a Relational Materialist Theory of the Beach." *Tourist Studies* 14 (3): 261–285.

Friedman, R. E. 1987. *Who Wrote the Bible?* San Francisco: Harper & Row.

Fuchs, C. 2002. "Some Implications of Anthony Giddens' Works for a Theory of Social Self-Organization." *Emergence* 4 (3): 7–35.

Garfinkel, H. 1967. *Studies in Ethnomethodology*. Englewood Cliffs, NJ: Prentice Hall.

Garland, E. 2008. "The Elephant in the Room: Confronting the Colonial Character of Wildlife Conservation in Africa." *African Studies Review* 51 (3): 51–74.

Gaventa, J. 2003. *Power after Lukes: A Review of the Literature*. Brighton, UK: Institute of Development Studies.

Giddens, A. 1976. *New Rules of Sociological Method*. New York: Basic Books.

Giddens, A. 1979. *Central Problems in Social Theory*. London: Macmillan.

Giddens, A. 1981. *A Contemporary Critique of Historical Materialism*. Berkeley: University of California Press.

Giddens, A. (1973) 1981. *The Class Structure of the Advanced Societies*. 2nd ed. London: Hutchinson.

Giddens, A. (1981) 1995. *A Contemporary Critique of Historical Materialism*. Vol. 1. Power, Property and the State. 2nd ed. London: Palgrave Macmillan.

Giddens, A. 1982. *Profiles and Critiques in Social Theory*. Berkeley: University of California Press.

Giddens, A. 1984. *The Constitution of Society Outline of the Theory of Structuration*. Berkeley: University of California Press.

Giddens, A. 1985. *A Contemporary Critique of Historical Materialism*, Vol. 2. The Nation-State and Violence. Cambridge: Polity Press.

Giddens, A. 1987. *The Nation-State and Violence (A Contemporary Critique of Historical Materialism)*, vol. 2. Berkeley: University of California Press.

Giddens, A. 1989. *Sociology*. Cambridge: Polity Press.

Giddens, A. 1991. *Modernity and Self-Identity*. Cambridge: Polity Press.

Giddens, A. 1994a. "Living in a Post-Traditional Society." In *Reflexive Modernization: Politics, Tradition and Aesthetics in the Modern Order*, edited by U. Beck, A. Giddens, and S. Lash, 56–109. Cambridge: Polity Press.

Giddens, A. 1994b. *Beyond Left and Right*. Cambridge: Polity Press.

Giddens, A. 1994c. "Risk, Trust, Reflexivity." In *Reflexive Modernization: Politics, Tradition and Aesthetics in the Modern Order*, edited by U. Beck, A. Giddens, and S. Lash, 184–197. Cambridge: Polity Press.

Giddens, A. 1997. "Risk Society: The Context of British Politics." In *The Politics of Risk Society*, edited by J. Franklin, 23–34. Cambridge: Polity Press.

Giddens, A. 1998. *The Third Way*. Cambridge: Polity Press.

Giddens, A. 2002. *Runaway World: How Globalisation Is Reshaping Our Lives*. 2nd ed. London: Profile.

Glasius, M. 2012. "Gramsci for the Twenty-First Century: Dialectics and Translatability. Edited by Marlies Glasius." *International Studies Review* 14:666–686.

Goldthorpe, J. H. 2002. "Globalisation and Social Class." *West European Politics* 25 (3): 1–28.

Goodman, D. 2013. "Sacred Scriptures, Secular Interpretations: The Bible as an Anthology of Philosophy, Psychology, Literature, and Religion." *Religious Studies Review* 39 (4): 223–232.

Goodman, D., and M. Redclift. 1991. *Refashioning Nature*. London: Routledge.

Goodman, N. 1978. *Ways of Worldmaking*. Indianapolis, IN: Hackett Publishing.

Gottfried, H. 1994. "Learning the Score: The Duality of Control and Everyday Resistance in the Temporary-Help Service Industry." In *Resistance and Power in Organisations*, edited by J. M. Jermier, D. Knights, and W. Nord, 102–127. London: Routledge.

Gramsci, A. 1971. *Selections from the Prison Notebooks*. Translated by Quentin Hoare and Geoffrey Nowell-Smith. London: Lawrence and Wishart.

Gramsci, A. 1975. *Quaderni del carcere*, edited by Valentino Gerratana. Turin, Italy: Einaudi.

Gramsci, A. 1977. *Selections from the Political Writings 1910–1920*, edited by Quintin Hoare, translated by John Mathews. New York: International. [first published as "Socialismo e cultura." Il Grido del popolo [January 29, 1916], reproduced in Scritti giovanili 1914–1918 [Turin, Italy: Einaudi, 1975]).

Gramsci, A. 1991. *Gefängnishefte: Kritische Gesamtausgabe*. Edited by K. Bochmann and W. F. Haug. Hamburg, Germany: Argument.

Gramsci, A. 1995. *Further Selections from the Prison Notebooks*, edited and translated by D. Boothman. London: Lawrence and Wishart.

Gramsci, A. 1996. *Prison Notebooks*, vol. 2, edited and translated by J. A. Buttigieg. New York: Columbia University Press.

Gramsci, A. 2000. *The Gramsci Reader: Selected Writings 1916–1935*. Edited by David Forgacs. New York. New York University Press.

Greenstein, E. L. 2009. "A Pragmatic Pedagogy of Bible." *Journal of Jewish Education* 75:290–303.

Gregory, D., D. Johnston, G. Pratt, M. Watts, and S. Whatmore. 2009. *The Dictionary of Human Geography*. 5th ed. West Sussex, UK: Blackwell Publishing.

Grossman, H. 2007. "Marx, Classical Economics, and the Problem of Dynamics." *International Journal of Political Economy* 36 (2): 6–83.

Gutting, G. 2005. *Foucault: A Very Short Introduction*. Oxford: Oxford University Press.

Guzzini, S. 2006. "Applying Bourdieu's Framework of Power Analysis to IR: Opportunities and Limits." Presented at the 47th Annual Convention of the International Studies Association in Chicago, March 22–25, 2006. Researchgate. net. https://www.researchgate.net/publication/237830294_Applying_Bourdieu's _framework_of_power_analysis_to_IR_opportunities_and_limits

Hall, D. 1989. *Worlds of Wonder, Days of Judgment: Popular Religious Belief in Early New England*. New York: Knopf.

Hall, K., and C. Macken. 2009. *Legislation and Statutory Interpretation*. Chatswood, Australia: LexisNexis Butterworths.

Haralambos, M., and M. Holborn. 1991. *Sociology: Themes & Perspectives*. 3rd ed. London: Collins Educational.

Harvey, D. 1996. *Justice, Nature and the Geography of Difference*. Oxford: Blackwell.

Heidegger, M. 1962. *Being and Time*. Oxford: Blackwell.

Hens-Piazza, G. 2002. *The New Historicism*. Minneapolis, MN: Augsburg Fortress Press.

Higgins, V., J. Dibden, and C. Cocklin. 2012. "Market Instruments and the Neoliberalisation of Land Management in Rural Australia." *Geoforum* 43:377–386.

Holmes, D., K. Hughes, and R. Julian. 2007. *Australian Sociology: A Changing Society*. 2nd ed. Frenchs Forest, Australia: Pearson Education Australia.

Homans, George G. 1975. "What Do We Mean by Social Structure?" In *Approaches to the Study of Social Structure*, edited by Peter Blau, 53–65. London: Gollier-Macmillan.

Horkheimer, M., and T. Adorno. 1972. *Dialectic of Enlightenment*. New York: Seabury.

Hughes, D. M. 2005. "Third Nature: Making Space and Time in the Great Limpopo Conservation Area." *Cultural Anthropology* 20 (2): 157–184.

Husserl, E. (1900/1901) 2001. *Logical Investigations*. 2nd ed. 2 vols. Edited by Dermot Moran. London: Routledge.

Husserl, E. (1907) 1999. *The Idea of Phenomenology*. Translated by Lee Hardy. Dordrecht, Netherlands: Kluwer.

Husserl, E. (1913) 1982. *Ideas Pertaining to a Pure Phenomenology and to Phenomenological Philosophy*. Translated by F. Kersten. The Hague, Netherlands: Nijhoff.

Husserl, E. (1931) 1960. *Cartesian Meditations: An Introduction to Phenomenology*. Translated by D. Cairns. The Hague, Netherlands: Nijhoff.

Husserl, E. (1931) 2002. *Ideas: General Introduction to Pure Phenomenology*. Translated by W. R. Boyce Gibson. London: Routledge.

Husserl, E. 1935. "Philosophy and the Crisis of European Man." Lecture delivered by Edmund Husserl, Vienna, May 10, 1935 [The Vienna Lecture] .

Husserl, E. 1962. *Ideas: General Introduction to Pure Phenomenology*. Translated by W. R. Boyce Gibson. New York: Macmillan.

Husserl, E. 1964. *The Phenomenology of Internal Time-Consciousness*, edited by M. Heidegger. Translated by J. S. Churchill. Bloomington: Indiana University Press.

Husserl, E. 1970a. *The Crisis of the European Sciences and Transcendental Phenomenology*. Evanston, IL: Northwestern University Press.

Husserl, E. 1970b. *Logical Investigations*, 2 vols., translated by J. N. Findlay. New York: Routledge & Kegan Paul.

Husserl, E. 1973. *Experience and Judgement*. Translated by J. S. Churchill and K. Ameriks. Evanston, IL: Northwestern University Press.

Husserl, E. 1977. *Cartesian Meditations*. Translated by D. Cairns. The Hague, Netherlands: Martinus Nijhoff.

Husserl, E. 1980. *Phantasie, Bildbewusstsein, Erinnerung.* Husserliana, vol. 23, edited by E. Marbach. The Hague, Netherlands: Martinus Nijhoff.

Husserl, E. 1991. *On the Phenomenology of the Consciousness of Internal Time (1893–1917).* Translated by John B. Brough. Dordrecht, Netherlands: Kluwer.

Husserl, E. 1997. *The Amsterdam Lectures, in Psychological and Transcendental Phenomenology and the Confrontation with Heidegger (1927–1931),* edited and translated by Thomas Sheehan and R. E. Palmer. Dordrecht, Netherlands: Kluwer Academic Publishers.

Husserl, E. 1999. *The Essential Husserl: Basic Writings in Transcendental Phenomenology,* edited by Donn Welton. Bloomington: Indiana University Press.

Husserl, E. 2001. *Analyses Concerning Passive and Active Synthesis. Lectures on Transcendental Logic.* Translated by Anthony Steinbock. London: Kluwer Academic Publishers.

Husserl, E. 2002. *The Shorter Logical Investigations.* Translated by J. N. Findlay. London: Routledge.

Husserl, E. 2005. *Phantasy, Image Consciousness, and Memory (1898–1925).* Translated by John B. Brough. New York: Springer.

Husserl, E. 2008. *Die Lebenswelt: Auslegungen der vorgegebenen Welt und ihrer constitution: Texte aus dem Nachlass (1916–1937),* edited by Husserliana XXXIX. Dordrecht, Netherlands: Rochus Sowa.

Husserl, E. 2014. *Ideas for a Pure Phenomenology and Phenomenological Philosophy. First Book: General Introduction to Pure Phenomenology.* Translated by D. O. Dahlstrom. Indianapolis, IN: Hackett Publishing.

Hutchinson, D. S., and M. R. Johnson. 2015. Protrepticus: "A Weblog of Research towards a Reconstruction of the Lost Dialogue of Aristotle." New Reconstruction, Includes Greek Text, January 25, 2015. http://blog.protrepticus .info/2015/01/new-reconstruction-includes-greek-text.html.

Ingarden, R. 1972. "What Is New in Husserl's 'Crisis.' " In *Analecta Husserliana: The Yearbook of Phenomenological Research.* Vol. 11. The Later Husserl and the Idea of Phenomenology —Idealism-Realism, Historicity and Nature: Papers and Debate of the International Phenomenological Conference Held at the University of Waterloo, Canada, April 9–14, 1969, edited by A. T. Tymieniecka, 23–47. Dordrecht, Netherlands: D. Reidel Publishing .

Jackson, P. 2008. "Pierre Bourdieu, the 'Cultural Turn' and the Practice of International History." *Review of International Studies* 34:155–181.

Jaensch, A. (Rev). 2014. "God Is Big Enough for Our Questions: Introducing Learners to a Critical Approach to Study of the Bible." *Lutheran Theological Journal* 48 (3): 186–197.

Jay, M. 1984. *Marxism and Totality: The Adventures of a Concept from Lukacs to Habermas*. Berkeley: University of California Press.

Jessop, B. 1990. *State Theory: Putting the Capitalist State in Its Place*. Cambridge: Polity Press.

Jessop, B. 2012. "Marxist Approaches to Power." In *The Wiley-Blackwell Companion to Political Sociology*, Edited E. Amenta, K. Nash, and A. Scott, 3–14. Oxford: Blackwell.

Jessop, B., and R. Wheatley. 1999. *Karl Marx's Social and Political Thought*. Vol. 6. London. Routledge.

Jönsson, E. 2016. "The Nature of an Upscale Nature: Bro Hof Slott Golf Club and the Political Ecology of High-End Golf." *Tourist Studies* 16 (3): 315–336.

Jori, A. 2003. *Aristotele*. Milano, Italy: Bruno Mondadori Editore.

Keel, O. 1978. *The Symbolism of the Biblical World: Ancient Near Eastern Iconography and the Book of Psalms*. Translated by T. J. Hallett. New York: Seabury Press.

Keen, R. 2009. *Exile and Restoration in Jewish Thought: An Essay in Interpretation*. London: Continuum International Publishing Group.

Kennedy, G. 1972. *The Art of Rhetoric in the Roman World 300 BC–AD 300*. Princeton, NJ: Princeton University Press.

Kennicott, P. 2004. "Bush's Capital, and Its Costs." *Washington Post*, December 19, 2004. http://www.washingtonpost.com/wp-dyn/articles/A9478-2004Dec17. https://www.washingtonpost.com/wp-dyn/articles/A9478-2004Dec17.html

Kinyua, J. K. 2013. "A Postcolonial Analysis of Bible Translation and Its Effectiveness in Shaping and Enhancing the Discourse of Colonialism and the Discourse of Resistance: The Gikuyu New Testament—A Case Study." *Black Theology* 11 (1): 58–95.

Kugel, J. L. 1997. *The Bible as It Was*. Cambridge, MA: Harvard University Press.

Laclau, E., and C. Mouffe. (1985) 2001. *Hegemony and Socialist Strategy: Towards a Radical Democratic Politics*. 2nd ed. London: Verso.

Laing, R. D. 1965. *The Divided Self*. Harmondsworth, UK: Penguin Books.

Layder, D. 1985. "Power, Structure and Agency." *Journal for the Study of Social Behaviour* 15:131–150.

Ledwith, M. 2009. "Antonio Gramsci and Feminism: The Elusive Nature of Power." *Educational Philosophy and Theory* 41 (6): 684–697.

Leggett, W. 2013. "Restoring Society to Post-Structuralist Politics: Mouffe, Gramsci and Radical Democracy." *Philosophy and Social Criticism* 39 (3): 299–315.

Lenin, V. 1917. *The State and Revolution: The Marxist Theory of the State & the Task of the Proletariat in the Revolution*. London: Aziloth Books.

Levene, N. 2011. "Does Spinoza Think the Bible Is Sacred?" *Jewish Quarterly Review* 101 (4): 545–573.

Levi-Strauss, C. 1963. *Structural Anthropology*. New York: Basic Books.

Liddell, H. G., and R. Scott. 1940. *A Greek-English Lexicon*. Oxford: Clarendon Press.

Lin, N. 2001. *Social Capital: Structural Analysis in the Social Sciences*. Cambridge: Cambridge University Press.

Lobo, C. 2010. "Husserl's Notion of Leib and the Primary/Secondary Properties Distinction." Presented at the 41st Annual Meeting of the Husserl Circle. Hosted by The New School for Social Research. Theresa Lang Center, New York City:86–102.

Lo Piparo, F. 1979. *Lingua, intellettuali, egemonia in Gramsci*. Laterza, Italy: Roma-Bari.

Low, N., and B. Gleeson. 1998. *Justice, Society and Nature: An Explanation of Political Ecology*. London: Routledge.

Löwy, M. 2002. "Marx, Weber and the Critique of Capitalism." http://europe -solidaire.org/spip.php?article2273.

Löwy, M. 2003. *The Theory of Revolution in the Young Marx.* Chicago: Haymarket.

Luhmann, N. 2004. *Law as a Social System.* Translated by K. A. Ziegert. Oxford: Oxford University Press.

Luke, T. 1997. *Ecocritique: Contesting the Politics of Nature, Economy, and Culture.* Minneapolis: University of Minnesota Press.

Lukes, S. 1977. *Essays in Social Theory.* London: Macmillan.

Luo, J. 2017. *Social Structuration in Tibetan Society: Education, Society, and Spirituality.* Lanham, MD: Lexington Books.

Lyell, C. 1832. *Principles of Geology.* Vol. 2. London: John Murray.

Marshall, G. 1997. *Repositioning Class: Social Inequality in Industrial Societies.* London: Sage.

Martin, J. L. 2003. "What Is Field Theory?" *American Journal of Sociology* 109:1–49.

Marx, K. 1844. "Economic and Philosophical Manuscripts of 1844." https:// www.marxists.org/archive/marx/works/1844/manuscripts/needs.htm.

Marx, K. 1849. "Wage Labour and Capital." *Neue Rheinische Zeitung*, April 1849.

Marx, K. (1858) 1974. *Grundrisse.* New York: Penguin Books.

Marx, K. (1867) 1976. *Capital.* Vol. 1. New York: Penguin Books.

Marx, Karl. (1894) 1981. *Capital.* Vol. 3. New York: Penguin Books.

Marx, K. 1947. *Misère de la philosophie.* Paris: Ed. Sociales.

Marx, K. 1962. *Manuscrits de 1844.* Paris: Ed. Sociales.

Marx, K. 1971. *Theories of Surplus Value.* Vol. 3. Moscow: Progress Publisher.

Marx, K. 1975. *Karl Marx: Early Writings*. Translated by Rodney Livingstone and Gregor Benton. New York: Vintage.

Marx, K. 1988. *The Communist Manifesto*, edited by Frederic L. Bender. New York: W.W. Norton.

Marx, K., and F. Engels. 1848. *Communist Manifesto*. 1st ed. Moscow: Progress Publishers.

Marx, K., and F. Engels. 1971. "Writings on the Paris Commune." In *The Second Draft*, edited by Hal Draper, 195-196. New York: Monthly Review Press.

Marx, K., and F. Engels. 1988. *Economic & Philosophic Manuscripts of 1844*. Translated by Martin Milligan. New York: Prometheus Books .

Marx, K., and F. Engels. 1989. *Collected Works*. Vol. 24. New York: International Publishers.

Marx, K., and F. Engels. 1998. *The German Ideology*. Amherst, MA: Prometheus Books.

Marx, K., and M. Nicolaus. (1858) 1993. *Grundrisse: Foundations of the Critique of Political Economy*. New York: Penguin Classics.

Mayr, E. 1982. *The Growth of Biological Thought: Diversity, Evolution, and Inheritance*. Cambridge, MA: Harvard University Press.

McCarney, J. 2005. "Ideology and False Consciousness' Marx Myths and Legends." April. https://www.marxists.org/archive/mccarney/2005/false-consciousness.htm.

McCarthy, C. 2013. "Said, Lukacs, and Gramsci: Beginnings, Geography, and Insurrection." *College Literature* 40 (4): 74–104.

Mcphee, R. D. 2004. "Clegg and Giddens on Power and (Post)Modernity." *Management Communication Quarterly* 18 (1): 129–145.

Meadors, G. T. n.d. "Power." http://www.biblestudytools.com/dictionaries/bakers-evangelical-dictionary/power.html.

Mensch, J. 2010. "The Question of Naturalizing Phenomenology." Presented at the 41st Annual Meeting of the Husserl Circle. Hosted by The New School for Social Research. Theresa Lang Center, New York City:63–73.

Merriam-Webster. n.d. Byzantine. https://www.merriamwebster.com/dictionary /Byzantine.

Mickunas, A. 2010. "Discursive Power." Presented at the 41st Annual Meeting of the Husserl Circle. Hosted by The New School for Social Research. Theresa Lang Center, New York City:3–14.

Miliband, R. 1969. *The State in Capitalist Society*. London: Weidenfeld & Nicolson.

Missler, N. 2012. "God's Supernatural Power." April. *Personal Update News Journal*. http://www.khouse.org/articles/2012/1051/print/.

Mitchell, N. D. 1999. *Liturgy and the Social Sciences*. Collegeville, MN: Liturgical.

Mizzi, P. (pastor). n.d. "The Almighty Power of God." http://www.tecmalta. org/tft135.htm.

Moraru, M. 2016. "Bourdieu, Multilingualism, and Immigration: Understanding How Second-Generation Multilingual Immigrants Reproduce Linguistic Practices with Non-Autochthonous Minority Languages in Cardiff, Wales." Doctor of Philosophy thesis. School of Modern Languages Cardiff University.

Morton, A. 2003. "Historicizing Gramsci: Situating Ideas in and beyond Their Context." *Review of International Political Economy* 10 (1): 118–146.

Mosedale, J. 2011. *Political Economy and Tourism: A Critical Perspective*. London: Routledge.

Mosedale, J. 2015. "Critical Engagements with Nature: Tourism, Political Economy of Nature and Political Ecology." *Tourism Geographies* 17:4.

Mumby, D. 1997. "The Problem of Hegemony: Rereading Gramsci for Organizational Communication Studies." *Western Journal of Communication* 61 (4): 343–375.

Mustafa, E., and V. Johnson. 2008. "Bourdieu and Organizational Analysis." *Theory and Society* 37 (1): 44.

Navarro, Z. 2006. "In Search of Cultural Interpretation of Power." *IDS Bulletin* 37 (6): 11–22.

Nicolaescu, A. C. 2010. "Dimitrie Cantemir Bourdieu—Habitus, Symbolic Violence, the Gift: 'You Give Me/I Give You" Principle.' " *Christian University* 1 (3): 1–10.

Nielsen, K., ed. (2009) 2012. *Religion and Normativity: Receptions and Transformations of the Bible*, 188. Aarhus: Aarhus University Press. *Book Reviews/Biblical Interpretation* 20:156–200.

Nietzsche, F. (1878–1880) 1986. *Human, All Too Human*. Translated by R. J. Hollingdale. Cambridge: Cambridge University Press.

Nietzsche, F. (1881) 1982. *Daybreak*, D. Translated by R. J. Hollingdale. Cambridge: Cambridge University Press.

Nietzsche, F. (1882–1887) 1974. *The Gay Science*. Translated by Walter Kaufmann. New York: Vintage.

Nietzsche, F. (1886) 1998. *Beyond Good and Evil*. Translated by M. Faber. Oxford: Oxford University Press.

Nietzsche, F. (1887) 1996. *On the Genealogy of Morals*. Translated by D. Smith. Oxford: Oxford University Press.

Nietzche, F. (1888) 1968. "The Antichrist." In *Twilight of the Idols and the Anti-Christ*. Translated by R. J. Hollingdale. Harmondsworth, UK: Penguin Books.

Nietzsche, F. (1889) 1998. *Twilight of the Idols*. Translated by D. Large. Oxford: Oxford University Press.

Nietzsche, F. (1908) 2005. *Ecce Homo: How One Becomes What One Is*. Translated by R. J. Hollingdale. London: Penguin Classic.

Nietzsche, F. 1969. *On the Genealogy of Morals*, edited by W. Kaufmann. New York: Vintage Books.

Nietzsche, F. 1976. *Portable Nietzsche*. London: Penguin Books.

Nietzsche, F. 1997. *Philosophical Writings*, edited by R. Grimm and C. Molina y Vedia. New York: Continuum.

Nietzsche, F. 2003. *Writings from the Late Notebooks*. Translated by K. Sturge. Cambridge: Cambridge University Press.

Nietzsche, F. 2005. *The Anti-Christ, Ecce Homo, Twilight of the Idols, and Other Writings*. Translated by J. Norman. Cambridge: Cambridge University Press.

Nietzsche, F. 2016. *The Will to Power, Book I and II: An Attempted Transvaluation of All Values*. eBook. Translated by A. M. Ludovici. London: Gutenberg.

Nietzsche, F. 2017a. *The Will to Power, Book I and II*. eBook. March 15. Prabhat Prakashan. New Delhi.

Nietzsche, F. 2017b. *On the Genealogy of Morality*. Translated by C. Diethe. Cambridge: Cambridge University Press.

Offe, C. 1984. *Contradictions of the Welfare State*. London: Hutchinson.

Omar, L. 2010. "Beyond the Antinomies of Structure: Levi-Strauss, Giddens, Bourdieu, and Sewell." *Theory and Society* 39:651–668.

O'Neil, M. A. 2015. "Leonard Cohen, Singer of the Bible." *Cross Currents*, March:91–99. https://onlinelibrary.wiley.com/doi/epdf/10.1111/cros.12112

Orosz, M. 2008. "Literary Reading(s) of the Bible: Aspects of a Semiotic Conception of Intertextuality and Intertextual Analysis of Texts." In *Reading the Bible Intertextually*, edited by R. B. Hays, S. Alkier, and L. A. Huizenga, 191–204. Waco, TX: Baylor University Press.

Oudshoorn, N. 1996. "A Natural Order of Things? Reproductive Sciences and the Politics of Othering." In *Future Natural: Nature, Science, Culture*, edited by G. Robertson, M. Mash, L. Tickner, J. Bird, B. Curtis, and T. Putnam, 122–132. London: Routledge.

Pakaluk, M. 2011. "Aristotle, Natural Law, and the Founders: Catholic University of America." Witherspoon Institute. https://www.nlnrac.org/classical/aristotle

Parsons, T. 1949. *The Structure of Social Action*. Glencoe, IL: Free Press.

Patnaik, A. 2012. "Commentary: The Contemporary Significance of Gramsci's Critique of Civil Society: 1089–7011." *Journal of Labor and Society* 15:577–588.

Peillon, M. 1998. "Bourdieu's Field and the Sociology of Welfare." *Journal of Social Policy* 27 (2): 213–229.

Poellner, P. 2007. "Consciousness in the World: Husserlian Phenomenology and Externalism." In *The Oxford Handbook of Continental Philosophy*, edited by Brian Leiter and Michael Rosen. Oxford: Oxford University Press. 409–460

Polka, B. 2015. "Modern Philosophy, the Subject, and the God of the Bible." *Sophia* 54:563–576.

Porpora, D. V. 1989. "Four Concepts of Social Structure." *Journal for the Theory of Social Behaviour* 19 (2): 195–211.

Postone, M. 1993. *Time, Labour, and Domination.* Cambridge: Cambridge University Press.

Poulantzas, N. 1978. *State, Power, Socialism.* London: Verso.

Prychitko, D. 2002. "The Concise Encyclopedia of Economics: Marxism." http://www.econlib.org/library/Enc/Marxism.html.

Rabinow, P., ed. 1997. *Volume 1, Ethics: Subjectivity and Truth.* Translated by Robert Hurley and Others. New York: New Press.

Rawolle, S. 2005. "Cross-Field Effects and Temporary Social Fields: A Case Study of the Mediatization of Recent Australian Knowledge Economy Policies." *Journal of Education Policy* 20 (6): 705–724.

Reay, D. 2004. "It's All Becoming a Habitus: Beyond the Habitual Use of Habitus in Educational Research." *British Journal of Sociology of Education* 25:431–444.

Reilly, E. C., and D. Hall. 2000. "Practices of Reading." In *A History of the Book in America: Volume One, The Colonial Book in the Atlantic World*, edited by Hugh Amory and David D. Hall. Cambridge: Cambridge University Press. 377-410.

Robbins, P. 2012. *Political Ecology: Critical Introductions to Geography.* 2nd ed. West Sussex, UK: John Wiley and Sons.

Ronald, E. K. 2012. "More Than 'Alone with the Bible': Reconceptualizing Religious Reading." *Sociology of Religion* 73 (3): 323–344.

Rummel, R. J. 1977. *Understanding Conflict and War*, vol. 3. *Conflict in Perspective.* Beverly Hills, CA: Sage Publications.

Ryan, G. E. 1983. *Ratio et oratio: Cicero, Rhetoric and the Scept—Academy.* Princeton, NJ: Princeton University Press.

Said, E. 1983. *The World, the Text, and the Critic.* Cambridge, MA: Harvard University Press.

Said, E. 1993. *Culture and Imperialism*. London: Chatto and Windus.

Said, E. 2000. *Reflections on Exile and Other Essays*. Cambridge, MA: Harvard University Press.

Salamini, L. 1981. *The Sociology of Political Praxis: An Introduction to Gramsci's Theory*. London: Routledge.

Savage, M. 2000. *Class Analysis and Social Transformation*. Buckingham, UK: Open University Press.

Sayer, A. 2005. *The Moral Significance of Class*. Cambridge: Cambridge University Press.

Scarso, D. 2013. "Beyond Nature and Culture?" *Limes: Borderland Studies* 6 (2): 91–104.

Schinkela, W., and M. Noordegraaf. 2011. "Professionalism as Symbolic Capital: Materials for a Bourdieusian Theory of Professionalism." *Comparative Sociology* 10:67–96.

Schmitt, C. (1985) 1922. *Political Theology: Four Chapters on the Concept of Sovereignty*. Cambridge, MA: MIT Press.

Scholz, S., ed. 2003. *Biblical Studies Alternatively: An Introductory Reader*. Upper Saddle River, NJ: Prentice Hall.

Schott, J. M. 2008. *Christianity, Empire, and the Making of Religion in Late Antiquity*. Philadelphia: University of Pennsylvania Press.

Scott, S. n.d. "Economy and Society in Marx Durkheim, and Weber."

https://www.scribd.com/document/140919999/Simon-.

Seddon, G. 1972. *Sense of Place*. Nedlands, Australia: University of Western Australia Press.

Segall, A., and K. Burke. 2013. "Reading the Bible as a Pedagogical Text: Testing, Testament, and Some Postmodern Considerations about Religion/the Bible in Contemporary Education." *Curriculum Inquiry* 43 (3): 305–331.

Sewell, W. H. 1992. "A Theory of Structure: Duality, Agency, and Transformation." *American Journal of Sociology* 98 (1): 1–29.

Sewell, W. H. 2005. "A Theory of Structure: Duality, Agency and Transformation." In *Logics of History*, edited by Gabrielle Spiegel 124–151. Chicago: University of Chicago Press.

Shakespeare, W. 1990. *Classics: The Complete Works of William Shakespeare— The Alexander Text*. Ann Arbor, MI: Borders Press.

Sheridan-Smith, A. M. trans. (1975) 1977. *Surveiller et punir* [Discipline and Punish]. Paris: Gallimard; New York: Pantheon Books.

Sherwood, Y. 2008. "The God of Abraham and Exceptional States, or The Early Modern Rise of the Whig/Liberal Bible." *Journal of the American Academy of Religion* 76 (2): 312–343.

Shurmer-Smith, P., and K. Hannam. 1994. *Worlds of Desire, Realms of Power*. London: Edward Arnold.

Simkins, R. A. 2014. "The Bible and Anthropocentrism: Putting Humans in Their Place."

Dialectical Anthropology 38:397–413.

Singer, C. 1931. *A Short History of Biology*. Oxford: Clarendon Press.

Skeggs, B. 2004. *Class, Self, Culture*. London: Routledge.

Smart, B. 1992. *Modern Conditions, Postmodern Controversies*. London: Routledge.

Smart, B. 2002. *Michael Foucault*. London: Routledge.

Smith, N. 1996. "The Production of Nature." In *Future Natural: Nature, Science, Culture*, edited by G. Robertson, M. Mash, L. Tickner, J. Bird, B. Curtis, and T. Putnam, 35–54 . London: Routledge.

Sokolowski, R. 2000. *Introduction to Phenomenology*. Cambridge: Cambridge University Press.

Sotirin. 1997. "Secretarial Bitching: The Ambivalence of Mundane Struggle." Presented at the Annual Convention of the International Communication Association, Montreal, Canada, May 1997.

Soule, M. 1995. "The Social Siege of Nature." In *Reinventing Nature? Responses to Postmodern Deconstruction*, edited by M. Soule and G. Lease, 137–170. Washington, DC: Island Press.

Soule, M., and G. Lease, eds. 1995. *Reinventing Nature? Responses to Postmodern Deconstruction.* Washington, DC: Island Press.

Sparks, K. 2008. *God's Word in Human Words: An Evangelical Appropriation of Critical Biblical Scholarship.* Grand Rapids, MI: Baker.

Spinoza, C. 2001. *Theological-Political Treatise.* 2nd ed. Translated by S. Shirley. Indianapolis, IN: Hackett Publishing.

Stone, L. 1983. "An Exchange with Michel Foucault." *New York Review of Books* 30 (5): 42–44.

Stones, R. 1991. "Strategic Context Analysis: A New Research Strategy for Structuration Theory." *Sociology* 25 (4): 673–695.

Stones, R. 1996. *Sociological Reasoning: Towards a Past-Modern Sociology.* London: MacMillan.

Strathern, M. 1980. "No Nature, No Culture: The Hagen Case." In *Nature, Culture and Gender*, edited by C. MacCormack and M. Strathern, 174–222. Cambridge: Cambridge University Press.

Suellentrop, C. 2004. "America's New Political Capital." *Slate*, November 30, 2004. www.slate.com. https://slate.com/news-and-politics/2004/12/what-is-political-capital-anyway.html.

Swinburne, R. G. 1995. "God." In *The Oxford Companion to Philosophy*, edited by Ted Honderich. Oxford: Oxford University Press.

TenHouten, W. 2018. "From Ressentiment to Resentment as a Tertiary Emotion." *Review of European Studies* 10:49–64.

Thompson, J. B. 1989. "The Theory of Structuration." In *Social Theory of Modern Societies: Anthony Giddens and His Critics*, edited by D. Held and J. B. Thompson, 56–77. Cambridge: Cambridge University Press.

Thrift, N. 1999. "Steps to an Ecology of Place." In *Human Geography Today*, edited by D. Massey, J. Allen, and P. Sarre, 295–322. Oxford: Blackwell.

Tzu, S. 1983. *The Art of War.* New York: Delacorte Press.

Vaccaro, I., O. Beltran, and P. A. Paquet. 2013. "Political Ecology and Conservation Policies: Some Theoretical Genealogies." *Journal of Political Ecology* 20:255–272.

Wacquant, L. J. D. 2014. "Homines in Extremis: What Fighting Scholars Teach us about Habitus." *Body & Society* 20 (2): 3–17.

Walton, J. 2011. *Genesis 1 as Ancient Cosmology*. Winona Lake, IN: Eisenbrauns.

Walton, J. H. 2012. "Human Origins and the Bible." *Zygon* 47 (4): 875–889.

Wark, M. 1994. "Third Nature." *Cultural Studies* 8 (1): 115–132.

Warren, Howard. 1921. *A History of the Association Psychology*. New York: Charles Scribner's Sons.

Weber, M. 1985. *The Protestant Ethic and the "Spirit" of Capitalism*. London: Routledge.

Werline, R. A. 2014. "Prayer, Politics, and Power in the Hebrew Bible." *Interpretation: A Journal of Bible and Theology* 68 (1): 5–16.

White, L., Jr. 1967. "The Historical Roots of Our Ecologic Crisis." *Science* 155:1203–1207.

White, R. 1985. "American Environmental History: The Development of a New Historical Field." *Pacific Historical Review* 54:297–335.

Wikipedia. n.d.-a. "Oligarchy." https://en.wikipedia.org/wiki/Oligarchy.

Wikipedia. n.d.-b. "Political Positions of the Democratic Party." https://en.m.wikipedia.org/wiki/Political_positions_of_the_Democratic_Party.

Wolfe, A. 2003. *The Transformation of American Religion*. New York: Free Press.

Wright, E. O. 1983. "Review Essay: Is Marxism Really Functionalist, Class Reductionist, and Teleological? In *A Contemporary Critique of Historical Materialism. Vol. 1. Power, Property and the State*. By Anthony Giddens. Berkeley and Los Angeles: University of California Press, 1981." *American Journal of Sociology* 89 (2): 452–459.

Yee, G. A., ed. 2007. *Judges and Method: New Approaches in Biblical Studies*. 2nd ed. Minneapolis, MN: Fortress Press.